1983

Reagan, Andropov, and a World on the Brink

ALSO BY TAYLOR DOWNING

Breakdown
Secret Warriors
Night Raid
The World at War
Spies in the Sky
Churchill's War Lab
Cold War (with Jeremy Isaacs)
Battle Stations (with Andrew Johnston)
Olympia
Civil War (with Maggie Millman)
The Troubles (as Editor)

1983

Reagan, Andropov, and a World on the Brink

Taylor Downing

DA CAPO PRESS

Da Capo Press
Hachette Book Group
1290 Avenue of the Americas, New York, NY 10104
www.dacapopress.com
@DaCapoPress; @DaCapoPR

Printed in the United States of America

Originally published in 2018 by Little, Brown in Great Britain
First U.S. Edition: April 2018

Published by Da Capo Press, an imprint of Perseus Books, LLC, a subsidiary of Hachette Book Group, Inc. The Da Capo Press name and logo is a trademark of the Hachette Book Group.

The Hachette Speakers Bureau provides a wide range of authors for speaking events. To find out more, go to www.hachettespeakersbureau.com or call (866) 376-6591.

The publisher is not responsible for websites (or their content) that are not owned by the publisher.

Print book interior design by M Rules.

Library of Congress Control Number: 2018934257

ISBNs: 978-0-306-92172-8 (hardcover); 978-0-306-92173-5 (ebook)

LSC-C

10 9 8 7 6 5 4 3 2 1

Contents

List of Maps

Prologue

At 8 a.m. on Monday, 6 August 1945 the city of Hiroshima was teeming with people. Citizens were streaming towards the centre of the city to their places of work. Trams and streetcars loaded with passengers clattered their way through crowded streets. The bridges over the six tributaries of the Ota river that flow through the city and out into the Inland Sea were packed with commuters. Eight thousand schoolgirls had been drafted in to the centre of the city to work on air raid defences. Tens of thousands of soldiers in the local barracks, stripped to the waist, were performing morning exercises. It was a beautiful summer morning, already warm, and a little humid, suggesting it would get uncomfortable later in the day. There was a bright blue sky above. There had been an air raid warning earlier but the all-clear had been sounded half an hour before. Few people noticed the three aircraft, tiny specks in the sky at 31,000 feet, one ahead of the two others. A doctor at home, two miles north of the city centre, wrote in his diary, 'Shimmering leaves, reflecting sunlight from a cloudless sky, made a pleasant contrast with shadows in my garden.'[1]

At 8.15 a.m. a blinding flash of what seemed like lightning lit up the sky followed almost immediately by a wall of heat. No one near the centre of the city survived to give an account of what happened next. A college student well away from the centre remembered, 'we felt a tremendous flash of lightning. In an instant we were blinded and everything was just a frenzy of delirium.'[2] The first atom bomb had been dropped by an American B-29 bomber and had exploded 1800 feet above the city centre.

Later calculations put the temperature at the hypocentre of the explosion, the point on the ground directly below where the bomb ignited, at between 3000 and 4000°C. Buildings were vaporised in an instant. At 600 metres from the hypocentre the heat was intense enough to scar granite, and at 1000 metres roofing tiles bubbled. People were incinerated and nothing was left except for small human-like shapes on pavements and walls where their bodies had temporarily blocked the severe heat. Up to 2000 metres from the hypocentre life and property were shattered, burned and buried under ashes. The destruction had taken place in two or three seconds. There was no escape.

Further out from the centre towards the suburbs there were survivors. But the hell that descended around them probably made many wish they had died instantly too. Fires were ignited up to 4000 metres from the hypocentre. The blast wave sent out from the bomb pulled down wooden buildings up to the same distance. Within seconds everything was covered in a thick fog of dust, smoke and ash. Men, women, children and babies were terribly burned, their skin blackened and blistered. Hair was burned right off scorched bodies. Some people were seen staggering about in agony. Others were on hands and knees crawling over bodies or body parts. Those a little further from the centre were still so badly burned that their skin began to peel off. As uninjured people from the outskirts came into the city to help they were met with hideous sights, not only of bodies piling up but of living, almost unrecognisable ghosts groping their way around, calling out the names of family members separated in the destruction and chaos. Most tram cars were just blackened wrecks, the passengers burned to cinders. Flames were whipped up by the winds into a firestorm that wreaked further devastation out into the suburbs. The ghastly smell of burning flesh filled the air. Hundreds, thousands crawled or jumped into water tanks that had been put up throughout the city to try to prevent fires spreading in the event of incendiary bombs being dropped. Others leaped into the rivers that were so much a feature of the city to try to escape the firestorms. But most of them were so badly injured that they did not survive long, and within hours vast numbers of blackened corpses started piling up along the estuary banks and the sea shore.

A later report calculated that of 76,000 buildings in the city of Hiroshima, 70,000 were damaged or destroyed. All the facilities of urban life, including the city hall, police stations, fire brigades, schools, roads, banks, shops, electricity and gas supplies, sewage systems, hospitals and medical centres, were destroyed. Ninety per cent of all medical personnel were killed or disabled. It is thought that about 70,000 people died in the first few hours after the bomb dropped.[3] The doctor who had been in his garden when the bomb exploded miraculously survived but was badly injured. He later wrote, 'Hiroshima was no longer a city but a burnt-over prairie . . . How small [it] was with its houses gone.'[4]

For the survivors, this was only the beginning of their horror. After a few days, even those who had escaped terrible burns started to sicken. They went down with nausea, vomiting, diarrhoea and fever. Blisters and ulcers began to appear on their skin, in their mouths and throats, and on their gums. They suffered from hair loss. The doctors did not know what they were witnessing and called this 'atom bomb sickness'. What they were seeing was the first ever case of mass radiation sickness. Victims were suffering from an extremely low white blood cell count and infections caused by gamma rays.

Few recovered. By the end of the year the total death toll from the bomb was estimated at 140,000, and after five years this had gone up to 200,000.

Three days after Hiroshima was hit, a second bomb was dropped. This was a plutonium implosion bomb, using a different fission process from the first. The target was Kokura, but when the B-29 arrived overhead heavy cloud cover obscured the city. So the plane flew on to its secondary target, Nagasaki. The same horror ensued on the ground after the explosion of this bomb. But Nagasaki was surrounded by steep hills so the loss of life was less severe. Probably about 40,000 died within hours, 70,000 by the end of the year, and 140,000 over the next five years.

The day before, the Soviet Union had declared war on Japan and the Red Army marched into Manchuria and then north Korea. Still the military faction in the Cabinet in Tokyo refused to consider capitulation. But on 10 August, Emperor Hirohito overruled his Cabinet and announced his intention to surrender. A few more days passed before final terms were agreed, and on 14 August the Second World War ended. But the atomic age had begun.

An official Japanese committee of scientists and physicians later compiled information on the damage caused by the two atom bombs. Many survivors were interviewed. Accounts that had been recorded by Japanese and US military and medical authorities who had visited the area in the weeks after the bombs exploded were assessed, and detailed calculations were made about the destructiveness of the bombs at different points from the hypocentre, and the different types of thermal burns victims had suffered. The committee defined the atom bomb as 'a weapon of mass slaughter' and concluded, 'The experience of these two cities was the opening chapter to the possible annihilation of mankind.'[5]

Four years after the atom bombs were dropped on Japan, at

dawn on 29 August 1949, a group of Soviet scientists and officials gathered at a desolate firing range in the remote steppe
of north-east Kazakhstan. Lead scientist Igor Kurchatov had
carried out extraordinary work of the highest national priority. Arriving from Moscow to join the scientists was a short,
bespectacled man with steely, penetrating eyes and receding
hair. A great deal of fuss was made of him. He was none other
than Lavrenti Beria, the sinister and all-powerful chief of the
secret police, the NKVD, Stalin's lead hatchet man. In 1945,
after the explosion of the American atom bombs, Stalin had
put Beria in charge of ensuring the Soviets speedily developed
their own bomb. Beria had allocated enormous resources to
the project and was now in Kazakhstan to observe the results.
Inwardly, he was not confident the scientists could pull it off.

Along with a smattering of senior generals, Beria, Kurchatov
and the other leading scientists gathered in an observation
bunker. The Americans had called their first atomic test,
carried out in the New Mexico desert, 'Trinity'. The Soviets
codenamed theirs 'First Lightning'. At exactly 7 a.m. a huge
white fireball engulfed the giant tower built to support the
bomb. As the fireball rushed upwards it turned orange, then
red, and sucked up thousands of tons of soil and rubble into a
vast mushroom cloud of smoke and debris. Inside the bunker
there was elation. Beria hugged and kissed Kurchatov. They
both knew that if the test had failed the punishment, even at
their level, might have been death.

Within hours a vast radioactive cloud formed in the
atmosphere and began drifting slowly eastwards across Asia
towards the Pacific. Four days later, an American B-29 flying
a routine weather mission over the north Pacific picked up
levels of radioactivity that were 300 per cent higher than
usual. Over the next few days more samples were gathered as
the cloud blew towards Canada. Analysis revealed that this
was without doubt the debris from a nuclear explosion of a

plutonium implosion bomb like the one used at Nagasaki. Initially, American intelligence experts doubted the veracity of this. Only a month earlier the CIA had concluded that the Soviets were unlikely to be able to explode a bomb until the middle of 1953. But within a couple of weeks the evidence was indisputable. President Harry Truman was told, and at the end of September he made a public announcement. The American people were dismayed but not hysterical. Everyone wanted to know, how had this happened so quickly?

The story of how the Soviets developed the highly complex technology necessary to produce an atom bomb is an extraordinary one. A huge secret laboratory was built 250 miles east of Moscow in an area that became known as Arzamus-16, entirely closed off to the outside world. An army of scientists were put to work. They were given every support they needed. Beria allocated huge numbers of labourers from the Gulag to the mining of uranium ore. The centralised Soviet command economy was well suited to a project like this as once a priority had been set, enormous resources could be martialled. In addition, the scientists benefited from information that had been supplied to them by spies working on the US atomic research programme.[6] But there was no doubting it. The American atomic monopoly was over. The Soviets had the bomb.

This led to a major policy review in the United States. American scientists were already discussing the possibility of developing a super-bomb that would release tremendous amounts of nuclear energy through the fusion of hydrogen atoms. Known as the H-bomb, this would be far more destructive than the Hiroshima and Nagasaki bombs. Behind this new project was nuclear physicist Edward Teller who argued that the Soviets would probably soon develop a hydrogen bomb and so it was essential for the US to take the lead in this next step in the nuclear arms race. He was heavily backed by the US military, and President Truman gave the go-ahead in January 1950, just a few months after news of the Soviet atom bomb had sunk in. Truman announced to the world that the US was starting to build a weapon that it hoped it would never use.

Just under three years later, on 1 November 1952, the US tested its first H-bomb on a tiny Pacific atoll called Eniwetok in the west Pacific. The bomb itself was huge at 82 tons and was housed in a gigantic refrigeration system that took six weeks to assemble. All the scientists and military figures observing the test were moved 30 miles back from the test site. The explosion produced a white fireball that was 3 miles in diameter. The wings of a B-36 flying at 40,000 feet, 15 miles from the explosion heated up to 93°C within seconds. Even 30 miles away the scientists reported that the heat was like standing next to the door of a hot oven being opened. A few minutes after ignition the largest mushroom cloud yet seen had sucked up 80 million tons of material from the atoll. The yield of the Hiroshima bomb had been estimated at the equivalent of 14,000 tons of high-explosive TNT, expressed as 14 kilotons. The yield of this new hydrogen bomb was measured at more than 10 million tons of TNT, or 10.4 megatons, roughly a thousand times greater. The world had now entered the thermonuclear age.

Nine months later, the Soviets tested their first H-bomb. Although its explosive yield was less, it was proof that the Soviet scientists had once again caught up. Further analysis of the radioactive cloud it produced detected elements of lithium. This indicated that the bomb was far smaller and did not need the giant refrigeration system the American H-bomb had required. It would be possible to drop this super-bomb from an aircraft.

On 1 March 1954, the US tested its first lithium H-bomb at Bikini Atoll in the Pacific. It vaporised coral on and around the atoll, turning it into radioactive calcium that was blown over a large area of ocean. The yield of this massive explosion was estimated at 15 million tons of TNT, or 15 megatons. Seven months later the Soviets responded by dropping from an aircraft a bomb with the equivalent yield of 20 megatons, nearly two thousand times more powerful than the Hiroshima bomb. The superpowers were trying to outdo each other in the ultimate and most terrifying arms race. American strategists began to talk not just about 'megatons' of explosive power but also about 'megadeath' as a unit for measuring one million deaths from a nuclear explosion.[7]

How, when or if such weapons would ever be used became the subject of much debate and strategic planning. In January 1954, under President Eisenhower, Secretary of State John Foster Dulles came up with the doctrine of 'Massive Retaliation'. Central to American thinking on nuclear policy was that the US would never carry out a surprise first strike. As the phrase had it, 'America doesn't do Pearl Harbors'. Instead, Dulles argued that the Soviet leaders would know that if they attacked the West they would be faced with a huge thermonuclear retaliation. The bombs would be carried by the heavy bombers of Strategic Air Command, and in the early 1950s its chief, General Curtis LeMay, drew up a list of 6000 separate targets within the USSR including airfields, military bases, nuclear power stations, oil fields and communication centres. Defence strategists calculated that a US nuclear strike might kill between 360 and 450 million people in the Soviet Union and China within hours.[8] In 1950, the US military had 298 atom bombs; by the end of the decade the number of nuclear warheads it possessed had risen to more than 18,000. At least twelve B-52 bombers were constantly in the air, 24/7, 365 days a year, flying patrols around the Atlantic and over the Arctic, each carrying three or four thermonuclear bombs. They were on continuous alert, ready to attack pre-assigned targets within the Soviet Union, China and the countries of the Warsaw Pact if they received the 'go-codes'. Dozens more bombers were waiting on fifteen minutes' stand-by at American bases around the world.

However, the rapid development of new technologies began to transform the situation. In May 1957, the Soviets launched their first intercontinental ballistic missile (ICBM). It could reach its target in a matter of minutes. If nuclear warheads could be made small enough to be carried by an ICBM then this offered an entirely new way of launching a nuclear attack. In October, the Soviets sent the first ever satellite called Sputnik, meaning 'fellow traveller', into orbit around the planet. Soviet missile technology was clearly getting ahead. A sense of deep humiliation in the United States led to talk of a 'missile gap', a 'technology gap', and behind that an 'education gap'. This was compounded a couple of months later when an American Vanguard missile, in a very public launch in front of the news cameras of the world, lifted a few feet off the ground then fell back and exploded. The British press mocked 'Oh, What a Flopnik'.[9]

In October 1961, the Soviets detonated the largest explosion ever triggered on Earth. Soviet leader Nikita Khrushchev boasted to the Communist Party Congress in Moscow a few days later that it was equivalent to 50 million tons of TNT – many times more than all the explosives used by all the participants in the whole of the Second World War. This represented a new generation of Soviet super-bomb. Khrushchev told delegates that he hoped 'we are never called upon to explode these bombs over anyone's territory'. Privately he spoke of the new bombs hanging 'over the heads of the imperialists, like a sword of Damocles'. This was his version of Massive Retaliation.

Yet at the end of the 1950s the US still had no overall strategic plan for the use of nuclear weapons. Pacific and Atlantic

Commands both had their own targets in addition to those of Strategic Air Command. In 1960, everything was brought together into one blueprint known as the Single Integrated Operational Plan (SIOP). In the event of an approach to nuclear war, this plan would offer the President a series of options ranging from launching a full-scale retaliation to hitting only primary targets.

The following year, the new young President John F. Kennedy launched a rethink of American nuclear policy. He was astonished to discover that Eisenhower had allowed senior US Air Force commanders to authorise the use of nuclear weapons. The reasoning behind this was that if a first strike had taken out Washington and the President was dead, there needed to be someone who could sanction a retaliation.[10] Kennedy changed the rules so that only the President could authorise the use of nuclear weapons. Along with this came a complex system of dual controls with electronic locks for those actually launching missiles in an attempt to prevent accidental launches. Secondly, Kennedy and his team began to revise the SIOP to manage the launch of nuclear weapons. The President rejected the concept of Massive Retaliation against the entire communist bloc as not being fit for purpose in the new era in which some of the threats were more local and fragmented. Kennedy, who confronted Khrushchev over Berlin and later over Cuba, wanted a system in which he could attack specific military targets or launch sites. He also wanted to be able to manage a selective retaliation that might withhold attacks on cities or even entire countries that were not belligerents. For instance, if the purpose of this more limited form of nuclear war was to bring the other side to the negotiating table then it would be pointless to destroy the political leadership, who were the only ones able to thrash out an armistice. This concept of a more limited form of nuclear war striking, say, only at the enemy's missile launch sites was known as 'Counterforce'.

Finally, as it was American policy not to launch nuclear weapons in a first strike, a system had to be devised by which the United States had sufficient nuclear capability held back so that it could survive a pre-emptive attack and still be able to retaliate. All of this was contained within Kennedy's new Single Integrated Operational Plan.

The new SIOP had only just come in when the scariest confrontation of the Cold War to date came with the Cuban missile crisis in October 1962. When the US discovered that Khrushchev was siting missiles in Fidel Castro's Cuba only a few miles from the Florida coast, it was clear that much of the US mainland would soon be within range of Soviet nuclear weapons. The military wanted to bomb the missile sites before they were finished but Kennedy insisted on restraint and launched a naval blockade of Cuba instead. For two weeks the tension was intense as each side tried to stare the other out. Khrushchev finally 'blinked' and agreed to withdraw Soviet missiles from Cuba after reaching a secret agreement with the US that American missiles would also be removed from Turkey, not far from the Soviet border. The crisis was acted out very much in public in the West. Constant television reports and speeches by the President and others brought the drama into everyone's living room. Americans nervously sought out the route from their workplace or home to the nearest nuclear air raid shelter. In Britain, people were concerned about whether it was safe to send their children to school. It seemed in the end that Kennedy had won a great victory when Khrushchev withdrew the missiles from Cuba because the quid pro quo of the American withdrawal from Turkey was kept secret. But undoubtedly Kennedy's restraint had saved the day. It is now known that several of the missile sites were operative and fully armed by the time the US discovered them. An attack on the sites would no doubt have provoked a nuclear retaliation against the US mainland, and this would almost certainly have triggered a nuclear Armageddon.[11]

Robert McNamara, Kennedy's Secretary of Defense, brought several strategists from the RAND Corporation, a defence think-tank, into the Pentagon. He came up with a new concept called 'Assured Destruction'. Neither side would attack the other because they knew it was suicidal: if one superpower attacked, the other had enough nuclear capacity to strike back, causing massive destruction. Someone added the word 'Mutual' to this new phrase, and 'Mutual Assured Destruction', better known by its acronym MAD, became one of the central tenets underpinning the Cold War. McNamara insisted it was far from madness, that it created a form of stability, as long as neither side perceived it had an advantage over the other.[12]

However, the technology continued to advance at a dizzying pace. In the mid-sixties the Soviets began to develop anti-ballistic missiles (ABMs) intended to intercept incoming missiles. This would have fundamentally shifted the nuclear balance and they caused great alarm in Washington. The problem was that organising a defence against a missile strike was dauntingly complex. In the late sixties the Americans developed the technology for multiple independently targetable re-entry vehicles (MIRVs). Missiles were developed to carry up to ten separately targeted warheads, each one capable of destroying a city or a military installation. Overnight this made the task of anti-ballistic missiles far more complex, and ultimately hopeless. If only a few missiles got through they could still cause widespread nuclear devastation.

Both sides were by now spending colossal sums on the development of weapons which publicly at least they said they would never use. By the late 1960s the Americans had clearly regained the lead in missile technology. Not only was the US able to send men to the moon and bring them home, but there was a new range of successful ICBMs known as Atlas and

Titan. These were stored in giant silos across the Midwest. A new generation of intermediate-range ballistic missiles known as Thor was located with NATO allies in western Europe. And an entirely new concept of submarine-launched ballistic missiles came in with Polaris. With all these weapons capable of transporting nuclear warheads, missiles could now be located across continents and in submarines nestling invisibly on the floors of oceans. In addition new radar systems were created to give early warning of the launch of missiles by the other side. Over the years, every innovation within the United States was matched by an equivalent development in the Soviet Union. A vast arsenal of nuclear weapons was created with the capacity to destroy all forms of life on planet Earth. Something had to give.

In the wake of the Cuban missile crisis, the United States and the Soviet Union had signed a Partial Test Ban Treaty to stop further atmospheric tests of nuclear weapons. This was a small first step on the long road of slowing up the arms race. In 1968 the Nuclear Non-Proliferation Treaty was signed by the US, the USSR and Britain, which had its own small nuclear capability, prohibiting the export of nuclear technology to other countries (France and China by this time also possessed nuclear weapons but did not sign). Both superpowers now accepted that some form of arms limitation was essential. Negotiations between the two continued at a snail's pace but eventually resulted in the signing of the Strategic Arms Limitation Treaty (SALT I) by President Richard Nixon and Soviet leader Leonid Brezhnev at a summit in Moscow in May 1972. Alongside this came a treaty to prevent the development of ABMs. The treaties effectively froze the nuclear arsenals of both superpowers while ensuring that Mutual Assured Destruction continued to be possible. In other words, each side still had more than enough nuclear weapons to destroy the other.

The SALT treaty ushered in a new era of détente between the superpowers that lasted for much of the 1970s. And in Europe, a newly prosperous West Germany recognised the existence of East Germany, ushering in what appeared to be a form of East–West reconciliation. In 1975 the Helsinki Accords were signed. Firstly they recognised the borders of post-war Europe; secondly they encouraged trade and cultural links along with scientific and industrial cooperation. A third basket of accords dealt with human rights issues as inserted by the American negotiators and included promises on the free movement of peoples and ideas. The Soviets hesitated but still signed, never intending to take much notice of this third area. President Gerald Ford, who had replaced Nixon after his resignation over the Watergate scandal, flew to Helsinki in person to sign. To symbolise this new unity between East and West the Soviet Soyuz and American Apollo spacecraft docked together in outer space. It looked as though peaceful coexistence between the two superpowers would at last prevail.

By the end of the 1970s people around the world had lived with the prospect of a nuclear holocaust for thirty years. Still technology continued to advance. Soviet defensive thinking had relied upon the fact that the leadership, who would take the critical decisions about retaliation in the event of an American first strike, would have time to evacuate to a huge underground city that had been built outside Moscow using a dedicated underground railway system. But what if an attack came suddenly, almost out of the blue? The Soviets knew that the latest American Pershing missiles, due to be located in Europe in the autumn of 1983, could hit Moscow six minutes after launch. This caused a new level of panic in the Kremlin. And in Washington it was accepted that Soviet submarines in the Atlantic could fire their missiles on targets like the US capital and again there would be only minutes between the point of detection and the moment of impact. Both sides concluded it might be necessary to launch their own missiles first in anticipation of an attack from the other, or at the very least on the first early warning that missiles were in the air, an option called 'Launch Under Attack'.

A key danger now arose. If one side thought it could get the upper hand in some form of limited nuclear war through a first strike that could take out the other side's launch capability, this would increase the likelihood of one superpower launching a surprise first strike to disable the other. By undermining the concept of MAD, this was creating a less stable, far more dangerous world. As the 1980s began some senior Soviet figures were beginning to fear that the superior technology of the United States would encourage them to think about a surprise first strike, a decapitation raid against the Soviet Union. These fears would gather momentum for some years to come.

The lesson from Cold War thinking on nuclear strategy and how and when to use nuclear weapons is clear. No matter how sophisticated the systems were, how thoroughly the structures governing the use of nuclear weapons had been prepared and the protocols rehearsed, it was always in the end an individual who had his finger on the button. There was always a single person who had to interpret the situation and ultimately decide what to do. Ronald Reagan was elected President of the United States in 1980. He summed it up: 'The decision to launch the [nuclear] weapons was mine alone to make. We had many contingency plans for responding to a nuclear attack. But everything would happen so fast that I wondered how much planning or reason could be applied in such a crisis. The Russians sometimes kept submarines off our east coast with nuclear missiles that could turn the White House into a pile of radioactive rubble within six or eight minutes. *Six minutes* to decide how to respond to a blip on a radar scope and decide whether to unleash Armageddon! How could anyone apply reason at a time like that? ... We were a button push away from oblivion.'[13]

This book highlights this lesson by telling the story of the 1983 war scare when the Soviets convinced themselves that the United States was preparing to launch a nuclear first strike against them. It is the story of how aggressive statements by President Reagan and other senior US officials were misinterpreted. It tells of how intelligence services will usually find evidence to prove whatever its masters want it to prove. It shows how minor and unpredictable events can rapidly escalate into major confrontations. And it climaxes with a night on which the Soviet nuclear arsenal was put on to maximum alert, when missiles were deployed to action stations in submarines and mobile launchers, when aircraft were put on stand-by and when silo commanders were preparing to launch dozens of missiles each one of which had hundreds of times the explosive yield of the Hiroshima bomb. If these missiles had been fired it would have prompted a nuclear exchange that would have destroyed much of North America, most of Asia, probably all of Europe. The fallout would have brought down a nuclear winter that would have covered Earth for years or decades to come. The death toll would have been counted in the hundreds of millions, dwarfing every conflict in human history. This is the story of the time when fingers really did hover over the nuclear button, when the world really was 'a button push away from oblivion'.

1983: Reagan, Andropov, and a World on the Brink aims to create a new and accessible narrative about what President Reagan called the 'really scary' events of that year. In addition to the memoirs and accounts of those who played a leading role in the events of 1983, it is based on an array of dazzling new material including that which a group of us at Flashback Television discovered in the making of a documentary on the crisis in 2007. Along with this is the mass of evidence revealed by the endeavours of the National Security Archive (NSA) in Washington in prising official top secret documents out of many government archives in the last couple of years.[14] Now at last it is possible to write an accurate version of the events around the 1983 war scare. No historian can any longer say that we do not know what went on in 1983. And no one can deny how this amounted to the most terrifying year of living dangerously.

The events described in *1983: Reagan, Andropov, and a World on the Brink* have several resonances in the world we live in today, not least that all systems are operated by human beings, and human beings are fallible. The book shows that the aggressive and confrontational tone of an American president can provoke unintended consequences. It also demonstrates the folly of having no exchange or dialogue with potential enemies. That is as true today between America, the West and, say, the leaders of North Korea, Iran or Islamic State as it was with the Soviet Union several decades ago. It shows how intelligence can be misused or just misunderstood. And it shows how dangerous the use or even the threat of the use of nuclear weapons can be without proper crisis management systems in place. In our multi-polar world of the twenty-first century, some people feel nostalgic about the era of Mutual Assured Destruction in the bi-polar world of the late twentieth century. I hope after reading this book that no one will want to return to the crazy world of 1983 at the brink of nuclear war.

In the summer of 1983, cinema audiences flocked to see the latest James Bond movie in which Roger Moore defeats a Soviet general who attempts to fire a nuclear weapon against the West.[15] People loved the film but believed that the storyline was entirely fictional, if not totally absurd. Little did they know that a few months later the Soviets would indeed be preparing to launch a real nuclear attack on the West. Sometimes fact is stranger than fiction.

1

Reagan

At noon on 20 January 1981, after being sworn in by Chief Justice Warren, watched adoringly by his wife Nancy, Ronald Reagan offered Americans a new start. Unlike all previous Presidents who had sworn the oath of office behind the Capitol overlooking a parking lot in the shade, the 40th incumbent performed his inauguration on the front steps of the grand building looking out towards the Mall, the tall Washington Monument and the Jefferson and Lincoln Memorials. As the new President began to speak, the grey clouds parted and the winter sun shone down on the gathering on the west side of the Capitol. Reagan promised to improve the economy, where inflation was running at 18 per cent. He said he would run down the massive national deficit and by cutting taxes he would 'lighten our punitive tax burden'. He said he would reduce the scale of central government, proclaiming in a memorable phrase that 'government is not the solution to our problem; government is the problem'. Striking the populist chord that had helped get him elected, he said he would govern for everyone, for the 'professionals, industrialists, shopkeepers, clerks, cabbies and truck drivers', to create 'a strong, prosperous America at peace with itself and the world'. He promised that America would have a 'greater strength throughout the world' and would again become 'a beacon of hope for those who do not now have freedom'. It was a simple vision, as though out of a Hollywood movie in which the world was divided between good guys and baddies. And he ended with a tale about a soldier who died on the Western Front in the First World War. On his body it was said that a pledge was found declaring 'I will work. I will save. I will sacrifice. I will endure. I will fight cheerfully and do my utmost as if the issue of the whole struggle depended on me alone.'[1] It was a classic Reagan moment in a classic Reagan speech, heavy on emotional rhetoric, full of optimism, light on substance and detail.

Just forty minutes later, the inauguration was upstaged by an event that moved Americans even more. An Algerian Airways Boeing 727 airliner took off from Tehran airport loaded with the fifty-two hostages who had been held for 444 days. It had been a long and humiliating crisis for America. The outgoing President Jimmy Carter and his team had patiently negotiated the release of these American hostages through Algerian intermediaries and had promised to return frozen Iranian assets to a special account in the Bank of England. But as a final rebuff, the Iranian authorities had kept the hostages waiting at the airport until the inauguration was over. The first announcement made by the newly installed National Security Advisor, Richard Allen, was of their release. And the glory fell to the new President. The sun truly was shining on Ronald Reagan that day.

Reagan had been born in 1911 into a neighbourly Midwestern farming community in Illinois. He grew to maturity in Dixon (pop. 8191) in small-town middle America: a few hundred houses along the banks of the Rock river bounded by dairy farms that spread into open country. Reagan's father, Jack, of Irish Catholic stock, was a shoe salesman with the gift of the gab. He was also an occasional heavy drinker who

David Hume Kennerly/Getty Images

At his inauguration Ronald Reagan was a few weeks off his seventieth birthday but looked energetic and younger than his years.

collapsed unconscious in front of his young son more than once. His mother, Nelle, was of Scottish extraction, and a year before the future President was born she joined an evangelical Christian sect called the Disciples of Christ into which she threw herself heart and soul. The family never owned the houses they lived in and many of Jack's jobs failed, leaving them struggling to make ends meet, although they never descended to soup-kitchen poverty. Nevertheless, Ronald, known as 'Dutch', grew into a tall, handsome and glamorous teenager, quite a star in Dixon in the 1920s, a good sportsman and a budding actor who was blessed with a photographic memory. Despite the hardships of his youth, he had an optimistic outlook, a strong Christian faith, enjoyed watching westerns and loved to tell stories from the adventure books he devoured, usually seeing in them a morality tale in which good always triumphed over evil.

After four years at Eureka College studying economics, he became a sports reporter in the booming world of radio. He had a great skill for vividly describing live sporting events like a baseball game even if he was not present, which was usually the case. Moving to Des Moines, the capital of and biggest city in Iowa, he became a radio celebrity, and this early fame encouraged him to take his next big step. In February 1937 he went to Hollywood. His good looks and relaxed, wholesome character impressed Jack Warner, who offered him a contract at Warner Brothers. He took his new career very seriously and always turned up on set on time and word perfect. Over the next few years he appeared in more than twenty films, few of which made much of an impact and most of which were described as B-movies. They were part of the huge output of the Hollywood studios which with a small army of contracted performers and technicians made movies as if on a factory production line. They were shot in about three weeks, usually ran for no more than an hour, and provided a curtain-raiser for the major 'A' feature. They also gave the studios the opportunity to try out fresh talent and to look for new stars.

In 1940, Reagan began to star in a set of films that took him into the premier league of movie stars.[2] In that same year he married actress Jane Wyman. Despite the fact that Reagan was nearly thirty and Wyman had been married twice before, the fan magazines described them as the Perfect All American Couple – two ordinary kids who had fallen in love. And when the war split them up it all seemed to play into the narrative. But Ronnie did not go off to fight in Europe or the Pacific. Instead he served with the 1st Motion Picture Unit of the Army Air Corps at Culver City, making training films. He returned home most weekends. During the war he also joined the board of the Screen Actors Guild and spent an increasing amount of time working on Guild business.

Until the end of the war, Reagan was a convinced Democrat

and an enthusiastic supporter of President Roosevelt. In 1945 he spoke against the use of the atom bomb and was hostile to the Ku Klux Klan. But in the post-war years Reagan realigned himself politically. The first of the Red Scares hit Hollywood in 1946 and Reagan began to spot communist sympathisers everywhere. He later wrote, 'The Communist Plan for Hollywood was remarkably simple. It was merely to take over the motion picture business ... for a grand worldwide propaganda base. In those days ... American films dominated 95 per cent of the world's movie screens. We had a weekly audience of 500,000,000 souls. Takeover of this enormous plant and its gradual transformation into a Communist gristmill was a grandiose idea.'[3] Elsewhere he wrote, 'Joseph Stalin had set out to make Hollywood an instrument of propaganda for his program of Soviet expansionism aimed at communizing the world.'[4]

The Second World War alliance between the United States, its allies and the Soviet Union fell apart very quickly in those post-war years. Old fears emerged in a new form as it seemed that Stalin sought to seize control of eastern Europe and, in Churchill's famous phrase, an 'Iron Curtain' descended across Europe. In the US, the FBI was the dominant agency in domestic intelligence and under its legendary conservative director J. Edgar Hoover it took the lead role in tracking down what it perceived to be the communist menace. It claimed to have found plots to infiltrate many aspects of American life and government. Hoover gathered a mass of evidence and leaked some of it to sympathetic Congressmen, knowing that it would not stand up in a court of law but that it would help to feed a growing hysteria about a Red Threat to the US. In April 1947 Reagan met FBI agents and gave them a list of names he believed were communists. Later he became an informer for the FBI, codenamed T-10. And in the same year he was elected president of the Screen Actors Guild.

In October 1947, the House Un-American Activities Committee

The Iron Curtain

Western Bloc
Eastern Bloc
Iron Curtain

(HUAC) began to take evidence on the communist threat to Hollywood. In public hearings, Reagan presented a moderate face and claimed that Hollywood in general and the Screen Actors Guild in particular could cope with the issue and purge itself of any communist agents. Behind the scenes he was passing on names to the FBI. Most of the writers, directors and actors subpoenaed to appear before HUAC gave evidence but a small number refused to answer questions about their political affiliations and claimed immunity under the First Amendment. A group of producers, directors and writers known as the Hollywood Ten were cited for contempt of Congress and given prison sentences of six months to a year. When they came out of jail the Hollywood studios refused to employ any of them – the first of several hundred figures who would be blacklisted over the coming years. Some of those listed never worked again. Others fled to Europe to work. Some could only get work by using pseudonyms. Reagan did nothing to help rehabilitate these film-makers and publicly even denied the existence of the blacklists.[5]

All of this was taking place while Reagan himself had to confront some major personal changes. Although he appeared in several movies he had difficulty in finding the parts he wanted to play. A new mood of realism was sweeping Hollywood, whose films were now darker than they had been pre-war. He did not want to appear in the more serious and challenging films of the day, unlike his wife Jane Wyman, who embraced several tough roles and won an Oscar for one performance, as a deaf mute who is raped.[6] Ronnie wanted to play the action adventure hero in pure entertainment movies but he was more often cast as the nice guy who stood up for the just cause. None of his films in these years was a box office success, and one of them has been listed among the fifty worst of all time.[7] In 1948 he and Wyman divorced – she sued him on the grounds of mental cruelty for not taking her views and thoughts seriously. All of this pushed him to take on a more political role. He became well known as an anti-communist crusader and devoted more time to the Screen Actors Guild. When in 1952 he married Nancy Davis, this seemed to encourage the trajectory. She had been an aspiring actress when they met but now devoted herself to supporting her husband and pushing him to be ever more ambitious. It was the part of dutiful and adoring wife that she now wanted to play, and she continued in this role, creating a truly close and loving relationship with her spouse, for the rest of her life.

By 1954 Reagan looked pretty washed up. He had broken his contract with Warner Brothers but had not found the parts he wanted elsewhere. In one notorious and frequently remembered film he was even upstaged by a chimpanzee.[8] He was short of money and his acting career looked as though it was over. Then salvation came in the form of a contract from

General Electric to host a television revue on CBS. In addition, when the show was not broadcasting he was required to
spend sixteen weeks each year making public relations tours
of GE plants across the country. It was a time when the big
corporations spent considerable sums to sell their new products and promote the consumerist American Dream. General
Electric's own slogan was 'Progress is our most important
product'.[9] From 1954 to 1962 Reagan spent the equivalent of
two years on the road visiting 139 GE plants and addressing
a quarter of a million of its employees.[10] The onscreen work
enabled him to become a confident performer in the new
medium of television and one of the most recognised faces in
America. And the talking engagements helped to forge him
into a fine speech-maker. The speeches were usually of a type,
including much corporate praise for GE and its products inter-
spersed with jokes, stories and warnings about the threat from
communism. Each one usually ended with a quip. He also
found that sounding off against the federal bureaucracy was
a good way to get the audience cheering.[11] Reagan was slowly
emerging as a prominent spokesman for the conservative
right wing, deeply imbued with a belief in individualism and
free markets styled as a passionate support for freedom, and
deeply hostile to communism and big government and what
he presented as creeping socialism, especially in the form of
high taxes and health care.

So for eight years GE helped Reagan to hone his skills and
spread his reputation across the country. In the 1964 presidential election he supported the hard-right Republican candidate
Barry Goldwater. But Goldwater was too extreme to win the
mass vote, and after one moving campaign speech by Reagan
many senior Republicans began to ask if the ex-actor would
not have been a better candidate. President Johnson was re-
elected in a landslide and began his Great Society reforms,
almost as significant as FDR's New Deal thirty years before,

although they ran out of steam and money against the backdrop of an escalating war in Vietnam.

Reagan was persuaded by some powerful friends to stand for Governor of California in 1966. Many believed he had little chance in a state where registered Democrats outnumbered Republicans by three to two. But with the help of a PR team, Reagan proved to be a proficient and appealing candidate. He came across well in homely television commercials and cast himself in the populist mould as the 'citizen-politician' who would bring new standards to government. But he was always short on detailed policy. When asked by a journalist what sort of governor he would be, he replied, 'I don't know, I've never played the part of governor.'[12] When his opponent, Democrat Governor Pat Brown, mocked his lack of experience, Reagan responded, 'The man who has the job has more experience than anybody. That's why I'm running.'[13] He won with a majority of just under one million votes.

Reagan's eight years as Governor of California gave him invaluable executive experience. He had a hands-off approach and made it clear that his leadership would rely on Cabinet-style government. He believed in finding good people to run the various departments and that they should formulate detailed policy. He would act like a chairman of the board and set the general direction. On any new subject he asked for a one-page typed summary of the arguments for and against. One member of his team later wrote, 'Reagan was a macro-manager and sometimes no manager at all.'[14] However, he also proved to be no right-wing ideologue but a leader who was willing to compromise. Although having called for a reduction of taxes and a scaling back of government, one of his first actions, in February 1967, was to request nearly one billion dollars in tax increases, the biggest hike in any state taxes at the time. Democrats thought this would undermine his credibility. Reagan answered that he was only solving problems he had inherited from the previous regime. His approval ratings continued to grow.[15]

He stood for a second term, canvassing again like an outsider 'citizen-politician', as though he had not been in charge for the last four years. He won with a majority of about half of what he'd had before. But it was convincing enough, and his second term proved more impressive. He argued that welfare payments had got out of hand, that there was no incentive for the poor to go to work, and asserted that teenage girls got pregnant simply to claim benefits. Then he negotiated a complex welfare bill that simultaneously gave more to the needy while bringing in anti-fraud controls and tightening rules of eligibility. The California welfare budget started to come down and the bill proved a model for many other states over the coming years. And Reagan kept the Californian Republicans united through eight tumultuous years.

By 1974 he had had enough of the role of governor and stood aside, probably with an eye to the presidential race two years later when Nixon would have completed his eight-year term. But Nixon resigned as a consequence of the Watergate scandal before almost certain impeachment, and Vice President Gerald Ford took over. Despite being up against an incumbent, Reagan stood against Ford in the 1976 Republican primaries, coming a close second. But then in the presidential election Ford was defeated by the Democrat candidate Jimmy Carter from Georgia. Reagan now looked favourite for the Republican nomination in 1980, but would America vote for the Grand Old Party that Nixon had discredited? Maybe the Democrats would be in power for eight years, or more?

The flow of events drifted in Reagan's favour over the next few years. Inflation grew while the economy stagnated with unemployment at 7 per cent by 1980 – a new formulation called 'stagflation' that seemed to go against the grain of post-war economic orthodoxies. Worse still, America seemed to be losing the Cold War. After the humiliation of withdrawal from Vietnam, that country along with neighbouring Cambodia and Laos fell to the communists. In Africa, Cuban-backed guerrillas had appeared in growing numbers and Angola and Mozambique fell to Soviet-backed regimes. Moscow further expanded its influence in Central America with the victory of the Sandinistas in Nicaragua. Most humiliating was the loss of the Shah of Iran, a long-term friend of America. For twenty-five years the Shah had led a process of Westernisation in Iran, and in return for major concessions to British and American oil companies received substantial oil revenues. But opposition to his corrupt regime led to his abdication in January 1979 and his replacement by the fundamentalist Islamic cleric Ayatollah Khomeini. The new, strict Islamic republic reversed the process of Westernisation and its leaders denounced the 'Great Satan' of America. The greatest insult of all came in November 1979 when militant students seized US embassy personnel in Tehran and took them hostage. An unsuccessful rescue attempt by the military resulted in an accident when a US helicopter crashed into a refuelling aircraft in the desert. It was the ultimate blow. President Carter not only looked weak but as commander-in-chief was blamed for the disaster. All of this gave Reagan an easy opportunity to beat the drum for a revival of American superpower military might.

The Committee on the Present Danger (CPD), a think-tank formed of established conservatives and ex-liberals, tried to alert America to what they perceived as a growing Soviet threat. They opposed the Cold War policy of détente that had brought the US and the Soviets closer in a series of cultural and political events culminating in the signing of the Helsinki Accords in 1975. But in the late seventies the Soviets began to introduce a new generation of SS-20 intermediate missiles and appeared to be going on the offensive in the Third World, supporting a variety of national liberation struggles. The CPD presented the Soviet Union as taking advantage of the US while its guard was down. In its publications it warned of a Soviet 'drive for dominance' and a desire for a 'Communist world order' for which it had undertaken an 'unparalleled military build-up'. It predicted that 'within several years [the Soviets will] achieve strategic superiority over the United States'. Moreover it warned that the Soviets had a different philosophy to the US and that the 'Soviet nuclear offensive and defensive forces are designed to enable the USSR to fight, survive and win a nuclear war'.[16] This claim was based on flimsy evidence of the existence of a Russian civil defence programme with plans to evacuate cities in the event of a nuclear exchange. But it helped to persuade many that the Soviets were limbering up for a fight. The CPD lobbied hard against the second round of Strategic Arms Limitation Talks (SALT II) saying that it was simply a way of appeasing the Soviets. CPD speakers crossed America and toured the television studios to sound the alarm.

In 1979, Reagan joined the executive board of the CPD. He admitted he was not well informed on issues of national security and the CPD influenced many aspects of his developing policy. In his speeches, Reagan picked up several CPD themes and began to warn about increased Soviet military spending. He claimed they had spent $240 billion more than the US on defence during the 1970s. He predicted the 1980s would be 'one of the most dangerous decades in Western civilisation'. He spoke of the Soviets threatening Iran, the Middle East and East Asia. When on Christmas Day 1979 the Soviets invaded Afghanistan, they played into his hands. Carter announced a series of trade sanctions, abandoned SALT II and launched a boycott of the Moscow Olympics the following summer. But once again he looked weak. Reagan's solution was to spend whatever was needed to match the Soviet build-up so the US could once again argue from a position of strength. In many election rallies he repeated the remark 'We are in an arms race, but only one side is racing.'[17] It all sounded very persuasive. Reagan now presented himself as a prominent Cold War warrior. And he seemed to offer a way to make America strong again after nearly a decade of retrenchment following defeat in Vietnam.

Reagan's principal opponent in the Republican primaries in 1980 was former CIA director and envoy to China George H. W. Bush. He accused Reagan of 'voodoo economics' in following the monetarism of Milton Friedman and calling for massive tax cuts. But when Bush was defeated at the party convention in Detroit, both men put previous hostilities aside and Bush joined Reagan as his vice-presidential running mate. The dream ticket helped deliver Texas to the Republicans and bring some foreign policy experience to the table. Uniting most parts of the GOP with the Christian evangelical right, Reagan now chose to fight the 1980 election on the issue of personality and leadership rather than on ideology. The White House, on the other hand, chose to paint Reagan as an ill-informed, empty-headed extremist. But they failed to notice that he had captured the mood of the country. Polls swung one way and then another, but when election day came Reagan won with 51 per cent of the votes cast; Carter took 41 per cent, and independents took the rest. Only half the electorate voted, but Reagan had won convincingly, especially in the south and west where new industries from defence to electronics prospered. Moreover, the Republicans won a majority in the Senate for the first time since 1954 and increased their standing in the House of Representatives.

Very much like Donald Trump on his arrival at the White House three and a half decades later, Reagan presented himself as an outsider coming in to shake up Washington. Across Defense, State, Intelligence and National Security as well as in the Treasury and many other federal departments, the newcomers swept away old ideologies and brought in new political ideas. As one Washington insider put it, 'For the first time in decades, an incoming President orchestrated a comprehensive battle plan to seize control of a city long believed to be in enemy hands ... between November and January [the transition team] deployed their forces for a political blitzkrieg.'[18] Alexander Haig, a former four-star general, NATO boss and Chief of Staff to Richard Nixon, was nominated for Secretary of State. Caspar Weinberger, who had worked with Reagan in California, was nominated as Secretary of Defense although he had no background in the defence business. James Baker, who had run Bush's primary campaign and who knew his way around the corridors of Washington, joined as Chief of Staff. His deputy was Reagan's long-standing adviser and PR guru Michael Deaver. The additional role Deaver had played since the days of the governorship of California was as a link to Nancy, who was close to her husband in all things and very protective of his interests. Deaver would speak regularly on the phone with the First Lady if she was not happy, sometimes up to a dozen times a day.[19] If Nancy did not think Ronnie was getting good advice or if an aide was slipping up, she would make her opinions felt via Deaver. One official who later became a key player in the administration wrote that over the years Deaver 'evolved into a faithful family retainer'.[20] Edwin Meese, another aide who had been with Reagan since 1967, joined the central White House team. Richard Allen, a prominent member of the CPD, was made National Security Advisor. Fifty members of the committee were given senior positions in the new administration. The Reagan team all shared the same broad objectives.

With everything in place, Reagan stepped out on to the western steps of the Capitol on 20 January 1981 to play the biggest role in his life. He was only a couple of weeks off his seventieth birthday and the oldest President ever at inauguration.[21] But he was lean and fit, and at six foot one he was still handsome, his hair black not grey and his face still bright not wrinkled. He looked the picture of health, and Americans like their leaders to look good. He had an unquenchable optimism too, along with an alluring smile and an attractive laugh. He had spent decades learning the part, years of travelling the country giving speeches, learning how to amuse but also to move an audience, and most importantly to express the mood of the crowd and to lead them where they might not even have known they wanted to go. He could also make people smile or laugh and was always ready with a quip from a vast supply of tales he seemed to be able to call upon. He had seamlessly moved through the media of the twentieth century, first making his name in radio, then going on to be a film star, and finally learning skilfully to use the art of television. Politically, he had begun as a liberal and a Democrat but for thirty-five years had been moving steadily to the right. He had helped the Republican party revive as a force that brought conservatives with many different outlooks together. He had learned to compromise in power and knew how to negotiate a deal. He was still a divisive figure in that many people thought him a fool with a simplistic world view, nothing better than an actor who read other people's lines. But he was now on the biggest stage and his performance would help to change the world.

Another transition was to take place the following year in very different circumstances, nearly 5000 miles from Washington on the other side of the Cold War divide.

2

Andropov

In the early hours of 10 November 1982, Leonid Ilyich Brezhnev, the seventy-five-year-old General Secretary of the Communist Party of the Soviet Union, died in his sleep. Nobody was surprised as he had been in ill health for many years and had grown visibly weaker over recent months. In line with custom, by the time the Politburo met ten hours later, a decision had already been made on his successor. Konstantin Chernenko had been Brezhnev's favourite and his choice, but the elderly clique who ruled the vast and powerful Soviet Union were not having it. Most of them regarded Chernenko as little more than a loyal courtier and spineless protégé of the deceased ruler. Marshal Dmitri Ustinov, the Defence Minister, was one of the most powerful figures in the Politburo. A stocky, tough-looking man who wore gold-rimmed spectacles and often displayed a chest full of medal ribbons, Ustinov had worked for Stalin during the war. He had built up the Soviet strategic bombing force and their intercontinental ballistic missile system from the 1960s. He had been Defence Minister for six years and had striven to ensure that the vast Soviet military machine had an overwhelming superiority of guns, tanks, rifles and other conventional weapons. Ustinov wanted a stronger ruler, someone who would reverse the disastrous trends of the last few years. He went for Yuri Vladimirovich Andropov, for fifteen years the head of the Committee for State Security, the KGB (Komitet Gosudarstvennoy Bezopasnosti), the chief secret policeman of the Soviet Union. When the twenty-one members of the Politburo met that afternoon, it had already been agreed that Andropov would take charge of the funeral arrangements, a key appointment. After just a few minutes it was Chernenko himself who nominated Andropov as General Secretary, and following this the other members agreed one by one. Andropov was unanimously acclaimed as the new leader. The Soviet people had not been consulted at any point during the transition and even the announcement of Brezhnev's death was not made public until after the Politburo had met and settled the succession.[1]

Andropov now found himself one of the most powerful men in the world. Unlike a US President, his term of office was not confined to a set number of years. Many Soviet leaders, like Stalin and Brezhnev, ruled until they died (all leaders of the Soviet Union were of course men, and there were very few women in senior positions within the Kremlin). Additionally, no Soviet leader was ever elected by the people. Power was passed from hand to hand within the tiny group who regarded themselves as heirs to Lenin's Great Socialist Revolution. Moreover, the head of state in the Soviet Union did not rule according to any sort of legal separation of powers. His authority was not limited by the judiciary nor balanced out with an elected legislature. Nor did he have to respond to the vagaries of public opinion. He was an absolute ruler. His writ had the full force of law behind it and would always be rubber-stamped by the Supreme Soviet – the USSR's version of a Parliament. In a one-party state all its members belonged to the same family and owed their allegiance to the General Secretary.

Yuri Andropov succeeded to the Kremlin leadership when he was
sixty-eight, but he was not as healthy as the photos made him look.

Stalin had demonstrated that he had power over life and death while presiding over an era known as the Great Terror: he personally signed authorisations leading to the deaths of hundreds of thousands of Soviet citizens. Indeed, in pure numbers, Stalin was a greater mass murderer than Adolf Hitler.[2] Soviet heads of state still held supreme power, even if by the early 1980s the days of the mass shooting of opponents in the back of the head were long gone. Every leader shared the same Marxist-Leninist outlook, an adaptation of nineteenth-century Marxist philosophy with twentieth-century Russian Leninism. This orthodoxy believed in the central role of the Communist Party and the supreme rule of the centralised state over all aspects of the political and economic life of the nation. Communist Party rhetoric spoke about ruling on behalf of the people, or the proletariat, but the people had no say over who would rule them and power in the nation was held by a self-perpetuating elite. Communism emphasised collective ownership in society and guaranteed full employment, free education and health care but gave no importance to individual human rights. Also central to the communist ethic was a belief in class-based confrontation and the need for continuous struggle with enemies either internal or external. By the 1980s this had come to be interpreted as a belief in the ultimate victory of the global communist revolution. But despite sharing the same general political beliefs, each leader defined his own era and imposed his own personality on his years in power. More than anything, the last decade of Brezhnev's rule had become one of dreadful economic torpor and lack of change. Brezhnev believed he could achieve all he wanted without change and had accepted stagnation as a form of stability. The world waited to see what Andropov's rule would bring.

In the 1970s and 1980s, Western observers of events behind the closed doors of the Politburo and the Central Committee of the Communist Party of the Soviet Union were known as Kremlinologists. They tried hard to figure out who was on his way up and who was on his way down in the secretive world of the Soviet hierarchy. The Kremlinologists were out in force at Brezhnev's funeral. The dignitaries at the funeral included Vice President George Bush and Secretary of State George Shultz, West Germany's President Karl Carstens, French Prime Minister Pierre Mauroy and British Foreign Secretary Francis Pym along with four princes, thirty-two heads of state and thirteen other foreign ministers. They all waited in line eager to shake the hand of the new Soviet leader. When a side door opened in the grand hall of the Kremlin many experts were expecting to see Chernenko emerge, but to their surprise a pale, stooping, elderly man in heavy glasses stepped forward. He appeared rather like an old-fashioned academic dressed in an ill-fitting shirt and tie, looking awkward and hesitant. This was only the first of many surprises.

At sixty-eight, Andropov was the oldest person ever to take charge in the Soviet Union, but a few years younger than his opposite number in the White House. Remarkably little was known about him in the West. Despite his role as head of the espionage and counter-espionage activities of the Soviet Union, he had rarely met with Western leaders and had kept a low international profile. Western intelligence agencies had extraordinarily little hard information about him. The CIA, for instance, were not even sure if his wife was still alive as she had not been seen at public functions for several years. His views on key aspects of Soviet policy were totally unknown. It was thought, entirely wrongly as it turned out, that he loved reading Western spy thrillers and spent much of his time at home listening to jazz. However, most of those who were granted an audience found that their first impressions of the rather shambling new Soviet leader were entirely misleading. Vice President Bush had a half-hour talk with him and later told the press that he found him 'self-confident, firmly in command, clear about policy positions, and quick and concise in making points'.[3] The West German President and his officials spent ninety minutes talking with Andropov the following day and were astonished at the contrast with Brezhnev. The old Soviet leader would spend ages slowly reading out a prepared statement that was patiently translated by his interpreter paragraph by paragraph. And when it came to answering questions, Brezhnev would defer to Andrei Gromyko, his Foreign Minister. A meeting with Brezhnev had become rather 'sad and embarrassing'. But Andropov was quite different. He spoke eagerly and with some passion, reacted quickly, and often started speaking again before his interpreter had finished.[4] The West Germans reported that a new broom was sweeping through the Kremlin.

Despite the scandalous lack of information about him in the West, Andropov had lived a full and remarkable life. He was born in 1914 into what could be called small-town Caucasus life. His father, Vladimir, worked on the railway at a tiny station on the line from Moscow to Baku on the Caspian Sea. His mother, Yevgenia, was the adopted daughter of a Moscow watchmaker. While he was growing up, the region known as Stavropol, in the basin of the Volga river, was going through the process of forced collectivisation of farming. It was a troubled time and would become even more so in the 1930s when Stalin began a policy of persecuting and imprisoning the richer peasants, or kulaks, who were seen as disloyal to the Leninist revolution. Millions would die as a result of the persecutions and the famine that followed. At sixteen, Andropov joined the Young Communist League, the Komsomol. This was not something done lightly or for career advantage. It clearly indicated that the teenage Andropov was an activist and a keen supporter of the communist system at a time of violence and deep division in the area in which he lived.

Andropov's parents died when he was in his teens and he moved away to the bigger industrial cities along the Volga, where he worked in a variety of jobs including telegraph clerk, cinema projectionist, and on the steamships that sailed up the river. He graduated from Rybinsk Technical College in 1936 and was secretary of the Komsomol at the college. He must have impressed because he went on to become organiser of the Komsomol Central Committee at the local shipyards, and in 1938 the First Secretary of the regional Komsomol committee. This was the time of the Five Year Plans that saw the Soviet Union dramatically turn in little more than a decade from a rural economy into an industrial powerhouse. To do this, workers without sufficient food and housing were forced to meet ever-increasing production targets. To these local pressures that at times were met by violent resistance were added immense political pressures from the centre. Stalin launched a major purge of the Communist Party that spread into the ranks of doctors, scientists, writers and intellectuals and finally the Red Army in a period generically known as the Great Terror. Millions of party members, senior military men and prominent figures who were classed as 'enemies of the people' perished in the purges or were sent to rot in freezing Siberian labour camps. Throughout these tumultuous times across the Soviet Union, Andropov remained a loyal and hard-working communist activist.

In May 1940, the party sent the twenty-five-year-old Andropov north to the newly created Karelian Soviet Socialist Republic. Here he met and married his wife, Tanya. The Soviet Union had just ended a short but bloody war with Finland known as the 'Winter War'. Stalin had been concerned with protecting Leningrad, only twenty miles from the Finnish border. He had demanded more territory and the Finns had resisted. When Stalin invaded they succeeded in holding up the Soviet advance for some months, revealing major short-comings in the Red Army. The creation of a new Karelian Republic following Moscow's final victory incorporated territory captured from Finland, and Andropov was made First Secretary of the Komsomol, an important and senior figure in the region.

In June 1941, three million German troops marched into the Soviet Union in the largest military invasion in history. Hitler spoke of his 'crusade' against Bolshevism. He called the Soviet state a 'rotten structure' that when kicked in would come 'crashing down'. The Karelian region was soon swept up in the war as the Finns (now allies of the Germans) sought to recover some of the territory they had lost. Across the Soviet Union superhuman efforts were made to resist the invading forces. In Karelia these involved building a new railway line in record time along the White Sea to the port of Murmansk and then sending partisan groups to operate in the forests and marshes behind enemy lines. Andropov's Komsomol was deeply involved in both ventures. Although Andropov did not fight with the partisans himself, he found or selected several thousand young communists to train in sabotage techniques. They were sent behind enemy lines after the Soviet regional capital, Petrozavodsk, fell to Finnish troops. The Komsomol also provided thousands of young workers for factories and timber yards. Men and women were called upon to work long, exhausting hours and to make Herculean efforts as the Soviet Union faced disastrous losses in 1941 and 1942. Andropov's work in swiftly and efficiently mobilising and encouraging young Komsomol members was clearly noted by the party grandees, who towards the end of the war appointed him the senior party official in the region, promoting him from the Komsomol to the main Communist Party structure.

At the end of the war, the Soviet Union lay in ruins. About 27 million soldiers and civilians had died in the struggle with Nazism. The devastation was enormous. Some 32,000 factories had been destroyed. As the German Army retreated it smashed everything in its wake including 65,000 kilometres of railway tracks, 70,000 villages and hamlets and about 100,000 collective farms. One third of the USSR's pre-war wealth had been destroyed.[5] The post-war challenge in terms of rebuilding the country was immense. But the centralised Soviet state soon got to work. The problems of Karelia were by no means the worst the nation had to face but they were still substantial. The old wooden buildings of the city of Petrozavodsk lay in ashes. Factories had to be rebuilt. Huge numbers of people needed repatriating. And in the paranoid world of the Stalinist state, security was a central problem, ensuring that all those who might have sympathised with the enemy were sought out and persecuted. Andropov played a leading role in the task of Karelian reconstruction and in January 1947, at the age of thirty-two, he became Second Secretary in the regional party hierarchy.

Andropov narrowly survived a purge of Karelian party officials in 1950 and the following year was transferred to Moscow on the specific order of the Central Committee of the party. Through his work in Karelia, some influential backers in the Kremlin had clearly picked him out as a rising star. After two years in Moscow his career took a new turn when he was transferred to the Ministry of Foreign Affairs, with specific responsibility for Moscow's relations with the countries of eastern Europe. In 1954 he was sent to Budapest as Soviet ambassador to Hungary. His time there included what was to be a critical moment for that country's future.

Stalin's death in 1953 marked a new era for the Soviet Union and its allies. Initially it looked as though control from Moscow was going to be eased up. Sensing that reform was in the air, East German workers came out on the streets to demonstrate and there were strikes in Czechoslovakia and Hungary. But the authoritarian communist regimes of eastern Europe soon restored order. In Moscow, a new set of leaders headed up by Nikita Khrushchev took power in the Kremlin, offering what seemed to be a new openness. The process of reform took a remarkable turn when in a late-night speech to the Party Congress in February 1956, Khrushchev denounced Stalin as a 'flawed leader' who was responsible for dreadful crimes and a reign of terror. It was like taking the lid off a boiling cauldron. For the people of eastern Europe at last there seemed to be an opportunity for change. In June 1956, workers in Poland began to demonstrate against working conditions and this soon turned into opposition to the state itself. Dozens of demonstrators were killed and hundreds wounded in a showdown with police. A new leader was installed, Wladyslaw Gomulka, whom it was hoped was well regarded enough to unite the nation. But popular expectations of change continued to grow. Eventually, Khrushchev himself flew to Warsaw and threatened to bring in Soviet troops to restore order. A modus vivendi was agreed. Some reforms would be allowed but Gomulka promised to be a good ally and supporter of the Warsaw Pact.

An even bigger demonstration of people power came a few months later in Hungary. Street protests again escalated into full-scale opposition to the state. The Hungarian leader called on the Soviet ambassador, Andropov, to help and he arranged for 30,000 Soviet troops to surround Budapest and restore order. But the violent confrontations that ensued only provoked the Hungarian people. As in Poland, a new leader was sought whom it was hoped would calm the situation. His name was Imre Nagy. But he stirred up the mix further, resulting in a major uprising against Soviet rule. Once again, in early November, Soviet troops, this time with tanks, were sent in. A bloody battle followed for several weeks on the streets of Budapest. Hundreds of Russian soldiers and thousands of Hungarian protesters were killed. The centre of the city was devastated. The Hungarians looked to the West for military support. President Eisenhower and his advisers, at the climax of a presidential election campaign, knew that realistically they could do nothing and Hungary was abandoned to its fate.

Andropov, as Soviet ambassador, played a central role throughout the crisis. He decided to shift allegiance to a new communist leader, János Kádár. With Soviet backing, Kádár slowly restored order. Tens of thousands of those who had taken part in the uprising were rounded up and 300 were executed, including Nagy, who was tricked out of his hiding place and arrested by the KGB almost certainly with Andropov's connivance. Despite Khrushchev's criticism of Stalin, nothing much seemed to have changed: the new Soviet leader had been quite willing to use force to suppress rebellious allies. Throughout one of the most severe crises in the post-war Eastern bloc, Andropov had ensured Moscow fully understood what was happening in Budapest and provided advice on which way the Kremlin should turn. For weeks he only ever left the embassy in an armoured car, but Andropov had shown that he could be cool in a crisis. A colleague said of him, 'He was so calm – even while bullets were flying, when everyone else at the embassy felt like we were in a besieged fortress.'[6] In addition, and most importantly to Moscow, Andropov had shown he would be supremely loyal in pursuing the interests of the Soviet state.[7]

But the uprising in Hungary left a profound impression on Andropov himself. He developed what was later called a 'Hungarian complex'. Looking out the window of his embassy he had been horrified to see officers from the Hungarian secret service being strung up from lampposts by the rebels. The events of 1956 left Andropov for the rest of his life with a sense of paranoia, haunted by the speed with which an apparently stable communist one-party society could collapse.[8]

A year after the Budapest uprising, Andropov returned to Moscow where he was picked out for further advancement. He was promoted to become a member of the Central Committee and was appointed head of a new international department whose duty was to coordinate relations with socialist countries not only in eastern Europe but in Asia as well, including North Korea and China. For ten years Andropov worked on this, helping to bring Yugoslavia back into the socialist fold and managing relations with Mao Zedong's China, which had sunk to a low point because of a fundamental difference between the two countries over the role of revolutionary communism in world affairs. The Soviet leaders were increasingly coming to believe that in the nuclear age the road to socialism did not necessarily have to come through war with the imperialists. To the Chinese this was crossing a vital line. Mao was committed to global revolution through violence if necessary and felt that Moscow was going soft.

Andropov travelled widely during these years, to Beijing, Belgrade, Bucharest, East Berlin and Hanoi. But he never left the socialist bloc or visited the West. Although now part of the senior party elite, he was very much second in command to Mikhail Suslov, First Secretary of the International Department, a key party ideologue. And of course also to the maverick Khrushchev, who liked to lead foreign affairs from the front, often deciding on initiatives without consulting his colleagues. These were momentous years in the Cold War that saw a growing split between Moscow and Beijing, the building of the Wall to divide Berlin, the test explosion of a new generation of thermonuclear weapons, and the Cuban missile crisis. Throughout these years Andropov took a moderate position, arguing against a complete falling out with China and in favour of modest reforms in the client states. But he was no liberal, and Khrushchev's fall in 1964 did not deflect his progress up the political ladder. He stayed loyal to the conventional orthodoxy of Marxism-Leninism, writing a series of articles for party publications with such catchy titles as 'Leninism Lights Our Way', 'Friendship of the Soviet Peoples: The Inexhaustible Source of Our Victories' and 'Proletarian Internationalism: The Communists' Battle Banner.'[9]

In May 1967 Andropov was appointed head of the KGB, and the following month he became a non-voting member of the Politburo. This move was part of the manoeuvrings that followed the removal of Khrushchev. Emerging as the new Soviet leader, Brezhnev wanted to replace the previous head of the KGB, a Khrushchev appointee, and put his own man in post. And making Andropov part of the central decision-making body helped to ensure that the KGB would be firmly linked to the party structure and not a separate empire within the state. The KGB was a huge organisation with perhaps half a million employees. It controlled the Soviet Union's spying and intelligence operations abroad. Every Soviet embassy included a KGB resident and often a sizeable staff. Its uniformed officials ran the country's immense border. The KGB also oversaw the biggest domestic security operation in the world with a huge network of paid agents supported by even more part-time informers. Its role was to keep a watch on party members at home and abroad and to spy on the activities of ordinary people. Every factory, almost every workplace, had its own KGB office from which officials kept an eye on citizens across the Soviet Union.

By the 1960s the physical terror associated with Stalin's era had gone. No longer were the 'enemies of the people' rounded up in the middle of the night, tortured in the Lubyanka and then shot with a single bullet in the back of the head. Even most of the labour camps that had once dotted the Arctic littoral, where millions more died from starvation and hypothermia, had been closed down. Andropov was not the first KGB head who saw his role more as a sort of spiritual or ideological guardian of the purity of the nation. This still meant that people were arrested, interrogated, imprisoned, could lose their job or be exiled from their family. Others who refused to recant were sent to psychiatric hospitals and treated as though insane. But killings were rare, except for spies, who would be put on trial and executed. During his leadership of the KGB Andropov brought in academic researchers to study trends and changes in attitude. But he was also strict on maintaining party discipline. In the collectivist state there was no respect for individual human rights. If a citizen failed to follow his expected duty he or she would still be harried and pursued. 'Dangerous citizens' were subject to permanent surveillance and possible deportation. No appeal was possible.

One of the first things Andropov did at the KGB was to study some of the files from the archives. From these meticulous records he got an idea of the terrible beatings, torture and killings that had taken place in secret. He was particularly interested in the case of the anti-Jewish purges of 1951–2 during which dozens of prominent Jews had been arrested and shot on Stalin's orders.[10] It's not clear what his feelings were about the details he discovered. He had himself lived through tumultuous times so he was probably not surprised by what he read. But he would have been barely human not to have been stunned by the scale of the horrors.

After only a year at the KGB, in 1968 he was faced with the events of the Prague Spring. Alexander Dubček was leader of the Slovak communist party who proposed a series of democratic reforms in Czechoslovakia. He eased censorship, pledged economic and political reforms and promised 'socialism with a human face'. Andropov, obsessed with the ghosts of 1956, saw evidence of Western plots everywhere. He feared Dubček would pull out of the Warsaw Pact, dismantle the internal security system and evict the KGB. He urged the Politburo to take a hard line on the reformers. In August, Moscow sent in Russian tanks and soldiers, as in Budapest twelve years before. There was no popular uprising as there had been in Hungary and order was soon restored. Czechoslovakia remained within the communist camp. But it painted a dreadful picture of the Soviet Union as once again suppressing the hopes and ambitions of its satellite peoples.

In 1973, Andropov was elected a full member of the Politburo. He joined the top elite at a time when the small group leading the Soviet Union was growing older and older. Men who had been in power for twenty or thirty years, who had few new ideas but were happy with the privileges that power brought them and their families, continued to govern. A long period of economic and political stagnation followed. Party Congresses saw no real debate about future policy, just the orchestrated clapping of senior figures by the massed ranks of local party secretaries. As the average age of Politburo members hit seventy, witty comments abounded. Before the Party Congress in 1981, a joke went around. 'How will the Party Congress be opened?' Answer: 'The delegates will be asked to stand while the members of the Politburo are carried in.'[11]

Andropov had a fine intellect and a powerful analytical mind. He read an enormous amount and owned a large library of books. He worked prodigiously hard. Literally tens of thousands of reports crossed his desk. He became very much an office-bound head of the security apparatus. He rarely travelled outside Moscow. Although he loved his family, his two children and grandchildren, he had precious little time to spend with them. Only very occasionally did he meet foreigners from outside the socialist bloc. He never gave interviews to the international press or appeared on television. He seemed happy with the image of the grey bureaucrat. But he transformed the international division of the KGB, stepping up spying activities on military and technical sites in western Europe and the United States to an extraordinary new level. A special section within the KGB was created to acquire information about Western computer technology. And he kept up the relentless pressure on dissidents such as author Alexander Solzhenitsyn and nuclear physicist Andrei Sakharov.

The third basket of the Helsinki Accords had called for the Soviet Union to respect the basic human rights of its citizens. A group of internationally known scientists and writers formed the Helsinki Monitoring Group to follow Soviet adherence to the Accords. These brave individuals, many of them taking advantage of their privileged status as highly respected scientists, hoped to expose internal human rights abuses to international opinion. They had no intention to confront the state, and certainly not to overthrow it. They held press conferences and occasional vigils. These attracted a lot of attention from Western reporters and television correspondents and created a bad press for the Soviet Union in the West. During 1978 Andropov ordered a clampdown, and several leading activists were put on trial. The courts handed down a string of punishments based on evidence supplied by the KGB. Yuri Arlov, a human rights activist, was sentenced to seven years' imprisonment. Anatoly Sharansky was convicted of treason and anti-Soviet activities and was sentenced to thirteen years. Anatoly Filatov was found guilty of spying for the CIA and was executed as a traitor. This was a far cry from the Great Terror of the 1930s but it was still enough to inflame opinion abroad and to prompt groups like the Committee on the Present Danger to denounce the entire Soviet state.

When the Moscow Olympics opened in July 1980, despite the US-led boycott eighty countries including Great Britain still attended the Games. It was the first time they had been held in the socialist bloc and, apart from the chance for the Soviet Union to show off on a global stage, it was a tremendous opportunity for young Russians to witness a great spectacle of world sport and perhaps even for sporting groups to meet young people from other countries. However, in the months before the Games Andropov's paranoia once again came to the fore. He deluged the Central Committee with warnings about 'impending ideological sabotage' brought about by having so many foreigners roaming around Moscow. He predicted 'possible terrorist acts' by foreign visitors and 'exceptional activity by Western secret services' under the cover of Olympic delegations. All of this was presented as a great threat to honest Soviet citizens.[12] As a consequence, tens of thousands of young Russian schoolchildren were evacuated from Moscow for the period of the Games to ensure they were not contaminated by foreigners, thereby missing out on the chance of a lifetime to be part of a great sporting and social celebration.

For fifteen years Andropov sat at the top of the organisation that spied on his own people and conducted extensive espionage operations abroad. But he was sufficiently clear-minded to realise that the Soviet Union was suffering from many inherent deficiencies. The economy was desperately held back by chronic low productivity. Both industrial and agrarian production needed substantial reform. Andropov picked out and promoted young men like Mikhail Gorbachev who had a clear vision of some of the changes that were needed. But Andropov himself would never be the man to bring about radical change. His thinking was still dominated by the core tenets of Marxist-Leninist belief. Whenever reform was needed, he would call for greater discipline within the party. No matter how frustrated he grew with the economic stagnation under Brezhnev, whenever a crossroads was approached he always chose the path of orthodoxy.

Such was the man who in November 1982 succeeded to the Kremlin throne.

3

Reagan Rearms

From the start of the Reagan presidency there were contradictions. Reagan talked tough in public speeches about the Soviet Union, but in private he sent friendly, personal, handwritten letters to the Soviet leaders. In public, he advocated a military build-up and called for confrontation with the USSR; in private, with his closest colleagues, he not only discussed the possibility of reducing the vast stockpile of nuclear weapons that had been accumulated by the superpowers, he even floated the idea of abolishing them altogether. It might seem that this epitomised a deeply divided White House and a President who did not know where he was going: the policy was always that of the last adviser who had left the room. In fact these contradictions were all part of Reagan's personality and outlook. There was no conflict in his mind between saying one thing for public consumption but hinting in private at an alternative route along which policy could develop. But there is no doubt that for the first two years of his presidency the confrontation 'school' that was heavily backed by the Committee on the Present Danger won out. Reagan believed the Soviet Union operated on different ethical principles to those of the democratic West, led by an ideology that called for global revolution and communist domination, and that any means justified these ends. He alleged that was why the Soviets were encouraging nationalist groups around the world in liberation struggles, often against American- or Western-backed regimes. He believed that arms reduction talks were a fraud that had allowed the Soviets to forge ahead while the West cut back on its armaments. He was persuaded that the Soviets were using détente as a cloak behind which they were building up the biggest strategic military superiority in history. But he was also convinced that the Soviet Union was a failed system that could no longer afford to win the arms race or bring military victory to conflicts like that in Afghanistan. He wanted to make clear to the Soviets that they had to change their ways, but he believed he could only do this from a position of strength, and that under his predecessors the United States had grown weak and vulnerable. This had to change.

From the first days of his presidency, Reagan accelerated the military build-up that had begun in the last year of the Carter administration. He inherited a defence budget of $183 billion for the fiscal year 1981–2 and proposed to double this to $368 billion by 1986 – almost one third of federal expenditure, or 6 per cent of GDP. He planned for total defence spending from 1982 to 1989 to increase to $2.7 trillion.[1] This amounted to the biggest peacetime build-up of military spending in American history. Just two days after the inauguration, in his first major policy statement, Defense Secretary Caspar Weinberger said his mission was to 'rearm America'.[2] Almost everything the Pentagon asked for, it got. The programme to build the B-1 bomber had been on the drawing board since the 1960s but was abandoned by Carter. A new version of this aircraft was given the go-ahead by the Reagan administration. The B1-B was a low-level penetration bomber that had many new stealthy features to reduce its radar cross-section to one-tenth that of the B-52 bomber, the US Air Force workhorse. One hundred of these new planes were ordered. In addition a new generation of ground-launched Cruise and Pershing II missiles were planned, all of which could carry nuclear warheads. In a plan inherited from Carter, many of these, including 108 Pershing and 464 Tomahawk Cruise missiles, were to be stationed in Europe. The Pershing II was the American answer to the Soviet SS-20s that had been located in eastern Europe and western Russia in the late 1970s. It had a range of nearly 1600 kilometres (1000 miles) and could hit a target with 45 metres of accuracy. The low-flying and highly manoeuvrable Cruise missile could be fired from land in Europe or from the sea or the air, and had an accuracy of 30 metres over a range of 2400 kilometres (1500 miles). Reagan also called for the development of a new 100-ton ICBM heavyweight known as the MX 'Missile Experimental'. However, this was one initiative that the administration struggled to get through Congress for several years, partly because of its cost, partly because of disagreements as to where it should be located, and partly due to environmental objections to transporting it around the US.[3]

A great deal of other new military technology came in during the early 1980s. Much of this was already in the pipeline but it was the Reagan administration that took the glory for its deployment. The M-1 Abrams Main Battle Tank, powered by a gas turbine engine, combined heavy defensive armour with speed. Thermal imaging and laser range-finding made its armaments accurate and deadly. Its rollout was intended to reverse the overwhelming superiority of the Warsaw Pact countries in terms of conventional battlefield armour in Europe. The twin-engine F/A-18 Hornet jet was both a supersonic fighter and a bomber. It incorporated a dazzling array of new computer guidance and targeting systems, some of which were reflected on to the cockpit glass in front of the pilot's eyes. Borrowing some of the technology of the B-1,

Lockheed developed in total secrecy another stealth bomber that was almost entirely invisible to radar. So complex was the technology required to design and build such a machine that research and development alone cost $6 billion, some of which was directed through the ultra-secret so-called Black Program. None of this research was published in academic journals and very few people even within Lockheed or the Pentagon knew much about it. Congress was not told on what the funds were being spent. When it became operational in 1982, the aircraft was allocated to an entirely new air base built in the Nevada desert and only flew at night. It was named the F-117 Nighthawk. When the public finally got to see the machine some years later it appeared so futuristic that it was described as looking like a flying version of Darth Vader.

The US Navy too saw huge growth during the Reagan presidency, with an increase from 479 to 610 vessels that were organised around fifteen mighty task groups. Each group included new Ohio-class submarines carrying twenty-four Trident missiles and was headed by a giant Nimitz-class aircraft carrier with a crew of more than 3000 that provided a full range of warfare capabilities including early warning, air defence, attack, anti-submarine operations, reconnaissance and electronic warfare.[4] In addition to this new high-tech capability, the administration also brought out of mothballs a few giant Iowa-class battleships whose heavy Second World War guns were supported with 1980s missile technology.

The US intelligence community also grew dramatically as a result of the Reagan rearmament. The National Security Agency, the signals gathering and interpretation centre based at an old army camp at Fort Meade in Maryland, had its budget increased by more than 150 per cent between 1980 and 1986, a growth unmatched since the Second World War. Its staff, a mix of military and civilian personnel, grew to nearly 27,000 by the end of the decade. The facility expanded so rapidly that two huge new buildings were constructed, and the network of winding roads that led to it became so gridlocked that a new freeway had to be built to ease access for the thousands of new employees.[5]

When Reagan became President he inherited a budget deficit of $909 billion. When he left office that deficit had grown to more than $2.5 trillion. He wanted to negotiate with the Soviets from a position of strength. He certainly achieved that.

Along with this colossal rearmament went new plans and thoughts about the use of nuclear weapons. Most new administrations want to rethink their nuclear policy, and the Reagan team was no exception. There was discussion about the concept of an early decapitation of the Soviet leadership with a nuclear strike against Moscow. It was thought that this would leave the Soviet military forces rudderless and unable to respond; the phrase used was 'like a headless chicken in a farmyard'. Rather at odds with this, there was also consideration of a limited nuclear war between NATO and the Warsaw Pact nations in Europe. It might be that both western and eastern Europe would be devastated but if the war did not escalate to the use of nuclear weapons against the USSR then the Soviets might not attack the United States.[6] Needless to say, public remarks along these lines led to a furore in European capitals.[7]

Reagan, like every President on taking office, had first to be introduced to the protocols for launching nuclear weapons should the need ever arise. As commander-in-chief of all US armed forces, the President had the constitutional authority to launch nuclear missiles through a set of special procedures that were part of the Single Integrated Operational Plan (SIOP) and the Red Integrated Strategic Offensive Plan (RISOP). These plans were triggered by the use of the nuclear 'football' carried in a briefcase by a military aide who was never more than a few paces from the President. They contained the various options for the use of nuclear weapons, the access codes and special authorisation codes. Just before his inauguration, the chairman of the Joint Chiefs of Staff, Air Force General David Jones, discussed with Reagan 'our nuclear forces and their relationship to the Single Integrated Operation Plan'. He was also given a short briefing by a White House military aide, Major John Kline of the Marine Corps, on 'the White House Emergency Plans'; Kline described 'some of the communications procedures that we would use in the event of an attack'.[8]

Ten weeks into his presidency, Reagan spent a Sunday afternoon, after church, thinking about nuclear armaments and the terrible ability of the USA and the USSR to destroy mankind itself. 'A war between the superpowers would incinerate much of the world and leave what was left of it uninhabitable forever,' he reflected.[9] But before he could develop these thoughts further, events intruded. The following day, Monday, 30 March 1981, Reagan went the short distance across town to the Washington Hilton Hotel to give a brief address to the National Conference of Building and Construction trade unionists. As he was leaving the hotel by a side door at 2.30 p.m. a young man stepped forward and called out 'Mr President'. Reagan looked up to wave and the man fired a revolver. Instantly, as the shots rang out, a Secret Service officer, Jerry Parr, leaped on the President and bundled him into his armoured limousine, which sped away leaving a mêlée on the street where police and other Secret Service officers were left restraining the gunman. He had fired a total of six shots, badly wounding the President's Press Secretary James Brady, along with a Secret Service agent who had shielded the President, and a policeman.

At first the President seemed only to be winded but after a few moments he said he was in pain, and Parr diverted his limousine to the George Washington University Hospital, six blocks from the White House. On arrival doctors thought that the President had suffered no more than a bruised or broken rib as a consequence of being manhandled into the limousine. But then the President collapsed on to one knee. He complained of not being able to breathe, and to the horror of the medical staff started coughing up blood. But they could find no sign of a wound. At this point James Baker, the Chief of Staff, and other White House officials arrived at the hospital suite. As the President's blood pressure dropped dramatically to a level at which many seventy-year-olds might struggle to survive, the pandemonium in the hospital emergency room mounted. Then, at last, the doctors found a small bullet wound in the left side of his chest, a few inches below his arm. The words were called out: 'The President has been shot.'

Having established where the bullet wound was, the medical team was soon able to stabilise Reagan. He was given a blood transfusion, and in an operation that lasted just over two hours the bullet was removed. It had hit his rib and punctured a lung. A doctor later said it had missed his heart by 'about an inch'. The situation was not so good for James Brady, who had a severe head wound. He survived but remained in hospital for three months and suffered permanent brain damage.

That afternoon another drama unfolded. The President had been shot and no one was sure who the gunman was or who he worked for. In the Situation Room, the secure headquarters in the basement of the White House, Secretary of State Alexander Haig temporarily took charge in the absence of the Vice President, who was in Texas and had been rushed on to a plane to fly straight back to Washington (he didn't arrive at the White House until just before 7 p.m.). Haig started to send out messages to allies around the world that the US government was continuing to operate as usual.

Also down in the basement, the Attorney General received reports from the FBI. The Treasury Secretary requested that Wall Street suspend trading. CIA director William Casey received intelligence reports from stations around the world. Then, while the Vice President was still in the air, intelligence was picked up that Soviet submarines off the US Atlantic coast were making strange moves. Maybe the attempted assassination and the actions of the submarines were part of a coordinated plot? One of those present described the situation as 'bedlam'.[10] Caspar Weinberger decided to put Strategic Air Command on alert. Crews were scrambled and missiles were readied.[11] But as quickly as it had blown up, the drama blew over. The Soviet submarines were not preparing to launch their nuclear missiles. The attempted assassin, John Hinckley Jr, turned out to be a lone gunman who had a crush on the actress Jodie Foster and imagined he could impress her by killing the President.

By early evening, the immediate crisis had passed. The President had recovered from his operation and was sitting up in bed smiling and joking. In a typical one-liner, he told his wife Nancy, who had been rushed to the hospital, 'Honey, I forgot to duck!' But that afternoon had revealed how quickly panic can take over the most ordered machine, how narrow was the line between stability and chaos, and most alarmingly, how concerns for national security can rapidly turn into a major international scare. For most Americans, however, it turned Reagan into a real hero, not just a Hollywood play actor. He had shown great bravery and the system had operated efficiently. The Secret Service had got him to hospital within minutes and the trauma team had stabilised him in a couple of hours. The attempted assassination had the unlikely outcome of prompting a bout of patriotic fervour in the US.

Having survived the assassination attempt, Reagan began to think once again about the future of the arms race. 'Perhaps having come so close to death made me feel I should do whatever I could in the years God had given me to reduce the threat of nuclear war,' he recalled later.[12] So while still recovering, he hand wrote a letter to Brezhnev. The State Department objected to parts of it and rewrote them. Reagan did not like the rewrites. In the end two letters were sent, one formal and one more personal with a few paragraphs about the 'real, everyday problems of people' along with pleas to release Anatoly Sharansky from prison and to allow a group of Russian Pentecostals who were holed up in the US embassy in Moscow to leave the country.[13] If Reagan had been expecting a warm response to his attempt at personal diplomacy he would have to try harder than this. A few days later he received what he called 'an icy reply' from Brezhnev.[14]

The attempted assassination put back the timetable in terms of Reagan's personal involvement in coming to grips with the nuclear launch protocols. But the Joint Chiefs, the heads of the armed forces, the principal military advisers to the President and the National Security administration continued to plan for a major exercise, to be called Ivy League 82, to rehearse the command and control of forces during a crisis in which the United States was hit by a major nuclear strike. In the build-up to this exercise, on 15 November 1981, Reagan flew on a specially adapted Boeing 747 known as the National Emergency Airborne Command Post. This aircraft was kitted out as a command centre from which the President could issue orders in the event of a nuclear attack that had devastated Washington and other parts of the US. It was nicknamed the 'Doomsday Plane' and was supposed to be able to remain airborne for seventy-two hours without refuelling. During the flight from Texas back to Washington Reagan received more briefings, but his staff concluded that he needed a further rehearsal of what to do in the event of a nuclear attack before the long-awaited Ivy League exercise, planned for March 1982.

So, at 2.11 p.m. on Friday, 26 February 1982, Reagan descended to the Situation Room for a 'special briefing'. The event was top secret and was excised from the presidential diary. Most probably the SIOP and the RISOP were once again discussed, the various options open to the President explained. In such briefings it was assumed that the Soviets had attacked first. The first main option in 1982 was to fire a retaliatory attack against nuclear launch sites in the Soviet Union. This would have been recommended if only a limited first strike by the Soviets had taken place, maybe against the US's own nuclear missile silos. The next option was to launch a larger-scale attack against a full range of military targets across the Soviet Union. In the event of the United States coming under a catastrophic nuclear attack, the most serious option was to retaliate against a wide range of economic and industrial targets. This would involve the launch of hundreds of intercontinental ballistic missiles and scores of bombers, and would lead to the destruction of many Soviet cities and massive civilian casualties, running at least into the tens of millions. An additional option that was still being refined in the early 1980s was to attack the political leadership and the command-and-control communications systems in an attempt to limit casualties, in other words, decimate the Soviet leaders and the ability of the Soviet military to respond. There were many additional variants, too.

If early warning systems detected the launch of Soviet missiles, the President could order a retaliation before the missiles had hit – the 'Launch Under Attack' option. The President could also order various 'Withhold Options'. So, if certain countries were not thought to be part of a strike against the United States, say Poland or Romania, they could be spared from attack. Despite the subject's enormous complexity, the special briefing did not last long. Reagan was back in the Oval Office by 3.23 p.m.[15]

According to Thomas Reed, who chaired the event, Reagan was given a further top secret briefing the following morning during which it was explained how he would receive information at times of nuclear crisis or war, how he would be protected personally, and how he would communicate his instructions to the armed forces. Along with this went an explanation of the times available to make his decisions. Reed later wrote that 'Reagan absorbed the discussions well. From his questions, we knew he was working to understand the incredible consequences of a nuclear exchange.'[16]

All of this was a prelude to Ivy League 82, which began on 1 March. This military exercise did not involve the deployment of thousands of troops or the use of hundreds of tanks and aircraft in pretend war games. It was a command post exercise in which the US faced a major nuclear confrontation and the players rehearsed the procedures involved with the National Military Command Center, the war room in the Pentagon that would advise the President in a crisis. It was held in conjunction with two other exercises: Nine Lives, which looked at issues surrounding the continuation and survival of the presidency during a nuclear war, and Rex 82 Alpha, exploring the evacuation and continuance of government in the event of nuclear war. The part of the President was played by former Secretary of State William Rogers, as Reagan would only be available for short periods of the war game, which was scheduled to last five days.

For a short time on the opening day Reagan sat in and watched the start of the exercise in the White House Situation Room. It began with a simulated warning of a missile attack. The conceit was that those present were on the Airborne Command Post flying over the US with a computer screen depicting events taking place below. Red dots began to appear on the map on the screen signifying where Soviet missiles had landed, lighting up first Washington then rapidly all the

major urban centres and military bases across the US. 'Before
the President could sip his coffee, the map was a sea of red,'
remembers Thomas Reed, who chaired the exercise. 'And
then, while he looked on in stunned disbelief, he learned that
the Soviet Air Force and the second round of missile launches
were on their way in. For the next half hour more red dots
wiped out the survivors and filled in the few holes in the sea
of red.' Reagan appeared stunned by the speed and scale of
it all. Reed concluded, 'I have no doubt that on that Monday
in March, Ronald Reagan came to understand exactly what a
Soviet nuclear attack on the US would be like.'[17]

That evening, Reagan again descended to the Situation
Room to participate in the exercise. He was given a full briefing on the SIOP options. It was explained how he would have
to call the Pentagon using special codes to identify himself
as the President. This seems to have been as intimidating

*A serious Reagan, who had just witnessed a simulation of a nuclear
attack on the US, with William Rogers who played the part of the
President in the rest of the Ivy League 82 war game, 1 March 1982.*

for Reagan as the earlier session. It was made clear to the President that 'with a nod of his head all the glories of Imperial Russia, all the hopes and dreams of the peasants in Ukraine, and all the pioneering settlements in Kazakhstan would vanish. Tens of millions of women and children who had done nothing to harm American citizens would be burned to a crisp.'[18]

For several days the exercises rolled out with senior military government officials playing their parts. During the Nine Lives exercise, the President was killed during a nuclear strike and potential successors were dispersed to hiding places around the country. During Rex 82 Alpha, parts of the Washington federal government structure were destroyed and the participants had to cope with a major communications collapse. By the fifth day, Reagan had retired to his ranch in California, but at the end of the exercise he made a conference call to the players and told them 'we pray to God that we never have to use the procedures we have tested [but] the nation is better off for what has been done'.[19]

Exactly what Reagan thought of these exercises is not known. They were top secret and he made no reference to them in his memoirs. But he had deeply held views about American nuclear strategy. He later wrote, 'Our dealings with the Soviets – and theirs with us – had been based on a policy known as "mutual assured destruction" – the MAD policy, and madness indeed it was. It was the craziest thing I ever heard of: simply put, it called for each side to keep enough nuclear weapons at the ready to obliterate the other, so that if one attacked, the second had enough bombs left to annihilate its adversary in a matter of minutes.'[20] After one briefing, Reagan was told by Pentagon officials that at least 150 million American lives would be lost in a nuclear war with the Soviet Union but it would still be possible to win such a war. Reagan was appalled and could not imagine what life would be like for the survivors. He wrote, 'Even if a nuclear war did not mean the extinction of mankind, it would certainly mean the end of civilisation as we knew it.' And he concluded, 'No one could "win" a nuclear war.'[21] Reagan also later wrote, with a strong sense of irony, 'As president, I carried no wallet, no money, no driver's licence, no keys in my pocket – only . . . [a] plastic-coated card which I carried in a small pocket in my coat, [which] listed the codes I would issue to the Pentagon confirming that it was actually the President of the United States who was ordering the unleashing of our nuclear weapons . . . secret codes that were capable of bringing about the annihilation of much of the world as we knew it.'[22]

Two months after the exercises, Reagan gave a speech at his old college in Eureka, Illinois to mark the fiftieth anniversary of his graduation. He talked about his hopes for the reduction of nuclear weapons by up to one third of all ballistic warheads. He also spoke about the horror of nuclear war and vowed that it was his duty as President to 'ensure that the ultimate nightmare never occurs'.[23] Whatever impression his words made in the US, in Moscow they had no impact whatsoever. The Politburo took no notice of the idea of reducing nuclear arsenals by a third. They saw this as nothing more than a 'propaganda cover-up for the aggressive militarist policy of the United States' and an attempt to roll back previous agreements that had agreed on nuclear parity.[24]

But participation in the war games did not diminish Reagan's core convictions about the Soviet Union. Even more fundamental than his dislike of nuclear weapons was his hostility to communism. Indeed, his view of the USSR had now been refined through months of what he had heard in defence and national security briefings. In a meeting at the White House on 26 March 1982, Reagan was briefed on the dire state of the Soviet economy. He wrote in his diary, 'They are in very bad shape and if we can cut off their credit they'll have to yell "Uncle" or starve.'[25] A new oil and gas pipeline from Russia to western Europe was being constructed that would earn billions of dollars for the USSR in fuel exports. The Reagan administration put immense pressure on its European allies not to sell the technology that was needed to build and manage the pipeline. In May, the administration issued National Security Decision Directive no. 32, which outlined a completely new form of aggressive stance towards Moscow. NSDD 32 stated that US policy was to weaken the Soviet Union's alliances (especially in Poland, where the trade union Solidarity had become a broad platform for opposition to Soviet control) by fostering nationalism in the Soviet satellite states, to force the USSR to 'bear the brunt of its economic shortcomings' and 'to limit Soviet military capabilities by strengthening the US military'.[26]

Reagan's undying belief was in the superiority of the Western democratic system over the totalitarianism of the Soviet state. In a speech to the joint Houses of Parliament in London in June, Reagan stated, 'The rate of growth in the Soviet gross national product has been steadily declining since the 1950s and is less than half of what it was then. The dimensions of this failure are astounding: a country which employs one fifth of its population in agriculture is unable to feed its own people ... Over-centralized, with little or no incentives, year after year the Soviet system pours its best resource into the making of instruments of destruction. The constant shrinkage of economic growth combined with the growth of military production is putting a heavy strain on the Soviet people.' Reagan was confident that the socialist system faced collapse and that the 'march of freedom and democracy' would 'leave Marxism-Leninism on the ash-heap of history'.[27]

Of course, not everyone went along with Reagan's

anti-communist crusade. In the mid-term elections in November 1982 the Democrats captured twenty-six seats in the House of Representatives, threatening the Republican majority. By early 1983 Reagan's opponents were still fiercely fighting the budget cuts that were necessary to fund the huge increase in defence spending. The Democrats wanted more to be spent on social and welfare benefits. Moreover, some Americans had started to protest about the growth in the number of nuclear weapons. They called for a halt to the testing, production and deployment of such weapons as the first step on the road away from the arms race and towards a peaceful future. Many Church leaders were coming under pressure to agree that the moral Christian approach to the global situation was to call for a nuclear freeze and oppose any further build-up of deadly arsenals.

In this context, on 8 March 1983 Reagan flew to Orlando, Florida to speak to a Christian organisation, the National Association of Evangelicals. The President believed that communism was anti-Christian, an ideology that lacked any sort of morality other than the right to pursue its own ends, and he had to persuade his audience what they were up against. He asserted that the Cold War was a spiritual struggle 'between right and wrong and good and evil'. Nancy had argued with her husband and tried to persuade him to lower the tone of his rhetoric. Reagan for once rejected her advice. In concluding his speech to the Evangelicals, the President called upon them to 'pray for the salvation of all those who live in that totalitarian darkness – pray they will discover the joy of knowing God. But until they do, let us be aware that while they preach the supremacy of the state, declare its omnipotence over individual man and predict its eventual domination of all peoples on the Earth, they are the focus of evil in the modern world.' He went on to tell his audience to reject the 'aggressive impulses of an evil empire'.[28]

Reagan had made his most outspoken attack yet on the Soviet Union. He had used the sort of apocalyptic language that was not usual for an American president. He had spoken of his struggle against communism and the Soviet Union in terms of a religious war, of a 'crusade for freedom'. He said that he wanted Andropov to take note of this speech.[29] By describing his rival superpower as an 'evil empire' he most certainly achieved that.

4

Operation RYaN

The Soviet leaders, too, were deeply worried about the consequences of a nuclear conflagration. In 1972, the General Staff
of the Soviet Defence Ministry had prepared a war game in
which Leonid Brezhnev and Prime Minister Aleksei Kosygin
were to take part. The exercise began with a report of the
imagined impact of an American nuclear first strike upon the
USSR. The Soviet military was reduced to one-thousandth
of its strength; 80 million Soviet citizens were dead; 85 per
cent of Soviet industry lay in ruins. According to a Soviet
general who was present, both Brezhnev and Kosygin were
visibly shaken by the scale of this destruction. As part of the
exercise, Brezhnev was called upon to launch three intercontinental ballistic missiles as retaliation. They were armed
with dummy warheads. When it came to the moment when
he had to press the button to launch the missiles, Brezhnev
apparently grew pale and his hand trembled. He anxiously
turned to the Minister of Defence who was standing alongside
for reassurance that this was not for real. 'Are you sure this is
just an exercise?' Brezhnev nervously asked.[1]

Brezhnev had come to power in the period following
Khrushchev's fall from grace, in 1964, when he was appointed
First or General Secretary. Kosygin became chairman of the

Council of Ministers, effectively Prime Minister, and Nikolai Podgorny became president. Three years later they appointed Yuri Andropov as head of the KGB. These four men ruled the Soviet Union for twenty years. Over that time, under immense pressure from keeping up with the relentless Cold War arms race, the Soviet economy struggled. It remained reliant upon heavy industry and the huge armaments business. All economic and industrial planning was still centralised, as in the days of Stalin. Minimum priority was given to consumer goods. Queuing became a way of life across the Soviet Union – for food, for the daily necessities, and for any of the rare luxuries that occasionally came along. There were department stores in most cities but they remained largely under-stocked and many of the goods on offer were beyond the prices the average citizen could afford.

There were new developments, of course. By the 1970s, for instance, small transistor radios were fairly cheap and widely available, although the stations citizens were allowed to tune in to were strictly limited. Standards of consumer service were appalling to Western eyes. Local officials were uncaring, incompetent and, if they were party members, sometimes arrogant. Housing was of poor quality, even when newly built. Owning a car was rare; Soviet cities were full of people on bicycles and packed into buses. The citizenry were kept in place by a system that, from the cradle to the grave, embraced a Marxist-Leninist ideology. Education was widely available; health care was free. Unemployment was officially non-existent. There was supposed to be no crime. Newspapers, radio and television were widely available but always controlled, only ever transmitting the party line. Entertainment and art were intended to encourage good socialist principles. The one commodity that was universally available and cheap was vodka. This too had its effect on productivity. The number of working days lost to drunkenness was uncounted by official statistics but colossal.

At the centre of the one-party system was the party elite, known as the *nomenklatura*. At the very top was the Politburo, supported by the Secretariat, and reporting to them were the party secretaries from every region of the Soviet Union, from the European border to the Asian Pacific coast, from the Arctic tundra to the deserts of central Asia. Beneath them was a vast party organisation that ran the factories and workplaces, the schools and universities, the hospitals and ultimately the shops and department stores. Keeping an eye on all this was the KGB, which was represented wherever groups of citizens met or worked. The elite who ran the system were afforded various privileges for themselves and their families that other citizens were not allowed. For instance, they were sent on holidays to pleasant resorts on the Black Sea coasts or in mountain retreats; they were given better health care, and priority access to televisions and cars. A strict definition of the *nomenklatura* was that it covered regime officials whose appointment had to be formally approved by the Communist Party. One estimate is that this comprised about 100,000 people.[2]

Brezhnev's foreign policy changed little from the late 1960s to the early 1980s. He favoured détente with the West while wanting to maintain Soviet authority, established by Stalin, over the regimes of eastern Europe. Brezhnev was proud of the various liberation movements that were taking part in national struggles across the Third World, as in Angola, Ethiopia, Nicaragua and El Salvador. Support for these took different forms but was always seen as ideologically based, with the Kremlin wanting to help the movements on the path to socialism. The Soviet leadership hoped this would bring about a triumph over capitalism without provoking a catastrophic nuclear war. Brezhnev had seen the devastation the Second World War brought to Russia and had no doubt that a nuclear conflict would be on a far more destructive scale and must be avoided. He believed the US leadership held the same view and that both sides saw nuclear war as suicidal.

However, by the late 1970s, while economies in the West were striding forward, reliant upon innovation, new technology and consumer spending, the Soviet economy was stagnating – a stagnation epitomised by the image of the man who led the country, whose regime wanted no fundamental change to the system. Brezhnev had been in his fifties when he became General Secretary. He had looked relatively youthful and vigorous. By contrast, in the late seventies he was not well and seemed old and frail. In his many television appearances the cameras often had to cut away from shots of him as he fumbled while trying to pin medals on those receiving awards, a common diet of Soviet TV. He began to slur his words in formal speeches. One story told of a senior meeting at which Brezhnev formally presided but during which he grew restless and began to fiddle with a felt-tip pen, with which he was obviously unfamiliar. Before long the pen began to leak and he covered his hand with ink. He called for an aide who returned with various wipes and he slowly began to clean his hand. Soon everyone at the meeting had lost interest in the speakers droning on and become entranced with watching the General Secretary as he tried to clean his ink-stained hands.[3]

Throughout the era of détente, the Soviet leaders, all of an age who had come to political maturity during the Second World War, had an ambivalent attitude to the West and most especially to the United States. This was as heartfelt as it was ideological. To them, the West represented an essentially individualistic, greedy, aggressive ethos, dominated purely by the creed of making money for personal gain. Marxism-Leninism, by contrast, was committed wholeheartedly to collective action for the good of everyone, even if the reality was far from the ideal. On the other hand, there was also a

Leonid Brezhnev ruled the Soviet Union for nearly twenty years.
In his final years he became something of a joke. Andrei Gromyko
looks over his right shoulder.

growing fear of the West. The Kremlin leaders sensed that its industrial and technological achievements had enabled it to stride ahead, particularly in the use of sophisticated new technology that was barely understood in Moscow. Russian visitors to America reported that almost every primary school in the US possessed a computer and that they were beginning to play a vital part in many aspects of life, from health care to consumer products, from the economy to defence. But the micro-chip was a rarity in the Soviet Union. There was no culture of openness to encourage its development. The availability of computers opened up a world of information technology enabling every user to access vast amounts of data. But this was totally against the grain of Soviet society. In the Soviet Union, owning even a typewriter or a photocopier was illegal unless approved and licensed by the state. The central bureaucracy controlled the publishing of every book and the content of all newspapers. There was absolutely no tradition of free exchange of ideas and information.

This combination of fear of the West and recognition of the developing gulf between Western and Soviet technology helped to generate a sense of paranoia in the Kremlin. Marshal Nikolai Ogarkov, First Deputy Defence Minister and Chief of the General Staff, said in a remarkably open interview to a Western journalist in March 1983, 'We cannot equal the quality of US arms for a generation or two. Modern military power is based on technology, and technology is based on computers. In the US, small children play with computers ... Here, we don't even have computers in every office of the Defence Ministry. And for reasons you know well, we cannot make computers widely available in our society. We will never be able to catch up with you in modern arms until we have an economic revolution.'[4] A senior KGB official summed the situation up succinctly: the 'ailing, ageing leadership, unable to move ahead with any domestic reforms, surrounded by surging Western nations economically and technologically and the advance of a very militant President in the United States, Ronald Reagan, verbally at least ... really scared them out of their wits.'[5]

As the paranoia spread within the Kremlin, the Soviet leaders turned to the KGB for reassurance. The vast organisation of the KGB was divided into a series of directorates, one for Internal Security and Counter Intelligence, one for Border troops, one to deal with Communications Interception and so on. The section dealing with Foreign Intelligence was probably the most prestigious and was known as the First Chief Directorate (FCD). In 1972 the FCD moved into brand-new buildings in Yasenevo, south-east of Moscow. It was a huge complex and consisted of an 800-seat conference hall, a library, a clinic, a well-equipped sports hall and a swimming pool.

Officers enjoyed lovely views over hills covered with birch trees, green pasture land and, in the summer, fields full of wheat and rye. Senior officials were brought by Zil limousine out to the complex and were driven to their own separate entrances and taken by private lifts to their grand offices, some of which were equipped with personal saunas or gyms. As very few of the other officers had cars, a fleet of buses travelled out from Moscow every morning. When work finished promptly at 6 p.m. everyone flocked on to the buses for the return journey, and the police obligingly halted the traffic on the outer ring road to speed them on their way.

In 1974, Andropov appointed as head of the FCD a man whose influence would be immense and who would eventually go on to direct the whole KGB. His name was Vladimir Aleksandrovich Kryuchkov and he would remain a key ally and adviser of Andropov. Kryuchkov had a round, lined face with narrow staring eyes. He was a workaholic who was described as having 'a tough, unsmiling Tartar exterior, thinly concealing a tough, unsmiling interior'.[6] What he brought to the FCD was a total belief in the fact that the West was constantly conspiring against the Soviet state. Like most in the Soviet leadership he had no understanding of how the American political system worked, with its different parts of government and its checks and balances. So, for instance, Nixon's forced resignation over Watergate totally bemused a man like Kryuchkov. The KGB view was that he had not been forced out by public indignation but by a conspiracy of the enemies of détente, probably the Zionists and the military-industrial complex who wanted to maintain arms sales. Accustomed to a command economy controlled from the centre, most Soviets could not imagine a system that operated successfully without regulation and control. As one senior Soviet diplomat put it, many of his colleagues were 'inclined to the fantastic notion that there must be a secret control room somewhere in the United States. They themselves, after all, are used to a system ruled by a small group working in secrecy in one place.'[7] Kryuchkov totally shared and perpetrated the view that most of what went on at a senior level in the West was underscored by a conspiracy of one sort or another.

During the late 1970s, confined to this closed mindset, the Brezhnev regime made a series of fundamental mistakes that helped to generate Western opposition and bring an end to the years of détente. Nothing created more alarm in the West than the Kremlin's decision to deploy a new generation of SS-20 'Pioneer' intermediate-range ballistic missiles in eastern Europe and western Russia. This decision was ill thought through and completely backfired on the Kremlin. The hawks in the US portrayed it as a stealthy plot by the Soviets to improve their nuclear standing while America was distracted with détente. But another Kremlin decision was even more disastrous for the Soviet Union and for its image in the West.

An SS-20 missile. These missiles could be launched from hidden sites across Russia at targets in Western Europe.

ullstein bild – ADN-Bildarchiv

Afghanistan had traditionally been an area of rivalry between the Russian Tsars and the Western powers. During the 1970s it became a battleground in the Cold War as a pro-Western regime was thrown out by a pro-Soviet group of Afghan army officers. This coup began a process of reform and of women's education that angered Muslim clerics who with encouragement from Iran and Pakistan began to support the Mujahideen, the 'soldiers of God', who openly fought the communist and 'ungodly' regime. Requests from Kabul for military help were sent to Moscow but in April 1979 the Politburo decided against sending in the army. Increasingly desperate pleas for assistance continued throughout the year and on the evening of 12 December, after another coup looked like making Afghanistan once again hostile to the Soviet Union, the Politburo met once more to consider military intervention. At this meeting Brezhnev was drunk and he failed to chair proceedings effectively. Only the inner circle of voting members were consulted. The Soviet military was against intervention but the hard-liners, who included Andropov, held sway. They argued that the victory of Islamic fundamentalism over socialism in Afghanistan would be a great blow to the prestige of the Soviet Union. Nobody stopped to think about the reaction in the West. Two weeks later, on Christmas Day, Soviet tanks and tens of thousands of motorised infantry crossed the border and within a few days had imposed a new pro-Soviet regime in Kabul.

In Washington, the administration that had been accused of being soft on the Soviets erupted in outrage. President Carter told Brezhnev on the hotline that the invasion of Afghanistan could be a 'turning point' in relations. He called for trade sanctions and suspended grain sales to the USSR. Carter saw Soviet aggression as a threat to the whole region, extending as far as the Persian Gulf and Middle Eastern oil supplies. In his State of the Union address in January 1980, Carter described the Soviet invasion as 'the most serious threat to peace since the Second World War'.[8] He called off support for the SALT II treaty and the US began indirectly to supply sophisticated new arms to the Mujahideen, who were described as 'freedom fighters' – a policy that left a disastrous legacy for the West in a country that would be fought over for decades to come. Many of the weapons would end up in the hands of the Taliban, who from the 1990s would offer a safe haven to Osama bin Laden and al-Qaeda.

Meanwhile, Soviet forces soon became mired in a conflict with a guerrilla army that they could not win but found very difficult to end. More than 600,000 Russian troops had passed through Afghanistan by the mid-1980s. The war became immensely unpopular at home. Hundreds, then thousands of young Soviet soldiers were sent home in body bags. They were usually brought back at night, out of the gaze of reporters or any publicity, in giant transport aircraft known as 'Black Tulips'. Their families were given very little information about what had happened to their loved ones and they were denied any sort of war memorial. The veterans, known as 'Afgantsies', were shunned by the public at home because of rumours of war crimes committed in Afghanistan and they faced a struggle with the Soviet bureaucracy for pensions and benefits.[9] The war dragged on for years and became known as 'Russia's Vietnam'. A senior KGB insider summed up what many felt when he said, 'We are bogged down in a war we cannot win and cannot abandon. It's ridiculous. A mess.'[10]

Right from the beginning of his presidency, Ronald Reagan had adopted a confrontational tone with the Soviet Union. In his first press conference he accused the Soviets of lying and cheating to achieve their ends. In answer to one journalist's question about whether the Soviet Union was still bent on world domination, he replied, 'The only morality they recognise is what will further their cause, meaning they reserve unto themselves the right to commit any crime, to lie, to cheat, in order to attain that.' He went on to say that 'we operate on a different set of standards'.[11]

In Moscow, the Kremlin had expected hostility from Reagan but they were upset and concerned by the immediately aggressive tone of this new administration. What the ageing leaders wanted most was to maintain a form of nuclear parity as had been the case for some time. The Politburo members were universally angry at their meeting on 11 February 1981 and took it in turns to denounce the new American President. The Soviet ambassador to Washington wrote that 'the collective mood of the Soviet leadership had never been so suddenly and deeply set against an American president'.[12] What alarmed the Kremlin even more than his harsh words was Reagan's agreement to continue with the deployment of Pershing II and Cruise missiles in western Europe. They did not see this as a response to their own wheeling out of the SS-20 missiles; instead it was interpreted purely as a belligerent act by the US, and it stirred up the fears the Soviet leaders had about Western technology. Moscow was well within range of a Pershing II missile fired from West Germany, so their presence was seen in the Kremlin as an attempt to tip the nuclear balance in favour of the West. If used in a first strike it would be almost impossible to react to an attack within the few minutes available to them, perhaps even to reach the safety of the nuclear bunkers that had been specially built for the leadership: they were a train ride away from the centre of Moscow. The effect of the imminent deployment was extremely destabilising, and one Soviet defence adviser later recalled that 'the only possible target of these missiles was our leadership in Moscow because Pershings could not reach most of our missiles'.[13] A new level of preparedness for a US first strike was going to be needed. If necessary, the Soviet Union would have to resolve to fire its own missiles first to avoid being taken by surprise and decimated.

ullstein bild – Poly-Press

The launch of a Pershing II missile, only six minutes'
flying time from the Kremlin.

Beyond Brezhnev and his immediate circle, by the early
1980s the rest of the Soviet leadership began to feel that the
international situation, what they called 'the correlation of
world forces', was turning against them (in the West this
was simply called the 'balance of power'). Andrei Gromyko,
the long-standing Foreign Minister, had to admit that 'The
international situation ... has taken a turn for the worse.'[14]
The Soviet leadership saw the US defence budget growing
at a staggering pace without apparently putting strain on
the expanding economy. They saw new weapons systems
being deployed that could give the US a first-strike capability.
And they felt the heat of what they believed was a renewed

aggressiveness in Washington. In a 1981 speech to KGB officers, Kryuchkov said, 'the political situation worldwide is going from bad to worse and there is no end in sight'.[15] As one leading CIA figure put it, the Soviet leaders all came from 'narrow backgrounds and worldview'; they were 'pedestrian, isolated and self-absorbed'; they were 'paranoid and fearful ... of their own people and of a world they believed [was] relentlessly hostile and threatening'.[16]

To Andropov, surveying this world from the Lubyanka, the perceived turn against the Soviet Union fuelled his sense of paranoia about the United States. In May 1981, not long after Reagan had returned to the White House after his recovery from the assassination attempt, a major KGB conference took place in Moscow. Brezhnev was present, and in a secret address he denounced Reagan's policies. Andropov went a lot further. He declared that the new American administration was actively preparing for war and, to the astonishment of many of those present, he claimed there was a strong likelihood of a nuclear first strike by the US. Andropov called for an entirely new intelligence initiative involving both the KGB and the GRU (the Glavnoye Razvedyvatelnoye Upravleniye, or Soviet military intelligence). It was to be called Operation RYaN, an acronym taken from the Russian words *raketno-yadernoye napadenie*, meaning 'nuclear missile attack'. The entire Soviet intelligence apparatus was to be set to look for signs of an imminent launch of nuclear weapons by the US and its NATO allies, in order to give the Kremlin time to prepare and to respond.[17]

The leadership was haunted by the dreadful memory of 22 June 1941 and the German surprise invasion of the Soviet Union, Operation Barbarossa. This was a painful, tragic experience for the USSR and still relatively fresh in the minds of the men who ruled the Kremlin. The lack of preparation for the Nazi attack had led to the deaths of millions, the capture of hundreds of thousands of Red Army soldiers, the occupation of much of western Russia and the Ukraine, and a terrible war that left the nation in ruins. The Kremlin leaders were determined never to be caught off guard again. Operation RYaN would give them the warning they needed of a future attack.

Nearly every Soviet embassy around the world had a KGB resident officer and a team reporting to him. These residencies varied in size. Britain was a key player in the Western alliance but the London KGB residency was not felt to be large, with twenty-three agents. Additionally, in London there were fifteen agents working for the GRU. The Washington embassy contained even more Soviet agents. The residencies sent regular reports on whatever topics the KGB Centre in Moscow asked for. Sometimes they contained little more than summaries of what was in the newspapers. But the residencies also worked undercover and ran agents in the field. These could be organisers of left-wing parties or workers' groups, local politicians or journalists, and occasionally a military insider. Sometimes these agents passed on information out of conviction, sometimes they were paid. Millions of dollars were built up in overseas accounts to facilitate this. It was essential to keep the reports flowing through to Moscow. And when there was nothing much new to say, there was a tendency to confirm whatever Moscow wanted to hear. It was thought to be a good station if a residency produced several reports a week, sometimes several a day. Promotion often depended on this. The Centre in Moscow often judged a residency not by the quality of the intelligence it passed on but by its quantity.

For Operation RYaN, agents in the USA, in Britain, in the other main NATO countries and in Japan were set the task of looking for particular signs or indicators that the KGB in Moscow thought would reveal preparations being made to launch a nuclear strike. Broadly speaking there were five principal categories: Political, Military, Intelligence, Civil

Defence and Economics.[18] Within the first category, the sort of indicators agents were told to look for were statements from political leaders suddenly changing in tone or becoming more aggressive. Agents were also told to monitor the whereabouts of these leaders: a sudden departure or change of schedule might indicate that an emergency was forthcoming. Within the military category there were many signs to search for. An increased state of alert might indicate that the US military or NATO forces were about to launch an attack. Any unusual activity or raised security around air bases or missile silos might suggest that preparations for a strike were being made. The agents monitoring civil defence were also told to look out for preparations of imminent war, which might include the evacuation of senior officials, the assembly of emergency blood supplies, or the emptying of hospitals of non-urgent cases in anticipation of a retaliatory attack. Economic factors might include changes in the banking sector or in the supply of money. Many of these indicators were put on the list as they were part of the Soviet Union's own preparations for a nuclear strike, and they naturally assumed the other side would act in the same way.

RYaN was known as a HUMINT (human intelligence) operation. There could be additional forms of SIGINT (signals intelligence), but in this instance the KGB and the GRU were relying on the observations of their agents on the ground. In some cases the indicators were minimal. The KGB resident in Helsinki, for instance, was simply asked to report back any signs of the evacuation of the US embassy or if American businesses were about to close. Elsewhere, in countries that were thought likely to take a more prominent role in a military strike, agents were asked to look out for any signs of mobilisation. They were told that this task was to take first priority in their 1982 Work Plans.[19] During the first year the number of indicators grew considerably, until the KGB had a list of 292 such 'signs of tensions'. The motto for the operation was summed up in the Russian words *Nie prosmotrite* – 'do not miss anything'.

The establishment of Operation RYaN was confirmed in the 1981 annual report of the KGB submitted by Andropov to Brezhnev. In this report, Andropov stated that the KGB had 'implemented measures to strengthen intelligence work in order to prevent a possible sudden outbreak of war by the enemy'. To do this, agents 'actively obtained information on military and strategic issues, and the aggressive military and political plans of imperialism [the United States] and its accomplices' and 'enhanced the relevance and effectiveness of its active intelligence abilities'.[20]

So many reports started to come in from its agents that the KGB in Moscow set up a computer program to process the flow of all the information. This would have been a simple and probably fairly primitive program that allocated relative weights to different categories of intelligence. A sign that military bases were going on to a maximum state of alert would, for instance, be given a higher weighting than information about the gathering of blood banks or the emptying of hospitals. The appeal of such a system was that it seemed to lend a scientific basis to the understanding and interpretation of several different and sometimes confusing items of intelligence. However, there was clearly scepticism about the ability of Soviet computer technology to cope with analysing data on this scale. The head of the East German foreign intelligence service wrote in an internal memo that previous Soviet experiences 'show us that a danger exists of computer application concepts not getting implemented'. He simply did not believe that the Soviets could build a sophisticated computer program.[21]

This might be a reason why in one of the top secret central rooms at the KGB Centre in Moscow an alternative way of displaying the intelligence collected was constructed. This was far more 'old technology' and consisted of a large Perspex board erected in the middle of the room. The board was made up like a matrix. Down the side were listed the five main criteria that were being observed; along the top were listed the principal countries being watched with a gradation for the severity of the indicators. Every time a new indicator was reported signifying preparations for the launch of an attack, a cross was made with a marker pen. At any time, senior KGB officials could get an idea of how dangerous the situation was simply by looking at the board and gauging how many crosses had been marked up. More crosses meant more indicators had been reported. It was simple, but the Soviet intelligence chiefs seemed to like it that way.[22]

Looking for indicators of war seemed perfectly reasonable. But like any intelligence agency, once this got down to the KGB agents on the ground the demands grew in scale and in absurdity. In London and Washington, agents were told to count the number of lights on in major government buildings like the Ministry of Defence or the State Department or in military installations. It was thought that officials working late would be a tell-tale sign of last-minute preparations for war. It did not occur to the KGB Centre that it might simply be a sign of cleaners going about their business in the early hours.[23]

Many agents believed the entire operation was ridiculous. In London, one senior KGB operative found he was inundated with requests to search out information for RYaN, such as counting the number of lights on in the Foreign Office and finding out the evacuation plans of senior civil servants and military officials in advance of a nuclear war. Like his fellow agents, he was totally cynical about the whole thing but had no alternative but to play along. 'We just paid lip service' to the instructions, he remembered. 'Let's pretend we are doing it and write reports about how well we are trying to study the Foreign Office,' he told his colleagues.[24] His name was Oleg

Gordievsky, and he would come to play a significant role in the drama that was to unfold.

Even the KGB office in Leningrad, the second largest Soviet city (today St Petersburg), received the warning that the world was at the most dangerous point since the Second World War, and all agents were told to look out for signs of an attack, perhaps through nearby Finland. Oleg Kalugin, the bureau chief there, used to listen, illegally, to the BBC World Service and Voice of America on the radio at home. He simply 'couldn't believe' what he heard from the Moscow Centre and asked himself, 'What on earth is going on?' He recalled that 'many residencies of the KGB and the GRU when they heard these warnings from Moscow that a nuclear attack was imminent . . . were very sceptical and took it as another example of Kremlin paranoia'.[25]

It was not only the KGB and the GRU that were required to pursue the objectives of Operation RYaN. There is clear evidence that agents in the Czechoslovak and Bulgarian intelligence services were also tasked with looking for signs of combat readiness in NATO countries and for indicators that suggested preparations were being made for war.[26] The foreign intelligence service of the German Democratic Republic, the HVA (Hauptverwaltung Aufklärung, or Main Reconnaissance Administration), was a branch of the East German secret service, the Stasi. Based in a vast complex of buildings along Normannenstrasse in the Lichtenberg district of East Berlin, it was thought to be far and away the most efficient spying agency in eastern Europe. Its head, Markus Wolf, was so elusive that he was dubbed by Western intelligence agencies as 'the man without a face'. The HVA too were required to search for RYaN indicators. Wolf was sceptical, writing later that 'our Soviet partners had become obsessed with the danger of a nuclear missile attack'. HVA agents were ordered to undergo military training and spend time on drills to prepare for war. Wolf wrote, 'Like most intelligence peoples, I found these war games a burdensome waste of time, but these orders were no more open to discussion than other orders from above.'[27] So, dutifully, the HVA also buckled down to find what they were asked to look for.

But no matter how dubious they were, no agent in any KGB residency or any Warsaw Pact intelligence service was willing to put his career at risk by speaking out and challenging the purpose of RYaN. Agents were required to report information even if they were cynical about its necessity or relevance. The more alarming the reports, the more the agents were congratulated for their diligence. A KGB agent in London heard a routine report on the BBC news about a drive for new blood donors and passed this on to Moscow. Headquarters came back saying this was particularly interesting as a sign of preparations for war and thanked the agent for his good work. Repeatedly, the Moscow Centre asked for reports and then became duly concerned by the information they received and demanded even more details. RYaN became self-fulfilling, a vicious circle. It told the Centre not what its agents on the ground thought was important, but what it wanted to hear. The panic in Moscow about the likelihood of a US-led nuclear first strike increased as the intelligence it was gathering confirmed its own fears.

To follow up on Operation RYaN, in August 1981 Brezhnev met secretly in the Crimea with the leaders of the Warsaw Pact nations. He asked them to sign an agreement that streamlined the decision-making process of going to war. This clandestine agreement effectively gave the Kremlin authority to order Warsaw Pact forces to take up battle stations without seeking authorisation from all the separate member states. Fearful that there would be too little time to react to a fast-moving situation or a NATO first strike, Moscow wanted the capability of acting quickly to mobilise its defences.[28]

When Brezhnev died and was succeeded by Andropov, the new leader's sense of paranoia over warlike US intentions advanced to centre stage in the Kremlin. One of Andropov's key backers in the succession was Defence Minister Ustinov, and he admired the KGB leader for his hard-line stance. Without doubt, establishing Operation RYaN helped Andropov to the throne. In his first public statement as General Secretary, Andropov took a defiant tone. 'We know very well,' he said, 'that peace cannot be obtained from the imperialists by begging for it. It can be upheld only by relying on the invincible might of the Soviet armed forces.'[29] It was clear where the backing for the new leader came from.

Andropov made no fundamental changes to the system he inherited. In domestic politics, in speech after speech, he called for further 'order and discipline' among workers and managers. This echoed the language of most communist leaders since Lenin. To those who heard his speeches on television this implied more belt-tightening, no letting up on the central control of the economy, a war against absenteeism, and more demands on working people. Working families were far more interested in increased wages, better housing, more consumer goods in the shops and cutting down on endless queuing.

However, with Andropov's call went out another message that marked a significant break with the Brezhnev era. Through the KGB's huge network of informers, Andropov knew of the vast extent of embezzlement, illegal gain and nepotism within the system. The new General Secretary made it clear that he would seek out and punish any form of corruption or organised crime. The press and media never discussed the existence of fat-cats who benefited from the system as regional party secretaries or factory managers but everyone knew that bribery, laziness and a form of black economy existed. Andropov brought this into the public domain for the first time. One of Brezhnev's old cronies, the Minister of the Interior Nikolai Shchelokov, was removed and charged with corruption, of using state money to buy luxury goods for his own and his family's personal use. The manager of the most important food store in Moscow was fired and put on a charge of criminal malpractice. All of this was widely reported and a message sent out to others: changes were needed. But Andropov's reforms tinkered at the edges and did not attack the central malaises of the Soviet economy.[30] And within months it was international affairs that took over his time and preoccupations. It will never be known how far he would have taken his domestic reforms had he not become so distracted.

In January 1983, Andropov made a major speech to the Warsaw Pact leaders. He was convinced that the deployment of the Pershing II and Cruise missiles, due later that year, was a 'new round of the arms race' that was quite different to previous ones. It was clear to him that these missiles were not about 'deterrence' but were 'designed for a future war', and were intended to give the US the ability to take out the Soviet leadership in a 'limited nuclear war' that America believed it could both 'survive and win in a protracted nuclear conflict'. In February, he set about sending out a new and more urgent list of indicators for Operation RYaN. Agents were instructed to keep up a continuous watch over US and NATO military bases where nuclear weapons were kept and from where they would be launched. They were also to observe key nuclear decision-makers and lines of communications. Once again, however, this perfectly rational list of indicators of imminent war was confused by demands that were pointless. Agents were told also to keep an eye on Church leaders: it was thought they would go into hiding or make some response if war was about to begin. It was another sign of how poorly the KGB Centre understood the West.[31]

When in early March 1983, four months into Andropov's new tenure, Reagan described the Soviet Union as an 'evil empire', Andropov was not only outraged but insulted. The Kremlin wanted at least to be taken seriously by the White House, to be given respect. The American administration seemed to be denying even this and trying to undermine their self-esteem. Andropov immediately denounced Reagan's speech. He said it was proof that the American President 'can think only in terms of confrontation and bellicose, lunatic anti-communism'. The Soviet media immediately picked up the baton, and *Pravda* was full of denunciations, calling Reagan a 'warmonger'.[32]

However, if Andropov thought this was as bad as it would get, he was wrong. Only two weeks after his 'evil empire' speech, Reagan came up with something that the Kremlin saw as even more threatening.

5

Star Wars

On 31 July 1979, while he was still thinking about launching his campaign for the presidency, Ronald Reagan paid a visit to the North American Air Defense Command (NORAD) centre at Cheyenne Mountain, Colorado. The NORAD centre was a vast underground bunker, a huge network of corridors, tunnels and meeting rooms channelling down to an enormous central control room, all of which in the early 1960s had been carved out of the granite rock below the mountain. It was constructed to resist a direct hit from a nuclear weapon and was protected by steel blast doors several feet thick. However, by the end of the 1970s even this immense structure would have been vulnerable to the latest Soviet heavyweight SS-18 missiles. NORAD was the command and control centre where reports from early warning radar stations around the world were monitored on a continuous basis. Added to this, data was collected from a host of observation satellites in space that were constantly watching hundreds of potential Soviet missile launch sites. Information from other ground stations and aerial observations were also fed back to here. Any sign of the launch of a ballistic missile attack on the United States or Canada would be first picked up at NORAD and would then be passed on to Strategic Air Command headquarters in Omaha, Nebraska, and to the National Military Command Center at the Pentagon which would alert the President. NORAD was the central link in the chain of communications that would begin the process of retaliation in the event of a Soviet nuclear attack.

Reagan's visit to this underground complex had been suggested by an old friend, a Hollywood screenwriter and producer named Douglas Morrow, who came along for the ride. They were accompanied by Martin Anderson, an economist and a former policy adviser to Reagan who would go on to work for him during the presidential election campaign. Their visit consisted of a series of briefings on the nuclear capabilities of the US and the Soviet Union and the methods for detecting an attack. Morrow's presence, however, was not the only link with Hollywood that day. Towards the end of their visit they were ushered in to the command centre, a huge room where a vast illuminated map of the United States extended along one wall. Incoming missiles would be tracked and displayed on this electronic board. The visitors agreed it looked more like a movie set than a military command centre and no doubt there were many jokes about James Bond and *Dr Strangelove*, in which the War Room had a huge wall map just like at NORAD.

The visitors talked with the NORAD commander General James Hill, and when Reagan asked him what would happen if the Soviets fired a missile at the United States, Hill explained that they could track its progress and project its exact point of impact. But by the time they could alert the officials in the target city there would only be a few minutes left. Nothing could be done to intercept the missile. There was no defence against a nuclear missile attack.

On the plane back to Los Angeles at the end of the day, according to Anderson, Reagan appeared extremely disturbed about what he had seen and heard. 'He couldn't believe the

United States had no defence against Soviet missiles.' Reagan shook his head and said, 'We have spent all that money and have all that equipment and there is nothing we can do to prevent a nuclear missile from hitting us.' He reflected on the terrible dilemma that would face the President if the US came under nuclear attack, and concluded, 'The only options he would have would be to press the button or do nothing. They're both bad. We should have some way of defending ourselves against nuclear missiles.' Anderson reminded him that under the ABM Treaty Nixon had signed seven years earlier the US had opposed the introduction of anti-ballistic missiles and their abolition had been enshrined in international law.[1]

A few days later Anderson prepared a short paper for Reagan on defence and foreign policy. In this he suggested that the situation was different now to Nixon's time and in the light of the Soviet military build-up perhaps it was time to revisit the concept behind the ABM Treaty. He proposed that one option was the development of a 'protective missile system' and suggested that the American people would probably find this far more acceptable than the 'satisfaction of knowing that those who initiated an attack against us were also blown away'. Defence and protection might be more popular than retaliation and revenge.[2]

The story of the visit to NORAD is revealing in that despite his many years in public life and as a state governor, Reagan had not appeared to grasp that strategic thinkers in both superpower nations had decided the best way to defend their countries was to have no defence. Instead, America's defence came through deterrence. The way to stop incoming missiles from lighting up the big board at the command centre was to threaten to destroy anyone who launched them. The stalemate that followed was at the heart of the Cold War, and by the late 1970s was seen as the natural order of things.[3] Moreover, Reagan did not appear to realise that there was no way of intercepting these missiles in mid-flight when they were travelling through space at several thousand miles per hour. Reagan was delighted by the idea of finding some sort of defence against Soviet missiles, but his political advisers thought that to turn his back on thirty years of national defence policy was far too revolutionary for a presidential candidate and would put off voters. It was thought that referring to nuclear missiles *at all* while on the stump could make him sound aggressive or might highlight his inexperience. Reagan was persuaded not to pursue the matter during the campaign he was about to launch. The idea of missile defence was quietly filed away.

Despite his silence on the matter during the election, Reagan harboured radical ideas about nuclear weapons. He had not fully agreed with the use of atom bombs on Hiroshima and Nagasaki in 1945. He rejected the entire policy of Mutual Assured Destruction which, as we have seen, he thought was 'the craziest thing I ever heard of'. He described it as 'like having two westerners in a saloon aiming their guns at each other's head – permanently'. He concluded this was not 'something that would send you to bed feeling safe . . . There had to be a better way.'[4] During his campaign Reagan did speak in private with his aides about abolishing nuclear weapons altogether but, as Anderson remembers, 'nobody believed there was the slightest possibility that this could ever happen'. His people humoured him. 'When Reagan began to talk privately of a dream he had when someday we might live in a world free of all nuclear missiles, well we just smiled.'[5]

After his election, as we have seen, Reagan talked tough about the Soviets and the need to rearm while at the same time trying to open a personal dialogue with Moscow. He had great faith in his ability as a negotiator and thought that if he were shut in a room with the Soviet leaders for a few hours he could probably work out some sort of deal about reducing nuclear weapons. But his attempts at personal diplomacy got nowhere and he felt he was coming up against a brick wall.

During his first year at the White House, the administration did reopen arms talks with the Soviets in Geneva, known this time as the Strategic Arms Reduction Talks (START). But arms control talks always take place within a broad geopolitical context. Whereas the SALT talks had proceeded in an atmosphere of détente, these new negotiations began amid a sense of growing confrontation. The US saw the Soviet Union effecting what it regarded as a vicious crackdown against the freedom movement in Poland, continuing its aggression in Afghanistan through its military presence, and driving forward its long-term attempt to destabilise Third World regimes and impose socialist governments around the world – all part of their aim for 'world domination', as Reagan saw it. In Geneva, the START talks began in a desultory way. Alexander Haig, Reagan's first Secretary of State, wrote, 'at this early stage there was nothing substantive to talk about, nothing to negotiate, until the USSR began to demonstrate its willingness to behave like a responsible power'.[6]

It was still a major part of US policy to try to reverse the installation of the new generation of SS-20 missiles in eastern Europe and western Russia. The deployment of the Pershing IIs and Cruise missiles with allies in western Europe was intended to counter this. In November 1981, after coming under pressure from Helmut Schmidt, the West German Chancellor, Reagan proposed a zero-zero option. That is to say, the US would agree not to introduce their new generation of nuclear warheads in Europe if the Soviets would withdraw theirs. Reagan later wrote that 'I viewed the zero-zero proposal as the first step toward the eventual elimination of *all* nuclear weapons from the earth'.[7] But as far as the Kremlin was concerned this was a non-starter. The Soviet leaders saw a US President who constantly denounced them and who was calling for the largest military build-up in peacetime history. The idea that they should dismantle their own missiles before the arrival of any US missiles, or before the missiles had even been built, was laughable. It was a completely one-sided proposal: they would withdraw their missiles; the United States would withdraw nothing. The Kremlin dismissed zero-zero 'as a formula for unilateral disarmament by our side and, frankly, an insult to our intelligence'.[8] Unsurprisingly, the proposal got nowhere.

From the early days of Reagan's presidency, the peace movement in Europe had grown in size and strength. During 1983, the year in which the Pershing II and Cruise missiles were due to be deployed in Europe, huge demonstrations were held in the capital cities of the countries where they would be located. In Bonn, West Germany, one 'anti-Euromissile' rally attracted about half a million supporters. They marched behind banners calling Reagan a warmonger and featuring grotesque figures satirising Uncle Sam. In October there were demonstrations in Rome, Paris and Brussels. Everywhere the protesters had the same message: 'No Nukes'.

In Britain, the Campaign for Nuclear Disarmament was already a potent force having been established in 1958 with its slogan 'Ban the Bomb'. Having gone into major decline during the years of détente, it experienced an enormous revival in the early eighties. A Women's Peace Camp was organised at the RAF air base at Greenham Common in Berkshire, where Cruise missiles were due to be stationed, with the idea that protesters would link hands around the base perimeter to prevent the weapons from being installed. Michael Heseltine, the new Defence Secretary from January 1983, spent almost as much of his time in office trying to counter the peace movement as he did planning for the deployment of the American missiles. As he travelled Britain giving speeches in favour of the new missiles he had tomatoes, eggs, a custard pie and even a brick thrown at him. He survived them all and felt his arguments helped to neuter the peace movement, that 'the propaganda victory was ours'.[9] But the numbers coming out on to the streets suggested otherwise.

In the US there were also protest rallies. One in New York's Central Park supposedly brought out 750,000 demonstrators, far larger than any anti-Vietnam War demonstration. Protest in the US galvanised around the Nuclear Freeze peace movement that called for a halt to the production, testing and deployment of nuclear weapons. It was designed not just to appeal to activists but to ordinary people who were worried by the arms race. During 1982 it picked up an increasing number of middle-class supporters including many church-goers. The National Council for Catholic Bishops drafted a pastoral letter to be sent to the nation's 51 million Catholics condemning the arms race and implying that even the policy of deterrence was immoral because it involved the use of nuclear weapons.

Barbara Alper/Getty Images

A huge crowd at a peace rally in New York's Central Park, June 1982. More people turned up than to most anti- Vietnam War demonstrations a decade before.

Many state legislatures and city councils passed motions in favour of a nuclear freeze. By the end of 1982 Reagan's popularity had gone into decline and his approval rating had dropped to 41 per cent, an all-time low for a new President in his second year. Much of this was down to a recession in the economy, but Reagan was increasingly seen as a hawk, even a warmonger. In one opinion poll, 57 per cent of Americans said they feared that Reagan would involve the US in a nuclear war. Reagan himself began to worry about his image.[10]

During the Ivy League 82 exercise, the President had been deeply shocked when he saw all those red lights come up on the map of America marking the hundreds of nuclear missile hits. It had been as though he had seen 'the United States of America disappear', wrote the strategist chairing the exercise. This had a real emotional impact on Reagan, leaving him feeling as though it was something that 'had really happened to him'. And 'It focused his mind on the need for protection from those red dots.'[11]

Edward Teller was the nuclear physicist who had been the key player behind the development of the H-bomb in the 1950s. By the early eighties he believed that nuclear weapons were about to advance to the next stage of their development with the ability to set off nuclear explosions in space that could direct X-ray laser beams to destroy powerful objects like incoming missiles. He called this the 'third generation' of nuclear weapons (the first being atom bombs and the second hydrogen bombs). On 14 September 1982, Teller, aged seventy-four, visited Reagan in the White House for a thirty-minute meeting. He outlined his vision of X-ray laser beams in space. If such an effective defence against missiles could be constructed then this would turn Mutual Assured Destruction on its head, he told the President: it would become instead 'assured survival'. Reagan asked if an American anti-missile system could be made to work. 'We have good evidence that it would,' Teller replied.[12] Reagan wrote in his diary that evening, 'Dr Teller came in. He's pushing an exciting idea that nuclear weapons can be used in connection with Lasers to be non-destructive except as used to intercept and destroy enemy missiles far above the earth.'[13] It's not clear if Reagan had fully understood the concept that had been put to him, as Teller's idea involved igniting nuclear explosions in space to power shortwave X-ray laser beams. However, the President had clearly been impressed by the fact that such a respected figure in the scientific community should propose a missile defence system in space.

Three months later, on 22 December, the President met with the Joint Chiefs of Staff in the White House. The meeting was mostly taken up with the issue of the MX intercontinental ballistic missiles, which was mired in dispute with Congress. At this point it looked as though they were not going to get approval. Searching for an alternative way forward, towards the end of the meeting Reagan asked the military chiefs, 'What if we began to move away from our total reliance on offence to deter a nuclear attack and moved toward a relatively greater reliance on defence?' According to Martin Anderson, the adviser who had been with Reagan on his visit to NORAD, one of the chiefs phoned the National Security Advisor, William Clark, later that day and asked, 'Did we just get instructions to take a hard look at missile defence?'

'Yes,' replied Clark.[14]

When the Joint Chiefs came back to the White House on Friday, 11 February 1983, they had done their homework. Admiral James D. Watkins, the naval chief, was an engineer by training and had commanded the US Navy's first nuclear-powered cruiser. He had met with Teller and other scientific experts and been impressed that new developments in computer technology, high-energy lasers and particle beams might make a defence against incoming missiles a possibility. He came up with a short presentation to make to the President.

It concluded that a form of missile defence would avoid the alternatives of either threatening a first strike or of simply absorbing a Soviet nuclear attack and was 'more moral and therefore far more palatable to the American people'.

Present at the meeting was Robert 'Bud' McFarlane, then deputy National Security Advisor. McFarlane was a quietly spoken ex-Marine with a cool, determined-looking face and a tall forehead. He had worked on Henry Kissinger's National Security Council in the Nixon years. Clark had brought him into Reagan's White House as his deputy. By early 1983 he had become deeply concerned that the opposition to the MX missiles had led to an American impasse, while he felt the Soviets were storming ahead building and deploying more and more heavy missiles. He had been wondering about the possibility of a new technological way forward. When the Joint Chiefs finished their presentation, McFarlane piped up. 'Mr President,' he said, 'this is very, very important. For thirty-seven years we have relied on offensive deterrence based on the threat of nuclear counter-attack with surviving forces because there has been no alternative. But now, for the first time in history, what we are hearing here is that there might be another way which would enable you to defeat an attack by defending against it and over time relying less on nuclear weapons.'

'I understand,' said the President; 'that's what I've been hoping.'

Reagan asked the Joint Chiefs if they all felt the same way. One after another they said they did. Watkins summed it up by asking, 'Would it not be better if we could develop a system that would protect, rather than avenge, our people?'

Reagan responded immediately to this point by saying, 'Don't lose those words.'[15]

That evening Reagan wrote favourably in his diary about the meeting, out of which, he said, had come 'a super idea'. He went on: 'What if we tell the world we want to protect our people, not avenge them; that we're going to embark on a program of research to come up with a defensive weapon that could make nuclear weapons obsolete? I would call upon the scientific community to volunteer in bringing such a thing about.'[16] Reagan's desire to find a way to abolish nuclear weapons had suddenly been spurred into action.

The Joint Chiefs assumed that a staff group would be allocated to pursue options. McFarlane imagined that the President would in due course expect a report. But Reagan was fired up and did not want to delay. He was scheduled to deliver a national television address about the defence budget on 23 March. Still reflecting on what he had heard from the Joint Chiefs, Reagan pushed his staff to come up with an announcement on missile defence. It fell to McFarlane to draft a section of the address that would call for a major research effort towards a form of strategic defence. McFarlane was anxious about moving forward so quickly and he advised the President that as this was such a radical shift from three decades of US policy he should run it by Congress and the chief NATO allies before making an announcement. Reagan ignored his advice. He was worried that the proposal would be argued to death before it had even seen the light of day. He did not mention the initiative to his Cabinet or to the commission that was at the time consulting on the development of the MX missiles. Secretary of State George Shultz only heard about the speech two days beforehand and made several major objections. Defense Secretary Caspar Weinberger was in Portugal for a meeting when he was told, and he expressed strong opposition to it. Several senior aides were only told on the day. Reagan rewrote parts of the speech in the light of Shultz's comments but was deaf to more fundamental objections. As McFarlane later remembered, 'He was so swept away by his ability to stand up and announce a program that would defend Americans from nuclear war, he couldn't wait.'[17]

On the day before the speech, in between other meetings, Reagan worked on some of the last-minute redrafting he had received from the State and Defense Departments. 'I did a lot of re-writing,' he wrote in his diary. 'Much of it was to change bureaucratic into people talk.'[18]

Reagan spoke live from the Oval Office at 8 p.m. on 23 March. Sitting in the East Room were all the Joint Chiefs and several eminent scientists, including Edward Teller, whose conversation with Reagan only six months before had launched the President on this new policy. Reagan began by saying, 'I've reached a decision which offers a new hope for our children in the twenty-first century.' He spoke about the policy of deterrence. 'It took one kind of military force to deter an attack when we had far more nuclear weapons than any other power; it takes another kind now that the Soviets, for example, have enough accurate and powerful nuclear weapons to destroy virtually all of our missiles on the ground.' He then rattled through a list of facts and figures about how the Soviets had updated their nuclear missiles and now, he claimed, had an overwhelming numerical advantage. He spoke about the Soviet threats in Angola, Ethiopia and Central America. He said a nuclear freeze 'would make us less, not more, secure and would raise, not reduce, the risks of war'. All of this was part of his conventional hard-line posture.

But as he built towards the main thrust of his address he said he wanted to share 'a vision of the future which offers hope. It is that we embark on a program to counter the awesome Soviet missile threat with measures that are defensive ... What if free people could live secure in the knowledge that their security did not rest upon the threat of instant US retaliation to deter a Soviet attack, that we could intercept and destroy strategic ballistic missiles before they reached our own soil or that of our allies? ... I call upon the scientific community in our country, those who gave us nuclear weapons, to turn their great talents now to the cause of mankind and world peace, to give us the means of rendering these nuclear weapons impotent and obsolete.'

He ended with this rousing call: 'My fellow Americans, tonight we're launching an effort which holds the promise of changing the course of human history. There will be risks, and results take time. But I believe we can do it. As we cross this threshold, I ask for your prayers and your support.'[19]

After the transmission of the speech, Reagan joined the party of senior defence officials in the White House for coffee. 'They all praised it to the sky,' he wrote in his diary. After they had gone he reflected on what he had said. To his diary he confided, 'I made no optimistic forecasts – said it might take 20 yrs or more but we had to do it. I felt good.'[20]

The speech was well received among Reagan's core supporters in the United States. Within days, the Strategic Defence Initiative (SDI) was dubbed his 'Star Wars' programme, named after the futuristic George Lucas movie set in space in which the force for good pits itself against an evil empire. This association no doubt helped to sell it to many Americans. Others saw it, like the 1977 film itself, purely as science fiction. There was, for instance, horror in the Pentagon, and the Joint Chiefs were astonished that such a half-baked concept should be given such prominence. And in liberal circles, SDI was not popular. It was thought that it would extend the arms race into space. The cost of designing let alone implementing a protective shield horrified many Democrat opponents and even some Republican supporters. The national debt was already racing upwards as a consequence of the huge increases in defence spending; SDI would add countless billions to the total. Reflecting the concerns of the mainstream liberal establishment, the *New York Times* declared that SDI was 'a pipe dream, a projection of fantasy into policy'.[21]

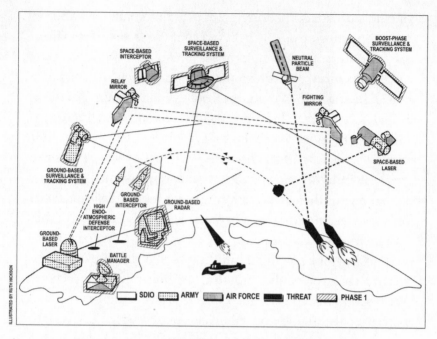

A diagram tries to explain Reagan's Strategic Defence Initiative in space, quickly dubbed his 'Star Wars' programme.

The speech brought together many currents of Reagan's thinking. He was concerned about the Nuclear Freeze peace movement and how this was affecting his image. By offering to lower the risk of nuclear war he would undermine the 'anti-nukes'. He wanted to try to find a technological approach where the United States would have a clear advantage over the Soviet Union. And if it was expensive, so much the better, as he knew the US could outspend the basket case of the Soviet economy. He wanted something that was essentially simple and catchy, not a proposal that was immersed in the complex abstractions of conventional strategic policy. But more than anything, he wanted to find a way out from the 'crazy' doctrine of Mutual Assured Destruction. Reagan's belief in his Star Wars policy would become a tenet of faith for the rest of his presidency. This was not something to be negotiated away or surrendered as a scoring point in a diplomatic exchange. It was something he deeply believed could save Americans from the horror of a nuclear holocaust.

The Kremlin was staggered by the speech. A defensive shield in space to protect the United States from incoming missiles, had it ever become a reality, would have fundamentally upset the nuclear balance. If the US knew that it could survive a nuclear attack, not only was thirty years of massive investment by the Soviet Union rendered instantly obsolete, it also meant that Washington was far more likely to *start* a nuclear war. In Moscow, where the Soviet leaders knew that America had a massive lead in computer technology, there was no way of knowing if building such a shield would take twenty years or twelve months. Leading physicist Yevgeny Velikhov was sceptical that the Americans could develop the necessary technology but his view carried very little weight as far as the leadership was concerned. Their belief in the great technological superiority of the US scored again. They treated the Star Wars idea as no 'pipe dream' but as a real and genuine threat.[22] SDI confronted the Kremlin with their own technological backwardness. Even talking about constructing a defensive shield was seen as a profoundly aggressive act.

Four days after Reagan's speech, Andropov responded. 'All attempts at achieving military superiority over the USSR are futile,' he said. 'The Soviet Union will never let that happen. It will never be caught defenceless by any threat. Let there be no mistake about this in Washington. It is time they stopped devising one option after another in the search for the best ways of unleashing nuclear war in the hope of winning it. Engaging in this is not just irresponsible. It is insane.'[23]

Just two weeks earlier, Reagan had called the Soviet Union an 'evil empire'. Now it seemed that the President was trying to overturn three decades of nuclear parity and make the US invincible. By appearing to suggest that the US could launch a first strike without any fear of retaliation, Reagan had created the Kremlin's ultimate nightmare. In his outrage, Andropov described Reagan's rhetoric against the Soviet Union and the communist system not only as 'irresponsible' but 'flippant'. He blamed Washington for failing to commit to the Strategic Arms Reduction Talks in Geneva by preferring to take unilateral action. Everything Andropov imagined about American aggression and willingness to go to war, all that had inspired Operation RYaN, seemed to be becoming a reality. Andropov was certain that this latest initiative brought nuclear war closer. And it was the United States that would start it.

6

Lack of Intelligence

The outrage expressed by the Kremlin leaders after Reagan's SDI speech clearly indicates how little Washington understood the Soviet mindset. Indeed, intelligence about the Soviet leadership and what they thought, how they saw the world and how in particular they perceived the United States, was shockingly inadequate. A CIA biographical profile of Andropov, compiled two months after he had taken over at the helm in the Kremlin, was lamentably poor in its assessment. It got the state of his health completely wrong, and it relied on a few bland judgements like the fact that as the ex-KGB chief he was 'probably better informed on foreign affairs, and on at least some domestic matters, than any other Soviet party chief than Lenin'. This showed little appreciation of how at the KGB he would have seen deep into the recesses of life in the Soviet Union, including the corruption and the organised crime he was trying to eradicate. Regarding his views on world affairs and his attitude to the United States, the report concluded that he had 'warned that a nuclear war would have catastrophic consequences and [had] spoken out in favour of East-West détente'.[1] With nothing more penetrating than this to inform them, it was not surprising that the White House should so completely misjudge the Soviet reaction.

When he became President, Reagan had appointed William 'Bill' Casey, a lawyer and long-term friend who had been his successful campaign manager, as head of the CIA. It would be from the agency in its substantial headquarters at Langley, Virginia, a short drive from Washington DC, that policy-makers in the new administration would receive their intelligence about the Soviet Union. Casey was sixty-seven when he took up his position. His appearance, grey-haired, balding and avuncular, betrayed a bulldog bark and a huge capacity for work. He pushed himself and those around him to their limits. Casey had been in the Office of Strategic Services (OSS), the US wartime intelligence service, during the Second World War. The OSS had collected intelligence and undertaken sabotage missions as well as training and supplying resistance groups to operate in Nazi-occupied Europe and Japanese-occupied Asia. Casey's great hero was 'Wild Bill' Donovan, who had led the OSS during the war and who stopped at nothing to achieve what he felt needed to be done. The OSS had many successes to its credit and in the post-war years metamorphosed into the CIA, as set up by President Truman in 1947. Casey left the world of intelligence after the war to pursue a legal career and was later appointed chairman of the Securities and Exchange Commission under Nixon. He built up a reputation as a no-nonsense intellectual who did not suffer fools gladly and who was constantly impatient to get things done. He read voraciously, could absorb complex papers quickly, and was demanding of everyone who worked for him. He had a tendency to bully staff, although he always respected anyone who could stand up to him and convince him he was wrong.

Casey returned to the world of intelligence in 1981. He came back with a strong sense that the intelligence community had grown too soft and become too academic in the years since the war. He wanted a far more aggressive approach to

understanding what the Soviets were doing, especially in the
Third World, how they were doing it and what they intended
to do in the future. He wanted to know where US interests
were being undermined by Kremlin-backed 'rebels' and more
importantly how this could be reversed. He expected intelligence analysts to prompt action, whether clandestine or overt.
He believed that Washington was already locked into conflict
with the Kremlin and it was his duty to drive this forward. As
one career intelligence insider saw it, 'Bill Casey came to [the]
CIA primarily to wage war against the Soviet Union'.[2] And
victory was the only acceptable outcome.

Ron Edmonds/AP/REX/Shutterstock

Reagan with William Casey, Director of the CIA. Casey felt he was at
war with the Soviet Union and there was only one possible outcome.

Within the first few months of his tenure he showed his
mettle. Alexander Haig wanted an intelligence assessment
on how far the Soviets supported terrorist groups to advance
their cause. He asked for this *after* he had already made a

public speech asserting that the Kremlin was behind a great deal of international terrorism. It was clear what the Secretary of State expected from the analysts at Langley. However, the first draft of their report concluded that the Soviets did not organise or direct terrorist groups and they discouraged the killing of innocent civilians. Casey exploded. He thought the report lacked rigour and was naive in its understanding of how the Soviets operated through allies and intermediaries around the world. He knew that all sorts of liberation fighters from across the Third World were trained and equipped at the Balashika training camp to the east of Moscow, even if the Soviets formally denounced the use of terrorist violence. There was 'blood on the floor' as the new director steamed against what he regarded as the 'fuzzy-mindedness' of his analysts. All CIA stations were instructed that they must start to produce monthly reports on covert Soviet action in their region. Rather like the KGB agents who thought that being asked to find evidence to support Operation RYaN was absurd, many CIA Soviet analysts played along but did not take this request to find evidence of covert Russian activity seriously.[3]

By the early 1980s the CIA had become large and bureaucratic. It moved slowly, not like the youthful, dynamic organisation Casey had been part of in the war that invented what it had to do and made up the rules as it went along. The CIA of the 1980s was bound by legislation and had to work alongside Congressional committees that were there to provide oversight. Casey was overtly impatient with having to report to Congress and made no attempt to hide his frustration at what he regarded as amateur interference in his work. There were four directorates. The directorate of Intelligence was where all the different forms of information gathered from many different sources – human, signals, electronic, imagery or open source (broadcasts, press reports, public speeches) – were analysed and interpreted in daily and weekly bulletins, and where in-depth intelligence estimates were produced on specific subjects as requested by policy-makers. Then there were directorates for Science and Technology, Administration and Operations. Each functioned as a distinct and at times separate entity to the others.

Operations was the directorate that ran spies in the field, recruited foreign agents and managed clandestine or covert ops. Rather like the British Secret Intelligence Service (MI6), on which it had been partly based decades before, it had become rather clubby. White middle- or upper-class males mostly from the East Coast liberal establishment dominated the agency, and they all shared the same values. It was the American equivalent of the British public school ethos, all rather closed and limited in outlook. By the 1980s the CIA was in need of new blood and some new ideas.

As the man who had done so much to help Reagan get to the White House, Casey had the President's ear and clearly influenced his thinking in the first years of his administration. In 1982, Reagan explicitly called for the US to support those groups fighting for freedom against communism wherever they were in the world in a policy that became known as the 'Reagan Doctrine'. Spearheading this, Casey took the CIA into battle on a variety of fronts: by supporting the Contras in Nicaragua, the Mujahideen in Afghanistan and the opposition to Gaddafi in Libya; by encouraging Solidarity in Poland; and by arming or equipping other groups in Africa, the Middle East and the Third World. But when it came to understanding the thinking of the Soviet leaders in the Kremlin the CIA had remarkably little to go on.

The CIA had good sources of intelligence on Soviet military affairs. For instance, Colonel Kuklinski, an officer on the Polish General Staff, passed on a tremendous amount of information to the agency about the military aspects of the

Warsaw Pact, a total of 30,000 Soviet documents over a ten-year period. He also provided detailed intelligence on the pressure the Soviets put the Polish government under when Solidarity emerged as a platform for opposition to communist rule.[4] Observation satellites provided first-grade imagery intelligence about Soviet air bases and military installations. And from military attachés and monitoring of tests and exercises, the CIA knew a lot about the capabilities of Soviet military equipment. In addition, the agency was able to make detailed intelligence estimates of the poor performance of the Soviet economy. In 1981 they had noted that a series of harvest failures along with shortfalls in industrial production had reduced the growth rate of the Soviet GNP to the lowest levels since World War Two. It was these detailed reports of the chronic state of the economy that enabled Reagan to describe it as a 'basket case'.[5]

However, in terms of allowing the US administration to appreciate the attitudes and intentions of the political leadership in the USSR the sources of information were very limited. Some of the doctors who treated the Soviet leaders came from the West and would sometimes pass on to the CIA what they knew about their health. Occasionally Western politicians, business leaders or journalists would meet with Kremlin officials and report back on what they found out, or any snippets they picked up. Beyond that, the CIA had for some time been intercepting radio traffic between the absurdly large Zil limousines used by Communist Party leaders to drive around Moscow. This provided some personal information but of a very limited kind. The senior party officials used to gossip on the radio to each other, discuss their favourite soccer teams and talk about the health of their rivals. Some of this was 'pretty graphic' but they rarely discussed political issues when out driving in their limousines.[6] What the CIA totally failed to pick up on in the early 1980s was the growing sense of unease among the men in the Kremlin. They despaired that they were losing the Cold War technological race, that their economy was failing, and that a new strident leadership in Washington was aggressive and increasingly threatening. On top of the normal levels of paranoia in the Kremlin, the Soviet leaders were experiencing a new level of anxiety. It was only years later that Robert Gates, deputy director of the CIA in the early eighties, summed up the Kremlin leaders by noting 'how pedestrian, isolated and self-absorbed they were'. He concluded that in retrospect 'We now know that those leaders entered 1983 even more paranoid than usual.'[7]

A Zil limousine leaves the Kremlin. All the Soviet leaders were driven around in such vehicles. For a while the CIA had them bugged.

Because there had been almost no dialogue between American and Soviet officials since the invasion of Afghanistan, there were no contacts through which either side could understand how the other was thinking. It was to be a near fatal omission.

In mid-February 1983, on the weekend following the critical meeting with the Joint Chiefs about the prospect of building a strategic defensive shield that had so excited Reagan, Washington was engulfed by a blizzard. Thick snow fell across the city bringing transport to a halt. The President and his wife abandoned plans to get away to Camp David for the weekend and instead invited Secretary of State George Shultz and his wife over to dinner at the White House. Shultz had taken over the State Department after Haig's resignation the previous June. Shultz was a product of some of America's finest academic institutions having taken a degree in economics at Princeton and a PhD at the Massachusetts Institute of Technology. He served in the Marines in the Pacific in World War Two and went on to spend part of his life in academia, and part of it working for the government as an economic adviser. He was given a senior appointment by Nixon in 1968 and four years later became Secretary of the Treasury. In 1974 he left Washington to assume the presidency of the Bechtel Corporation, a huge multinational engineering and construction company based in San Francisco where he was also a professor at the Stanford University Business School.

Shultz was known as an effective boss and a shrewd worker of the federal bureaucracy. He could be quite impass-ive when listening to presentations, giving no sign of what he thought – a reaction that led to his nickname, 'the Sphinx'. But he had definite views on most subjects, although he was very much a pragmatist. He was a big man, calm in a crisis, and with his rich, deep voice could be reassuring when speaking to the media. When he arrived at his new depart-ment he was appalled at the state of US–Soviet relations and he regarded their improvement as his principal task. He later wrote that 'Relations between the superpowers were not simply bad; they were virtually non-existent.'[8]

After their dinner during the snowstorm, Reagan and Shultz had a heart-to-heart. Reagan told Shultz how hostile he was to the concept of Mutual Assured Destruction. He asked him to think about 'How much better it would be, safer, more humane . . . if we could defend ourselves against nuclear weapons.' Shultz replied, 'Maybe there was a way, and if so, we should try to find it.' Realising that two years into his presidency Reagan had not spent time with a single senior Soviet official, he suggested that he should meet the Soviet ambassador to Washington, Anatoly Dobrynin. The White House staff were totally opposed to such a meeting. Nancy thought it a good idea. Her husband agreed.[9]

Dobrynin had been the larger-than-life Soviet ambassador to Washington for nearly twenty years. He was a big, broad-shouldered man who looked as though he liked the finer things in life. He had an infectious smile and the diplomat's charm but was totally loyal to his Kremlin masters. He was uniquely placed at the centre of US–Soviet relations, well respected by the most senior figures in the Kremlin but also highly regarded in Washington. He had played a central role in the Cuban missile crisis, providing a secret back channel for Robert Kennedy to make contact directly with Khrushchev in Moscow, bypassing the normal diplomatic procedures. Dobrynin had seen all the Presidents since Kennedy come and go. He had got on well with Nixon and Kissinger during the days of establishing détente, but in the late seventies he had taken a strong dislike to Carter who he thought was using human rights as a way of rattling the Kremlin. He had hoped that the anti-Soviet sentiments Reagan had voiced during his election campaign would transform into a more pragmatic view when he moved into the White House. So he was horrified by Reagan's outspoken assault on the Soviet leaders in his first press conference, when he called them criminals, liars and cheats. He later wrote that he was 'genuinely puzzled by the new president's fierce anti-Soviet attack'. He reflected, 'it had been quite impossible for me at that moment to imagine anything much worse than Carter. But it soon became clear that in ideology and propaganda Reagan turned out to be far worse and far more threatening.' In a meeting with the new Secretary of State, Haig told the ambassador that Reagan had not intended to offend anyone in Moscow with his words but that this outburst was just an expression of his deep convictions. As far as Dobrynin was concerned 'this clarification only made things worse'.[10]

Dobrynin had paid regular visits to the State Department for many years. Usually he went in by the main entrance when making an official visit. But on other occasions, when the American diplomats did not want his visits to be public, he was driven to the back door through a basement garage. Haig had made it clear that he was no longer interested in private meetings or in keeping the back channel open. From now on, all Dobrynin's visits would be through the front door and in full public view.

In the first eighteen months of the Reagan administration, Dobrynin had several meetings with Haig. But the Secretary of State had used these sessions simply as a means of chiding Moscow for what were seen as infringements here or there around the world. He did nothing to try to understand where the Soviets were coming from or how they were reacting to the arms build-up and to Reagan's hostile remarks. When Shultz became Secretary of State and Brezhnev was replaced by Andropov, Dobrynin hoped there would be an opportunity to improve relations between Moscow and Washington.

When at 5 p.m. on Tuesday 15 February Dobrynin arrived at the State Department for a routine meeting, Shultz told him that he had a surprise in store: the President wanted to talk with him. They drove together in Shultz's car to the East Gate of the White House, where official visitors were rarely received. They went not to the President's office in the West Wing but to the second floor and the President's private apartment. Coffees were served. Everyone left the three men, Reagan, Shultz and Dobrynin, alone. The meeting was quite intense. Reagan insisted that America wanted only peace with the Soviet Union. Dobrynin replied by pointing out that the Soviet people felt surrounded by US military bases and that the huge rearmament programme currently under way was seen as 'a real threat to our country's security'. Reagan said the threat to world peace came from Soviet aggression in the Third World and its belief in the future global victory of communism. However, Reagan assured the ambassador, 'We believe in our future and will fight for it.' The banter went back and forth with neither the President nor the Soviet ambassador ceding any ground. The meeting lasted for two hours, an unusually long time for Reagan, whose attention span was notoriously short. The President remarked in his diary, 'Sometimes we got pretty nose to nose.'[11]

The only substantive thing to come out of the meeting was an agreement that the Soviets would at last grant exit visas for the group of seven Russian Pentecostal Christian fundamentalists who were holed up in the basement of the US embassy in Moscow. Dobrynin later said that after two years in office, the Kremlin bosses were astonished to hear that the only concrete request by the President when he met Dobrynin was the release of the Pentecostals, 'as if this were the most important issue between us'.[12] In many ways the meeting confirmed that neither side really understood the other. For Reagan and for many Americans, the issue of these Christians and their desire to leave the Soviet Union was of fundamental importance. The fate of individuals was a vital part of political discourse. To the Soviet leadership, looking at a President who had spent much of his life mounting an anti-communist crusade and whose ideology was deeply opposed to theirs, it was an irrelevance.

Shultz later placed great importance on this meeting. But its significance lay only in the long term. In the short term it completely failed to provide Reagan with any deeper understanding of his adversary, or any greater grasp of how the Kremlin leaders were responding to his own anti-Soviet rhetoric. Reagan said he liked and admired Dobrynin, to the extent that he was surprised that he and his wife could 'stick with the Soviet system'.[13] But Reagan's personal feelings did not in any way intervene in his own political trajectory. He had said from the beginning of his presidency that negotiations with the Soviets could only proceed when the US had built up a position of strength. That point was fast arriving. Three weeks after his secret and unofficial meeting with Dobrynin, Reagan described the Soviet Union as the 'evil empire'. And two weeks after that he called for his new Strategic Defence Initiative. He had no sense of how these speeches offended the Soviet leaders or of how SDI particularly was seen as a way of undermining decades of Soviet policy, potentially giving the US an ultimate advantage. It was Robert Gates at the CIA who later reflected that to the Kremlin leadership, SDI seemed to offer Reagan the opportunity of launching a first strike of nuclear weapons without fear of retaliation and that this was 'a Soviet nightmare come to life'.[14]

7

Double Agents

In June 1982, a KGB officer arrived in London from Moscow to take up the post of Counsellor in one of the key residencies where Soviet intelligence agents were to look for RYaN indicators. His name was Major Oleg Gordievsky.[1] He was a short, slight man with glasses and nothing about him to make him stand out in a crowd – as required by an agent who would need to move around a foreign country anonymously. With him came his second wife Leila and his two young daughters, Maria (two) and Anna (nine months). He arrived during the climax of the Falklands War during which the local KGB team had strongly sided with the Argentines, hoping that they would give 'the arrogant Britons a bloody nose'.[2] Instead it ended in victory for Britain with its superior military technology and highly motivated army and navy.

Gordievsky was amazed by the atmosphere he found at the London embassy, a large set of buildings in Kensington Palace Gardens at the west end of Hyde Park. It was a place that was riven with animosities and rivalry. The ambassador presided over a daily conference every morning. He was long-winded, pompous, and made so many critical comments that he ended up annoying everyone. Many officials set up meetings first thing as a way of avoiding his ponderous sermons. The

KGB resident (the head KGB official) hated the ambassador, and the feeling was reciprocated. Gordievsky's direct boss, the resident, Arkady Guk, was ignorant about Britain, could not read English well and was a poor judge of character, which was not helpful in a spy. He was boastful and liked to throw his weight about to try to impress others, and he was a conspiracy theorist who was convinced that the West was constantly plotting to destroy the Soviet system. Guk was also an alcoholic who ended every day with a few large vodkas from the embassy shop where it was sold very cheaply, after which he would open up and tell anyone he met stories about his past escapades – again, not good form for a spy. Within the embassy, the GRU men from the Soviet military felt superior to both the KGB agents and the diplomatic staff. Cliques formed between groups of agents in different sections and embassy staff, all of them in competition with each other for the ear of the ambassador or the resident, or to curry favour with their bosses in Moscow.[3]

Everyone was paranoid about listening devices they were sure had been planted by the British secret service. Because the KGB went to great lengths to eavesdrop on conversations in the British and American embassies in Moscow it was assumed the British must be doing the same to them. It was believed that the British secret service had set up listening devices in the neighbouring Egyptian and Nepalese embassies that could hear conversations through walls and had even dug a tunnel underneath the embassy from which they could listen in to what was being said above. Computers and electric typewriters were banned because it was thought they could be bugged. Even manual typewriters were not supposed to be used as it was thought that the sound of the keys being struck could be recorded and decoded. There were signs in block capitals on every wall warning 'DON'T SAY NAMES OR DATES OUT LOUD'. Guk was obsessed with the Underground and told all his agents to use it as little as possible because he believed the advertising panels along the walls were glass-fronted booths in which members of the British security service sat, spying on the KGB as they went about their business. It was believed that the gardener who came in to tend the roses was a British spy, and that there were cameras on the roofs of the houses where agents lived, recording their movements. Again it was said that because this was done in Moscow, the British were bound to be doing it in London too. All this was fuelled by Soviet fears about the superiority of Western technology, which made the officers believe that of course the cunning British could develop microphones that were able to hear through walls and listen in from tunnels, and could decipher text from the sound of a typewriter typing. On arrival, Gordievsky found the paranoia, intrigues, underhand attacks and denunciations in the London embassy were 'on a scale that made the Centre in Moscow seem like a girls' school and turned life into a nightmare'.[4]

However, in this case the Soviets had reason to be paranoid. Not because they were being watched as they travelled on the Underground or listened to through neighbouring walls, but because Gordievsky, who seems to have aroused absolutely no suspicions, had a secret life. He was a double agent who had been working for British intelligence for eight years. He had joined the Soviet Foreign Ministry after university and been posted to Berlin, soon after the Wall had gone up. In 1963 he transferred to the KGB, and three years later, after training in Moscow, he was sent to the Copenhagen residency. Living in the West, he saw a world that was entirely new to him and slowly he began to change his views as he realised that economic prosperity went hand in hand with political freedom. He started to see the Soviet Union as a 'vast, sterile concentration camp'. The Soviet military invasion of Czechoslovakia in

August 1968 pushed him over the edge. He began to hate the communist state with 'a burning passionate hatred'. Knowing that his flat was bugged by the Danish security service he started talking openly about his opposition to the Soviet Union, dropping hints that he might be willing to work for Western intelligence. Finally, in 1973, he was approached by MI6 agents in Copenhagen. After a series of secret meetings, he agreed to work for British intelligence but made it clear that he wanted no payment for the information he provided, nor did he want to do anything that would bring harm to any of his colleagues. The MI6 agents accepted his terms and he began to copy hundreds of documents which he passed over at lunchtime meetings to his minder. Instead of feeling bad about what was nothing less than treachery, he felt relief and growing satisfaction that he was helping a little to undermine the totalitarian state he had come to despise.[5]

The British Secret Intelligence Service was delighted when in the summer of 1982 the agent they had recruited in Copenhagen was posted to London. On his second night in the city, Gordievsky called a telephone number he had memorised and was relieved to hear a recorded message from his minder. They met a few weeks later and it was explained that he was to have a new contact, who was introduced to him at his next meeting. This was a senior and rapidly rising figure in MI6 by the name of John Scarlett. Young, tall, elegant and already going bald, Scarlett looked like a successful business-man, but he had been First Secretary in the British embassy in Moscow and spoke Russian well. Gordievsky took to him immediately and described Scarlett as 'highly intelligent' and 'a first class intelligence officer, but also truly kind, full of emotion and sensitivity, honest both personally and in his ethical principles'. Accompanying Scarlett to each meeting was a slightly older woman named Joan who would be his case officer. She was in her fifties with ash-blonde hair and a welcoming smile. Joan also impressed Gordievsky with her skill as a listener and the speed with which she absorbed information. He again found her very understanding, and wrote that she had 'a face that seemed to embody all the traditional British qualities of decency and honour'.[6]

It was agreed that Gordievsky would meet with Scarlett and Joan once a month. But before long he had so much intelligence to impart and so many issues to discuss that meetings were arranged far more regularly. Eventually, they met weekly. The meetings took place during Gordievsky's lunch break. Almost everyone in the Soviet embassy used to leave the building to have lunch. Gordievsky would say he was off to see a contact. He would take documents with him and drive to a flat in Bayswater. There he would cover the diplomatic number plates so as not to attract attention. The meeting would never last more than fifty minutes. Often there was a secretary present as well. She would photograph the documents Gordievsky had brought. There was considerable risk in this as no one was allowed to take documents out of the embassy, so Gordievsky had to ensure he was always the last one to leave for lunch and the first to return. It soon turned into a smooth and regular operation, and Gordievsky passed on thousands of documents to MI6.[7]

KGB activity in foreign embassies was separated into a set of different lines, and Gordievsky was deputy head of the PR Line that dealt with collecting political, economic and strategic military intelligence. The job was to meet with MPs and well-informed journalists, gathering information and always looking to recruit new contacts who could supply more information over a long period of time. Gordievsky had to take over as the liaison with several long-established contacts on the left. The KGB had links to members of the Labour Party, the trade unions and the peace movement. These had been of potential value in the 1960s when Labour had been in government but most of the contacts were now growing old and were very much on the margins of politics, and some of them had no real information to pass on. Some were pensioners, but still the Moscow Centre insisted on keeping them on. Gordievsky was cynical about most of the contacts he was asked to pursue, feeling that it was rare to elicit anything of real political or economic value that he could report back with. He knew that good work was being done by Line X, which specialised in technological intelligence, but had no idea who their contacts were as each line within the KGB kept the names of its contacts secret from every other section. But still it was necessary to keep up a steady flow of reports to the Centre. It was quite common for officers to build up their contacts or exaggerate the interest of what they found simply to keep feeding the Centre's insatiable appetite. One of the contacts Gordievsky inherited from his predecessor was Ron Brown, a Scottish Labour MP and ex-trade union organiser. However, Brown had such a strong Scottish accent that Gordievsky could barely understand anything he said. When they met, he had no idea whether he was being given a rundown on events in Parliament or a description of the weather in Scotland. Nevertheless, after each meeting he would still put together a lively report, possibly including some gossip he had read in the newspapers, to keep the Centre happy.

There were various 'active measures' the residency in London were engaged in. Many of these related to the mission set by the Centre to try to prevent the deployment of Pershing II and Cruise missiles in western Europe, the weapons so feared by Moscow. As Britain's Campaign for Nuclear Disarmament (CND) was a well-established protest group, the London residency naturally showed an interest in the group's leadership. But the CND leaders were reluctant to meet with Soviet officials for fear of being compromised and thereby losing support. In any case, CND was riding a wave of popularity in the early 1980s and needed very little support from Soviet agents. Despite this, in July 1982, after a huge rally held in London organised by CND, Guk proudly boasted to Gordievsky and another colleague, 'It was us, the KGB residency, who brought a quarter of a million people out on to the streets!' The two men nodded politely, and when Guk had gone, his colleague turned to Gordievsky and exclaimed, 'Whoever heard such nonsense?'[8]

But top of the list of priorities at the KGB residency in London, as in all major KGB residencies, was Operation RYaN and the search for indicators that the West was about to launch a nuclear attack on the Soviet Union. The Moscow Centre expected their residency in London to feed them with a mass of details about preparations for war. As a major player in NATO and because of its close links to the US, what happened in Britain was of great interest to the Kremlin. The London residency was swamped with demands about RYaN from the Centre but Gordievsky found that nearly all the agents were sceptical about the operation. Living in London and travelling around the country, they were not at all worried about the risk of a nuclear war. Nevertheless, no one wanted to question their bosses in Moscow or risk his career by failing to appear keen, alert and responsive. So they all assiduously reported back on everything they were asked to, even if they did not believe in it. Reports confirmed to the Centre, for instance, that the opening of a new motorway really had a strategic function: to transport troops and equipment from one city to another. If the army was spotted driving weapons and equipment along the roads of Britain this was reported back as signs of a preparation for war. Reports that confirmed Margaret Thatcher as a puppet of the capitalists and a stooge of American imperialism went down particularly well. Every day information was sent to Moscow answering requests and every fortnight a full report listed all the indicators of imminent war that had been spotted.[9] This did nothing but encourage the paranoia in the Kremlin.

Even Guk, convinced as he was that conspiracies were raging around him, found some of the requests ridiculous. When asked to find out about the evacuation routes senior government and military officials would take in the event of a build-up to war, he allocated the task to a junior officer who had no car and no authority to travel outside London without permission of the Foreign Office. He probably made up most of his reports in order not to lose face. Gordievsky believed all this showed up 'the yawning gap between the perceptions of the Centre and conditions at the front'.[10]

In his regular meetings with his MI6 handlers, Gordievsky began to tell them about Operation RYaN. At first, Scarlett was totally disbelieving. He thought the Centre's demands were so crass and completely out of touch with the real world in Britain and the West that they could not be real. But slowly, as Gordievsky passed on more and more information about the indicators of nuclear war they were being asked to report on, it began to appear to Scarlett that perhaps Moscow really was fearful of a nuclear attack by the West. As Scarlett related the information he was picking up from Gordievsky to others in MI6, the penny slowly began to drop in British intelligence circles that Moscow was genuinely scared of the West and the aggressive stance being taken in America. But this was happening a long way from Washington. Would anyone in the American intelligence community have any interest in what a lone double agent was reporting in London?

The successful infiltration of the other side's political and military establishment was not unique to the West. Despite its sometimes absurd fumblings, the KGB and the other Soviet bloc intelligence agencies notched up some notorious successes. The Arctic fringe and the Barents Sea to the north of Norway and the Soviet Union was becoming an area of growing interest to Moscow in the mid-1970s. The naval base near Murmansk was the headquarters of the Soviet Northern Fleet and there were several nuclear submarine bases nearby. NATO firmly believed that in the event of a conventional war, the Soviet Union would seize Norway and operate its submarines from the Norwegian fjords as the Northern Fleet tried to break out into the Atlantic. It was a truism believed wholeheartedly that 'the battle of the Atlantic must be fought in the Norwegian Sea'.[11] When Western oil and gas rigs started drilling in the Barents Sea, the naturally suspicious KGB thought they were all equipped with devices to monitor both the surface ships and the submarines of the Soviet Navy.

The KGB already had a relatively low-ranking Norwegian official who had been working as an agent for them since the 1950s, Gunvor Galtung Haavik. Haavik was an elderly secretary in the Norwegian Foreign Ministry who had fallen in love with a Russian prisoner of war during the Second World War. She had been passing documents to the KGB for decades when Gordievsky, then in Copenhagen, tipped off MI6 about her existence. She was arrested during a handover of documents to her controller in January 1977. The KGB came to the conclusion that a mole within the KGB had probably named her.[12] In Moscow, the head of the Counter Intelligence Department called together seven senior officials from the Scandinavian section, including Oleg Gordievsky, and announced that it looked as though someone was leaking information. He added that it was possible 'that the traitor might be here in the room at this moment. He could be sitting here amongst us.' Astounded at this, Gordievsky pinched himself sharply in the thigh through his trouser pocket, to try to stop himself from blushing. He left the meeting feeling physically sick. But in this instance the finger of suspicion did not point to him.[13]

Meanwhile, the KGB in Oslo was cultivating another, younger contact. Arne Treholt was in his thirties, a striking, flamboyant rising star in the Norwegian Labour Party with well-known anti-American views, when he was first approached by the KGB. He agreed to supply information in return for money. His controller in the late 1970s was Gennadi Titov, known as 'the Crocodile'. Titov was very unpopular with most KGB operatives as someone who would do anything to advance his own career. He went against the grain of most officers, who regarded themselves as suave and sophisticated, with his crude jokes and rough language that relied on the constant use of obscenities. But he was good at flattering his bosses and Kryuchkov, the head of the First Chief Directorate, promoted him. Titov's flattery also seduced Treholt, who developed into a major asset for the KGB, not only passing on a great deal of information about NATO plans in the Barents Sea, but also becoming 'an agent of influence' – that is, he began to influence decisions to which he was a party in favour of the Soviet Union. He was a member of the delegation that negotiated the delimitation of the Barents Sea in 1977 between the Soviet Union and Norway. In Norway the agreement was severely criticised for being pro-Soviet.

Treholt became a gold mine of information for the KGB when he was part of the Norwegian delegation to the UN in New York, and then between 1982 and 1983 when he was at the Norwegian Defence College where he had access to top secret NATO material. His time at the college was later likened to that of 'a fox let loose in a chicken farm'. Partly as a consequence of information supplied by Gordievsky, Treholt was put under surveillance by the FBI and the Norwegian security service. He was arrested in January 1984 at Oslo airport about to leave for Vienna, where he used to meet Titov. In his briefcase he had sixty-six classified Foreign Ministry documents. At his trial the following year he claimed that he was simply trying to build bridges between East and West. The court found he had been paid about one million Norwegian kroner during the years he had been passing on intelligence and gave no credence to his claims to be a bridge builder. He was sentenced to twenty years in jail for treachery.[14]

An even brighter jewel in the espionage crown was an agent run by the HVA, the foreign intelligence division of the East German secret service, the Stasi. In 1968, Rainer Rupp was a student radical in Mainz, West Germany, long-haired and dressed like a hippy. Like so many students during that year of protest, Rupp frequently took part in demonstrations against the war in Vietnam and against West German government policies. He believed the West German state was becoming a puppet of the 'American imperialists' and too bourgeois. He grew increasingly hostile towards his home country, which he thought was 'rotten' and had not thrown off the legacy of its recent past, with ex-Nazis employed in powerful positions in government, in business and in the universities. He became increasingly angry and violent towards the society he was living in.[15]

After one big demonstration against the West German government, Rupp and some of his friends went to a local bar in Mainz for a beer and some soup. When they found they did not have enough money between them to pay the bill, an elderly man named Kurt on an adjoining table offered to pick up the tab. Afterwards, a grateful Rupp walked back with Kurt towards his student residence and they discussed politics. He realised that this man, old enough to be his father, was one of the few people of that generation who he felt shared his own view that the right wing was on the rise in West Germany. They met again to talk politics, and after a few meetings Kurt told him that he was working for the Stasi, suggesting that Rupp visit East Germany to see for himself what it was like. Kurt said to him, 'Sometimes a single man can be worth a whole army.' Rupp was very taken by this thought. He did not realise that he was in the process of being recruited into East German intelligence.[16]

Rupp felt he had been brainwashed, like all West Germans, into thinking the east of his country was run by an evil dictatorship. So after his conversation with Kurt he agreed to visit East Berlin, and while there he was asked to do some work for the Centre for Documentation. This was an organisation that was collecting documents about Nazi crimes and the rise of neo-Nazi groups in the West. Rupp became totally committed to this work and went about it with vigour. He did not at this point know that the centre he was working for was an arm of the foreign intelligence division of the East German secret police, the HVA.

As his work hunting down Nazis in the West continued, Rupp made more trips to East Berlin. He met a wider group of intelligence officials who realised they were dealing with a talented potential agent. He spoke fluent French and English and had a high IQ and a good grasp of political economy. During these visits he was asked to go on some courses to learn how to cipher and decipher messages, how to use micro photography, how to conceal and pass on mail through safe drops, and how to evade someone trying to follow him. It's not clear at what point Rupp realised who he was working for, but by the early seventies he certainly had no doubts that he was being trained as an East German spy to work in the West. A plan was put to him: he was told that he would be of value to the East if he could get a job within the European Community (the forerunner of the EU). So, looking to head in that direction, he went to Brussels to study economics. There he became a 'sleeper' for East German intelligence.

One evening in Brussels, Rupp was introduced by friends to a bright young English girl named Ann. They got on well immediately and before long were lovers. Ann Bowen had

grown up in Dorset in south-west England. She was the
daughter of an army major and on her father's recommen-
dation got a job as a secretary in the Ministry of Defence in
London. From there she was posted to Brussels as part of the
British military mission to NATO. Ann was not at all political,
but listening to Rupp talking about economics and politics she
began to see the world differently, and felt her eyes opening
to the reality of the war in Vietnam and the struggle between
communism and capitalism. Going against all protocols, Rupp
told his British girlfriend that he was working for the Stasi.
Apparently, she did not react much to this. But when Rupp
was next in East Berlin and told his controllers what he had
done, they were horrified. They believed she would report
him and he would be arrested, so they told him not to go
back. Rupp decided he would return and crossed the border
with his 'teeth chattering', expecting to be arrested at any
moment. He was convinced that if she had not betrayed him
the relationship would succeed. She had not reported him.
They were married in 1972. And in another turn of events,
Ann then agreed to work for the Stasi too. Rupp later said he
forced her into this, although she never claimed that herself.
So the spying couple continued to live and work in Brussels,
reporting back to their controllers with titbits of information
Ann would bring home from NATO that Rupp would photograph and then hand over to the HVA.[17]

A few years later a job came up at the headquarters of the
planning section at NATO in Brussels. The post called for an
economist who was good at languages and had German and
English. Rupp applied without much hope of getting through
the long application process, which included sitting an exam.
He later discovered that seventy people applied for the job, but
to his amazement he came first in the examination and was
offered the position. In 1977 he joined the staff of NATO. He
was delighted and, still as angry as he'd been in his student

days, was clear from the first that 'NATO was my enemy and I went into it to destroy it'. If Rupp was happy with getting this new job, the HVA were elated to have an agent now at the heart of the enemy's military machine.

Rupp proved excellent at his job. He was hard-working, fast, and had the ability to absorb a lot of information. He was also very popular with his fellow workers who saw him as nothing other than a dedicated, efficient and very capable colleague. He was soon promoted to senior analyst within the Political Affairs Directorate. He was directly involved with military planning and the annual defence budget, and sat on the Defence Planning Council where he would meet with senior ambassadors and defence ministers. On several occasions he sat in on meetings with Caspar Weinberger. He was on the distribution list for detailed assessments of NATO's policy regarding arms control, the aftermath of the war in Vietnam, American plans for the siting of new missiles, and so on. He was so well respected that in 1982 he was promoted again, this time to the senior position of head of the Current Intelligence Group. This group was at the nerve centre of NATO. It was where all the intelligence from the different member states about the Warsaw Pact nations and the Soviet enemy, along with details of NATO facilities, capabilities and plans, was gathered. Every morning it issued an Intelligence Summary that was sent to the Secretary General, the various NATO command organisations and the Defence Planning Council. Rupp therefore had access to a mammoth amount of top secret material about NATO and its plans. He was even privy to documents that were given the highest level of security classification and marked with the words 'Cosmic Top Secret'.

At first, Rupp took documents home with him and in the seclusion of his cellar he photographed them. Sometimes Ann assisted him. But before long he grew more confident and took a tiny, specially made micro camera with him to work.

He knew he was taking a risk. If he was discovered taking photographs of documents in his office, or if the tiny camera was found on him, he would be exposed. Carrying top secret documents home in a briefcase was also not allowed. But these were risks he thought worth taking. He took the camera and film in and out of the office smuggled inside various daily items such as the handle of his squash racket. It was quite normal to take a sports bag in and out of work so no one gave it a second thought when they saw Rupp arriving at his desk carrying his squash kit. He had his own private office with a second desk in the corner. He would use his spy camera to photograph documents on this desk, having propped his bag by the door so that anyone arriving would knock into the bag and be held up for a few seconds, giving Rupp time to hide the camera in his top pocket and appear quite normal when the person came in. He said that after a while all this became so routine that his heart 'did not beat any faster' when he was carrying out his espionage.

One of his most spectacular revelations was in early 1983 when he managed to photograph an entire copy of the NATO MC 161 document. This was a detailed annual survey of the strengths and capabilities of the Warsaw Pact countries, matched by a line-by-line analysis of all NATO assets and the precise location of missile sites and conventional forces, a sort of Warsaw Pact versus NATO balance sheet. It also contained an economic appraisal of the principal members of the Warsaw Pact. This document had the highest level of classification, 'Cosmic Top Secret', and could not be removed from the registry at NATO headquarters, where it was marked 'For Authorised Eyes Only'. To this day, Rupp will not explain how he got hold of the document and managed to make a copy. When it got back to East Berlin it was, of course, very welcome: it was invaluable to know exactly how your enemy rated your strengths and weaknesses, as well as his own comparative military and technological capabilities. But the HVA chief became thoroughly depressed as he read the document because it seemed to reveal all of the Eastern bloc's shortcomings and suggested they were 'locked into a precipitous spiral of decline'.[18] But had there ever been a conventional war in Europe, the knowledge revealed in this document could have given a decisive advantage to the Warsaw Pact nations.

Getting the images Rupp had taken out of the country posed a problem. The Stasi devised an ingenious system of smuggling film inside an ordinary can of Tuborg or Carlsberg lager. The beer was still in the can but at the bottom there was a tiny dry container into which the film was inserted through a pinhole. If the carrier was stopped and any suspicion fell on the lager can, he simply pulled it open at the top in the normal way to reveal it was full of beer.

Rupp could no longer travel to East Berlin, and as a senior Western defence official he was prohibited from travelling to anywhere in the Eastern bloc. So he would pass over his information and the photographs he had taken to couriers who came to Brussels, or sometimes he met them in other cities in western Europe, in Switzerland or Austria. Again, these drops posed a risk, but he was regarded as so trustworthy that he was never followed.

Nevertheless, Rupp had to be constantly on his guard. When he joined NATO he felt passionately hostile towards the entire organisation. Had he let slip a chance remark that revealed his true feelings he could have blown his cover in an instant. But after a few years this early 'romanticism' or 'youthful enthusiasm' had gone and he came to a 'modus vivendi' within himself. 'All I had to do was to switch on my brain before I opened my mouth,' he later recalled. He had a mathematical mind and likened it to 'operating in a binary system' where you just had to 'switch the mode' in which you were thinking to fit the current circumstances. He did occasionally begin to feel lonely 'out there at the invisible front', as he put it, but he always had his wife behind him who by this time shared the same basic political views and who supported him throughout. And one of the couriers to whom he passed documents was a visiting Professor of Political Science from the East, and Rupp always enjoyed their conversations. As a Marxist-Leninist, he felt that his discussions with the professor helped to recharge his batteries and enabled him to return again in disguise to 'the front'.[19]

When Reagan announced his Strategic Defence Initiative in March 1983, Rupp was asked to join a working group to assess the NATO response. Although his controllers in East Berlin were naturally keen on this, Rupp put on a clever show that he was too busy to take on this extra responsibility. But, of course, when his boss tried to persuade him he finally agreed to the additional workload. First of all he was sent to Washington for two weeks of intensive briefings on the technical background to the planned Star Wars programme. This convinced him that the whole project was unfeasible, and he passed this on to East Berlin. Back in Brussels, he began to hear the different European concerns about SDI. The British Prime Minister, Margaret Thatcher, was particularly opposed to it as by potentially shielding the United States from incoming missiles she believed the Americans were putting Europe at a higher risk. A nuclear war, she feared, might be more likely as it would be confined to Europe. The French had their objections too. The West Germans, although wary, thought they should line up behind Washington in support. Every stage of these discussions was duly reported back to East Berlin.

The HVA were naturally delighted with their agent at the very heart of NATO and they gave him the codename 'Topaz', the glittering jewel.[20] All the information they acquired from him was passed on to the KGB in Moscow. The KGB regarded itself as the senior intelligence service within the socialist bloc and required its junior members to share what it knew. The HVA was happy to do so but saw itself not just as a junior partner but as one of the most successful intelligence agencies of the Cold War. The head of the organisation, Markus Wolf, later proudly wrote that the HVA was 'the most efficient and effective such service on the European continent' and that they were able to capture 'many of the strategic and technical secrets of the mighty armies arrayed against us'. Through Rupp, Wolf knew of the precise sites in western Europe where all the Pershing II and Cruise missiles were going to be located along with all their detailed technical specifications. Wolf also later became well known for having penetrated the office of Chancellor Willy Brandt and so could boast that he 'knew more about the secrets of the Federal Republic of Germany than the chancellor in Bonn'.[21]

1983 was certainly proving to be a dangerous year. The fact that each side had a direct insight into the strategic planning of the other through its spies was going to have a major influence as events unfolded. But regardless of the amount of intelligence that was being gathered, it was military issues that were about to take the foreground.

8

PSYOPS

The Sea of Okhotsk is an expanse of ocean in the remote north-west Pacific. It lies between the semi-Arctic Russian island of Sakhalin in the west and the Kamchatka peninsula in the east, a land of tundra, forests and mountains jutting south into the Pacific from the easternmost tip of the Soviet Union. Around the Sea of Okhotsk are several naval bases, and Soviet submarines used the sea not only for trials but as one of the places from where, in the event of war, they would fire submarine-launched nuclear missiles against the American mainland. To the south, where the Okhotsk meets the Pacific, is a chain of islands known as the Kuriles. These islands were Japanese until the Second World War but since 1945 have been occupied by the Soviet Union. Although still claimed by Japan, the Kuriles played an important role in Soviet defence as they guarded the exit points of their navy from its bases into the Pacific, and as a consequence there were many Soviet military bases located along the island chain. Since the Second World War, the Soviet Union had regarded the Sea of Okhotsk as its own, almost like an inland sea, inaccessible to others. Then in April 1983 a huge US naval task force sailed into it.

The USS *Enterprise*, known as the 'Big E', a giant 93,000-ton nuclear-powered aircraft carrier, had appeared in the Sea of

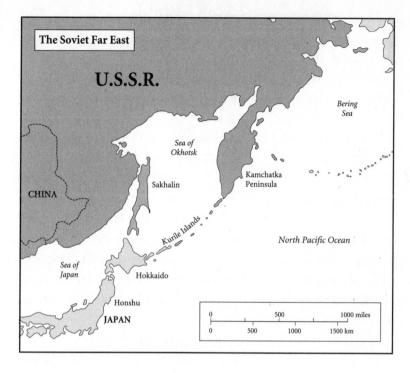

The Soviet Far East

U.S.S.R.

Bering
Sea

Sea of
Okhotsk

Kamchatka
Peninsula

CHINA

Sakhalin

Kurile Islands

North Pacific Ocean

Sea of
Japan

Hokkaido

Honshu

JAPAN

| 0 | | 500 | | 1000 miles |
| 0 | 500 | 1000 | 1500 km | |

Japan in February to take part in annual exercises conducted with the South Korean Navy. At the end of the exercises she moored at the Japanese port of Sasebo and carried out a number of ceremonial duties as crowds came out to admire the empress of the seas. On 26 March she set sail along with the rest of her task force. The sailors on board thought they were heading back to the United States. Instead, *Enterprise* made a rendezvous with two other carrier groups, centred around the *Midway* and the *Coral Sea*, to carry out an exercise known as FleetEx 83. This involved 40 ships, 23,000 men, more than 300 aircraft, and included vessels from the Canadian Navy. Admiral Lang, the commander-in-chief of US forces in the Pacific, said, 'It was the largest fleet exercise conducted by the Pacific Fleet since World War Two.'[1]

East Asia had recently witnessed one of the biggest build-ups of Soviet forces anywhere in the world. In 1965 there were eighteen Soviet Army divisions in the region; by 1982 this had grown to forty-seven divisions. Most of these were assembled along the Chinese border where there had been isolated clashes in the late sixties. In the same period the Soviet Air Force in the area grew six-fold, so that by the early eighties there were 2400 combat aircraft in the region with 800 fighters and 350 bombers, including the latest addition to the Soviet Air Force, the Tupolev Tu-22M 'Backfire' supersonic bomber. There was a major Soviet air base at Petropavlosk in the south of the Kamchatka peninsula. Here there was also a submarine base, where nuclear missile-carrying Delta-class submarines could head out into the vast openness of the Pacific. The other principal Soviet naval base in the area was at Vladivostok, which hosted the headquarters of the Soviet Pacific Fleet. This was the home of the largest of the Soviet Navy's four fleets and the 40,000-ton aircraft carrier *Minsk*.

The US Pacific Fleet too had grown dramatically as a result of President Reagan's military build-up in the early eighties. The US was also in the process of reinforcing its air bases in Japan, South Korea and on the Pacific island of Okinawa with squadrons of newly deployed F-16 fighters. South Korea was defined as a 'zone of vital interest', putting it on the same footing as western Europe in terms of US defence. The entire region, although remote from the Soviet heartland and thousands of miles from the USA, was rapidly becoming an armed camp at the edge of the world.

For the two weeks of FleetEx 83 the three giant American carrier groups sailed up and down the Sea of Okhotsk parallel to the Siberian coast, as if taunting the Soviet airfields, naval bases and military garrisons there. Accompanying them were B-52 bombers and AWACs (advanced warning aircraft) which were packed with radars and electronic listening equipment that could monitor Soviet communication systems. During FleetEx 83, the navy conducted anti-submarine warfare exercises in an area where Soviet nuclear missile-carrying subs were known to patrol. One night the *Midway* shut down all its electronics as emissions could be picked up by Soviet monitoring stations and used to locate the carrier. Silent and invisible to the Soviets, the *Midway* sailed south and suddenly turned up near the Kamchatka peninsula where according to one American analyst the Soviets 'were clearly surprised'.[2]

The following day, aircraft from the carriers carried out a mock attack on a Soviet military installation at Zeleny in the Kurile islands. Two days later the Kremlin issued a formal complaint to the US embassy in Moscow claiming this was a major provocation, asserting that American jet fighters had flown 20 miles into Soviet airspace and had remained for several minutes over their sovereign territory. The navy said there had been a navigational error. But it is clear this was no error. FleetEx 83 had been planned as a provocation to see how the Soviets would react and if they would respond, and to assess whether the Americans could trick the Soviets into not knowing where they were or what they were up to. It was designed to taunt the Soviet military, and it succeeded. Two days after the mock attack at Zeleny, the Soviet Air Defence Force in the Far East was put on high alert. They would stay on that footing for the rest of the spring and summer.

FleetEx 83 was an example of a new type of American military adventure known as psychological operations, or in military jargon PSYOPS. Admiral James D. Watkins told the Senate Armed Services Committee the following year that it was vital to adopt a policy of 'aggressive defence' that was to be characterised by 'forward movement, early deployment of forces, [and] aggressiveness on the part of our ships'. He explained, 'Kamchatka is a difficult peninsula. They [the Soviets] have no railroads to it. They have to resupply it by air. It is a very important spot for them and they are as naked as a jaybird there, and they know it.'[3]

This was by no means the first aggressive naval exercise of this sort. Two years earlier an armada of eighty-three American, British, Canadian and Norwegian ships led by the carrier USS *Eisenhower* managed to cross the 'Greenland-Iceland-United Kingdom Gap' without being noticed by the Soviets. The GIUK Gap was an imaginary line drawn across the north Atlantic from Greenland to Scotland where in the event of war NATO naval forces would line up to try to prevent the Soviet Northern Fleet from breaking out of its bases into the north Atlantic. Using a variety of concealment measures such as reducing electronic emissions and by actively jamming Soviet radar signals, the American-led armada sailed through these waters without being spotted even by a Soviet low-orbit satellite that was specifically intended to monitor the north Atlantic. At the end of the exercise, four ships peeled off from the armada and sailed north through the Norwegian Sea and around Cape North into the Barents Sea. For nine days they remained near the Kola peninsula, along which there was another series of important Soviet naval bases used by its nuclear-powered submarines. The idea seemed to be to force the Soviet Navy into defensive bastions in order to protect their ballistic missile-carrying submarines, a core feature in their strategic nuclear defence.[4]

Since the 1960s the US had been flying what were effectively spy missions along the Soviet borders to collect communications and electronic intelligence. The Soviet surface-to-air missiles (SAMs), the cornerstone of their air defence, were directed by different types of radar that sought the range, bearing and height of intruders and then operated as fire control systems for the missiles themselves. The US Air Force, flying RC-135s, specially adapted Boeing 707s packed with electronic recording systems and laden with antennae, could monitor how these Soviet radars operated and could identify changes, updates or improvements in their capabilities. An operation known as Rivet Joint flew up to eighteen RC-135s out of bases in Alaska, Okinawa, Greece, and from Mildenhall in England. The aircraft could remain in an area of airspace for hours at a time, often flying figures of eight, continuously recording and intercepting radar signals and electronic messages from the ground below. These flights were always careful to avoid actually penetrating Soviet airspace and would assiduously remain just outside. They also operated in the Middle East monitoring the activities of the different national air forces in that conflicted region. The information they recorded, generically known as SIGINT (signals intelligence), was sent back to the National Security Agency, the huge data-gathering and interpretation centre at Fort Meade, Maryland. The RC-135s could also listen in on Soviet Air Force communications. As they eavesdropped on the talkback between a Soviet fighter pilot sent up to follow them and his ground controller, one RC-135 crew were once amused to hear the pilot fail to identify the four-engine RC-135, instead counting eight engines and telling his controller that he must be following a B-52 bomber. The amusement of the RC-135 crew turned to panic when they thought the Soviet fighter was about to attack them. Instead, he was recalled to base by a doubtful controller.

This sort of activity had been going on for several decades, but the huge increase in military spending begun by the Reagan administration ushered in an entirely new campaign of psychological military warfare. The intention was to actively probe the Soviet defences, test out their early warning systems, assess their response times, and measure all this against US methods of operating stealthily. Ultimately it was about finding weak points in the Soviet defences and keeping those manning them constantly on their toes, trying to guess what the US forces would do next, to the point of exhaustion. The US Navy, which was at the forefront of the military build-up under Reagan, took the lead in some of these operations. At both extremities of the USSR, whether in the Arctic north-west or on the fringes of the northern Pacific, the navy served notice that it had the right to intrude into what the Soviets had come to regard as their own private seas. PSYOPS of course remained top secret, with only a small number of White House and Pentagon officials knowing the full picture. Former Under Secretary of Defense Fred Ikle recalled, 'It was very sensitive. Nothing was written down about it, so there would be no paper trail.'[5]

But it was not just the US Navy that carried out these operations designed to spook the Soviets. Sometimes the US Air Force would send bombers over the North Pole to observe the Soviet radars coming on. Other aircraft would probe the European or Asian peripheries of Soviet airspace. They would fly along or very near to the borders monitoring the speed of the response. There might be several flights a week, then they would stop operations, only to start up again a few weeks later. Dr William Schneider, former Under Secretary of State for military assistance and technology, saw the classified 'after action reports' and remembered how 'A squadron would fly straight at Soviet airspace, and other radars would light up and units go on alert. Then at the last minute the squadron would peel off and return home ... They didn't know what it all meant.'[6] These operations exposed gaping holes in Soviet oceanographic surveillance and in their early warning systems. Slowly they wore down those organising and manning Soviet sea and air defences. As one top secret US analysis of secret operations concluded, 'These actions were calculated to induce paranoia, and they did.'[7]

These operations clearly rattled the Kremlin leadership as well. Already worried about the Americans and their claim to be able to create a technology that could undermine the nuclear balance of power, these regular incursions only added to their unease and sense of military weakness. Andropov himself grew so frustrated that he issued an order to the Soviet Far East Air Defence Command that any unidentified aircraft carrying out border intrusions should be shot down.[8] This 'shoot-to-kill' policy was to have tragic consequences later in the summer.

American attempts to undermine the Soviet Union did not stop with the military. High on the Soviet shopping list for new technology it did not have the capacity to produce for itself were computer systems to operate the brand-new pipeline that was being constructed to transport natural gas from the vast gas fields in Siberia across the deserts of Kazakhstan and western Russia into Europe. The sale of this gas in western Europe would bring in billions of dollars of hard currency. The efficient operation of such a pipeline required sophisticated software to control the pumps, valves, compressors and storage facilities.

While the pipeline was under construction, on 19 July 1981 Reagan met with the French President, François Mitterrand, at an economic summit in Ottawa. At a side meeting Mitterrand astonished Reagan by telling him that the French intelligence service had recruited an agent in the KGB Centre in Moscow. This man, Captain Vladimir Vetrov, had been given the codename 'Farewell' by the French and he worked in the Science and Technology Directorate. He had passed on to the French thousands of documents recording the existence of a group of agents forming part of an operation called Line X, whose *raison d'être* was to copy and steal Western technology that was needed in the USSR. Mitterrand offered to pass on all that they had gathered to the new administration in Washington.

The following month the Farewell dossier arrived at CIA headquarters. Thomas Reed, who would work on Reagan's National Security Council, remembered that 'It immediately caused a storm. The files were incredibly explicit. They set forth the extent of Soviet penetration into US and other Western laboratories, factories and government agencies. They made clear that the Soviets had been running their R&D on the back of the West for years.' They chronicled what Reed described as a 'massive transfer of technology in radars, computers, machine tools and semiconductors from the US to the USSR'.[9] In addition to documents listing the names of agents and the details of the thefts, the dossier also outlined a wish list of new forms of technology the Soviets sought to acquire or pilfer from the West.

Dr Gus Weiss was another National Security Council member who was given clearance to go through the Farewell files. He was equally astounded at the scale of the Soviet operation. But he spotted an opportunity for getting their own back. Instead of simply closing Line X down, he came up with a remarkable idea for turning it to America's advantage. 'Why not help the Soviets with their shopping? Now that we know what they want, we can help them get it,' Weiss proposed. But there would be a catch: the CIA would add some 'extra ingredients' to the software to ensure that it would go wrong at some point. In effect this would be what is known as a 'Trojan horse', burying a few lines of rogue software into an operating system that would make it go 'berserk' at some future date.[10]

Weiss took the idea to William Casey at the CIA in December 1981. He loved the concept as it fitted with his overall belief that the CIA should be more active and aggressive. Casey discussed it with Reagan during a routine meeting the following month and the President gave his go-ahead. No records were kept of the operation. Just as with the PSYOPS, there would be no paper trail.

Using the information gleaned from the dossier, software that would malfunction for use in stealth aircraft, space systems, the operation of chemical plants and even a tractor factory was shipped to the Soviet Union. It is not recorded

how these disrupted military devices and industrial operations in the USSR but there must have been a lot of perplexed
Soviet computer scientists scratching their heads over the
breakdown of their systems over the next few years. However,
the spectacular results of another 'Trojan horse' soon became
very apparent.

For the maintenance systems of their new pipeline, the
Soviet gas authorities turned to a Canadian firm to supply
the software that was needed. The CIA intervened in the
deal and inserted some malware. The pipeline was opened
and for some time ran very efficiently, bringing in the promised dollars from sales in Europe. Then, one day, a section of
remote pipeline mysteriously blew up. The explosion was so
huge that it was picked up by surveillance satellites in space.
NORAD was alerted that a possible missile launch had taken
place. But there were no missiles located where the explosion
had been spotted. The air force believed a nuclear device had
been set off and the chief of intelligence rated it at 3 kilotons.
But no electromagnetic pulse had been picked up, and one
would have been sent out even from a small nuclear explosion.
The National Security Council staff in the White House were
just about to go into an emergency crisis meeting when Guy
Weiss came down the corridor and told them not to worry.
Because the operation had been so secret he was not able to
explain the details, but he made it clear that he knew about the
cause of the explosion and there was no reason to be alarmed.
Fortunately there had been no casualties, but the supply of gas
was disrupted for some time with a negative impact on the
Soviet economy.[11]

This combination of PSYOPS and diseased software left the
Soviet leadership feeling increasingly jittery. But the extent
of their anxieties was not appreciated in Washington or elsewhere in the West. It needed someone at a senior level to meet
with the Soviet leadership outside the normal and formal

world of diplomatic exchanges and report back on how the Kremlin were thinking. In May 1983, a unique opportunity for this arose.

Averell Harriman had been President Franklin Roosevelt's special envoy to Britain in the dark days of World War Two. He had travelled with Churchill to Moscow to meet Stalin in 1942, and the following year he became American ambassador to Moscow. He had grown close to Stalin, or as close as any American 'imperialist' had ever been allowed to get. During the 1960s and 1970s he had carried out a number of diplomatic missions for different Presidents and taken part in a series of personal meetings with Brezhnev. By the early 1980s Harriman was widely respected in Washington as an elder statesman but was also still remembered in Moscow as a friend of the Soviet Union. In May 1983, at the age of ninety-one, he arranged a personal trip to the city to see how the place had changed since his first visit forty years earlier and made a request to see Chairman Andropov.

In advance of his trip to Moscow, Harriman visited George Shultz in the State Department to be briefed for his visit. They agreed that Harriman should present himself to Andropov very much as a 'private citizen' and not an emissary from Washington. Shultz explained that the President had had a two-hour meeting with the Soviet ambassador, Anatoly Dobrynin, only recently and that Harriman should press for expanded contacts with Dobrynin in Washington. Shultz also advised Harriman that since he had 'talked with the Soviets more than anyone else' he should use his knowledge of the Soviet leaders to 'size up' how Andropov behaved and estimate whether or not he had a genuine desire 'for a better relationship with the US'. Shultz said it was fair to say that at present they had a 'lousy relationship' with Moscow and that the President wanted it to be more 'constructive'. Harriman told Shultz that he much regretted the President's confrontational tone and concluded by saying, 'I do wish the President could be more careful.'[12]

Harriman travelled to Moscow, and in advance of his meeting with the General Secretary he met with the Soviet expert on the United States Georgy Arbatov, who told him that in the Kremlin his visit was being seen as 'the first real meeting between the United States and the Soviet Union since the start of the current Administration'. Arbatov tried to impress his American visitor that the view in Moscow was that relations with the White House had dropped to a new low.

At 3 p.m. on 2 June, Harriman and his wife[13] were ushered into Andropov's office in the Communist Party headquarters. Harriman explained that he was on a private visit but that he had a State Department translator with him. The visit lasted for eighty minutes and began with Andropov, in the Soviet style, reading out a prepared statement to his visitor. It gives a unique insight into Andropov's thinking just two months after the outrage caused by Reagan's Star Wars speech. Andropov admitted that there were 'grounds for alarm' given the current state of US–Soviet relations and he was worried that they could 'become still worse'. He feared the threat of a nuclear conflagration 'that could happen through miscalculation'. He said he felt that Reagan was 'moving towards a dangerous "red line"'. In a clear reference to the so-called Star Wars programme, Andropov remarked that 'The engendering of new types of arms complicates our task.' He summed up his point of view when he said, 'In these conditions we can simply have no confidence in the present Administration and certain people should really give that a lot of thought.' He made no specific reference to the psychological operations that were being carried out against his armed forces but it was obvious from what he said that he was seriously riled.

In the conversation that followed it was clear that Andropov felt the Soviet Union had been slighted and was always being asked to make gestures towards better relations with America but that it was never the other way round. At one point he became heated and insisted that 'He felt the Reagan administration was demanding one-sided actions by Soviets and refusing to act reciprocally.' Harriman tried to point out that many people in the US wanted peace and good relations with the Soviet Union. He talked about Dobrynin and his important role as a bridge builder in Washington. But his words did not quell Andropov's concerns in the slightest.

In the report he wrote of the meeting for the State Department, Harriman noted that Andropov's hands seemed to be shaking during part of the conversation. He concluded that 'The principal point which the General Secretary appeared to be trying to get across ... was a genuine concern over the state of US-Soviet relations and his desire to see them at least "normalized," if not improved. He seemed to have a real worry that we could come into conflict through miscalculation.'[14] Four times during the course of their meeting Andropov had referred to the prospect of nuclear war. For a first meeting at this level since Reagan had come to power, he hoped that this clear and repeated message would be taken back to the White House: the President's sabre rattling was causing real distress. But would anyone listen?

9

Shootdown

The international passenger lounge at Anchorage airport, Alaska, was busy on the late night of Wednesday, 31 August 1983. As was routine on many such evenings, two Korean Air Lines jumbos were parked up, en route to Seoul. One aircraft, flight KAL 007, had flown in from New York; the other, flight KAL 015, had come from Los Angeles. While the aircraft were refuelled and readied for their long, eight-hour overnight flight to the Korean capital, passengers were allowed to disembark, enjoy a little shopping or just relax in one of the bars or cafés. Alternatively, if they wished they could stay on board. On this particular night there were various VIPs travelling in the first class sections. Senators Jesse Helms and Steve Symms and Congressman Carroll Hubbard were on board the flight from Los Angeles to attend the thirtieth anniversary celebrations of the US–South Korea Mutual Defense Treaty. Senator Helms wandered around the lounge, probably looking to catch up with another VIP who was on the flight from New York, Congressman Larry McDonald of Georgia, chairman of the far right-wing John Birch Society. But McDonald had had a terrible journey from Atlanta to New York, had been delayed by bad weather and had missed his intended flight and was re-ticketed on to KAL

007. Exhausted, he decided to remain on board, probably sleeping through the stopover.

Both flights, as per usual, were due to fly in tandem on to Seoul less than half an hour apart on the international air route known as Romeo 20 across the north-east Pacific. Both flights picked up fresh crews in Anchorage to fly the second leg. The crew of the first leg on KAL 007 had reported a VHF radio malfunction, and while engineers were fixing that the new crew arrived on the flight deck. The crew were as experienced as any on Korean Air Lines. Captain Chun Byung-in was in charge of the flight. He was a tall, stocky man, larger than most Korean males. He had been a fighter pilot in the Korean Air Force and was known then as an aggressive, bold flier. He had joined KAL in 1972 and was one of their most experienced pilots, having clocked up 6600 hours flying Boeing 747s, and had been flying the Anchorage to Seoul route for five years. He had just received a commendation for his long accident-free record. He had also been picked out to fly the South Korean President on three international journeys – a highly prestigious honour. He was one of the best-known pilots in Korea and certainly one of the most respected.

Chun's co-pilot that night was Son Dong-hui, who had also flown in the Korean Air Force for twenty years. He had 3400 hours' flying time on 747s. The flight engineer was Kim Eui-dong, another experienced flier with 2600 hours of flying experience in 747s. With them were a crew of twenty stewards and stewardesses. In addition another six KAL pilots and flight engineers were on board as passengers returning to Seoul after flights around the world. They were in first class. The flight was not particularly busy that night and about one third of the seats were empty. The total number of passengers and crew aboard was 269.

What happened as the crew prepared their aircraft for

Photograph by YONHAP, Camera Press London

KAL captains. Captain Chun Byung-in, in command of KAL 007,
was the airline's most famous pilot and stands in pride of place on
the right of Cho Choong-Hoon, President of KAL.

its 4000-mile flight to Seoul has been the subject of intense
speculation and debate ever since. The fact is, we will never
know how or why the flight veered so massively and tragi-
cally off course that night. The aircraft's flight data and voice
recordings, the so-called 'black box', were not analysed at the
time.[1] Of the many speculations, perhaps the most likely is
that the flight engineer put the wrong information into the
aircraft's navigation system at Anchorage. Flight KAL 007
was flying with the most modern and sophisticated airline
navigation system available at the time, in the era before
GPS came in. The inertial navigation system (INS) consisted
of three separate computer systems all linked to a gyro-
scope. This resulted in incredibly accurate readings of the
latitude the aircraft was flying at: the slightest variations of
speed, wind or direction could be picked up, and the route

to the destination continually re-computed. Even if two of the systems were to fail (which had never been known to happen), the third would continue to fly the aircraft. However, although the INS was a brilliant device, a series of latitude and longitude details had to be entered manually at the start of the flight. According to the rule book, the captain should call out the coordinates and the flight engineer would programme all three computers with the necessary data, beginning with the position of the aircraft at its starting point on the runway and then going through all the waypoints on the route. However, this was a long, laborious business that would slow up the process of pre-flight checks that pilot, co-pilot and engineer had to carry out, and official protocols were rarely followed. It was usual for the flight engineer to enter all the coordinates by himself.

The first computer he would set up would always be the captain's. It was this computer that directed the auto-pilot that actually flew the aircraft. If Kim Eui-dong mistakenly input the longitude as W139 degrees instead of the actual start point of W149 degrees, a process known as 'finger-slipping' in the trade, then the start point for the flight would have been recorded as about 300 miles to the east of the plane's actual position. Later simulations using this start point give a route similar to that followed by KAL 007 that night. However, the INS was designed to prevent such a simple error from occurring. Assuming the engineer input the correct longitude on the second computer, an amber error light would come on to highlight the discrepancy. But it is probably human nature to imagine that the first computer had been set up correctly so it must be this second computer that was wrong, and the system in use with KAL allowed the opportunity to override the error indicator. If the engineer did this and, again, entered the correct longitude on the third flight deck computer, then with the override set this would not have indicated an error.

It was theoretically possible, therefore, to set the INS with different coordinates and with the main computer that flew the aircraft being incorrectly programmed.[2]

This was only the start of the procedures. The engineer then had to enter the next seven waypoints into each of the three INS computers. These are stations along the route at which the crew are supposed to report their position. On route Romeo 20 from Anchorage to Seoul, the first waypoint was at Bethel in Alaska, 346 miles away. The next six points were purely geographical coordinates across the sea with fancy names: NABIE, NUKKS, NEEVA, NINNO, NIPPI and NOKKA. At the last of these the aircraft would be near Japan and have entered the zone covered by Tokyo Air Traffic Control. Having reached that point, the engineer would then input the final waypoints to Seoul, ending at Kimpo airport. It was highly unlikely that the INS computer system could fail. So assuming the crew were using it that night – and it would have been totally bizarre for them not to – then some form of human error in operating it must have taken place.

Flight KAL 007 was due to take off at 3.20 a.m. local time, with a flying time of eight hours and twenty minutes, arriving at Seoul just before 6 a.m. Korean time. However, on this night the headwinds along Romeo 20 were less strong than usual so the departure time was put back by thirty minutes. The following KAL flight, 015, was to take off twenty minutes later and would follow 007. In the intervening time Captain Chun carried out his last-minute checks and made a series of strange modifications to his flight plan and to the amount of fuel carried on board. The scribbles he made alongside the flight plan suggest that as a loyal KAL pilot he was trying to slightly shorten his route in order to save on petrol and therefore reduce costs to the airline. The manifest that Chun signed before departure shows that he had taken on less fuel than usual, thus reducing the weight of the aircraft. But the reality was that Chun had taken on 7900lb *more* fuel than was required. There is no simple explanation for such a peculiar error from an experienced pilot who was known to be pains-taking in his preparations. Was it just an untypical mistake? Or was it a sign that Chun knew he was going to be taking a detour that night and would need extra fuel?[3]

KAL 007 eventually took off from Anchorage at 4 a.m. local time, with KAL 015 taking off only fourteen minutes later. From the outset, 007 began to deviate slightly north from its correct route. By the time it reached Bethel after fifty minutes of flying it should have been just south of the waypoint but in fact it passed about 12 miles to the north. Either ignorant of this or trying to mislead, 007 reported back that it was passing Bethel, and headed out over the Pacific.

Flying long-haul flights at night for thousands of miles over featureless ocean is known to be among the most boring jobs for flight crews. By the early eighties computers did most of the flying and had taken the fun out of aviation. The three men on the flight deck simply had to keep awake and double-check what was going on. There was nothing else to do or to see. Although they were well rested, keeping alert for hour after hour could not have been easy. Many crews have described helping to pass the hours by playing cards, or reading, or with some other distraction. It is also entirely possible that Captain Chun, having flown KAL 007 for the first thirty minutes or so, did what KAL captains were encouraged to do in the era before threats of terrorism closed off the flight deck from the rest of the aircraft and went back into the cabin to welcome the first class passengers. He would have known that he had a Congressman on board and would have wanted to speak with him. In addition there were the three KAL captains and three flight engineers also in first class. They were friends and colleagues, and Chun might have enjoyed chatting with them while being served some Korean delicacies by the first class cabin crew. This is purely surmise, but all communications with KAL 007 from its departure were with the co-pilot, Son Dong-hui, indicating that it was possible that Chun was not on the flight deck.

Whoever was in command of KAL 007, the aircraft slowly drifted hundreds of miles off course. As it did so, a series of extraordinary coincidences occurred. The aircraft had some difficulty in communicating with Anchorage Air Traffic Control so instead of messaging direct it communicated through its sister aircraft KAL 015 flying behind it. This was not an unusual procedure, and as 007 reported back its position incorrectly to 015, this information was passed back to Anchorage without question. There was a lot of chatter between the two aircraft, the normal sorts of things air crew talk about: future shifts, good restaurants, sporting fixtures. But no one on 015 picked up that 007 was no longer ahead of it but drifting way off course. This in itself is remarkable. Furthermore, all KAL jumbos were fitted with air-to-ground navigational radar. But, astonishingly, no one on 007 seemed to notice that as it crossed the Kamchatka peninsula it was crossing land when it should have been over sea. Or, later, that the Kurile islands should have been to the aircraft's north, but were in fact to the south. The only partial explanation for these failures is that Korean Air Lines crews paid great deference towards their captains. As Chun was the most experienced and highly valued captain in KAL, it might have been that his co-pilot and engineer did not at any point want to challenge him if he were on the flight deck or call him back to see what was happening if he were in the cabin chatting with colleagues. The later ICAO report concluded there had been 'a considerable lack of alertness and attentiveness on the part of the entire flight crew'.[4] This was putting it mildly. Whatever was going on was an outright dereliction of flying duties. Unless, of course, the crew were deliberately flying on a different course but reporting that they were proceeding perfectly normally down Romeo 20.

A few hours before KAL 007 took off from Anchorage, another aircraft had taken to the skies of the north-west Pacific. Cobra Ball was a top secret US operation active since the 1960s, its remit to monitor Soviet missile tests. Many of these missiles were fired from the west of the Soviet Union and travelled up to 7000 miles before landing on the Kamchatka peninsula or in the adjoining Sea of Okhotsk. By 1983 the Cobra Ball monitoring process was being carried out by RC-135 aircraft equipped with two high-resolution cameras to photograph the re-entry of the missiles into the Earth's atmosphere. Each aircraft also carried computer systems that could detect and record the automatic signals sent by the missiles to the ground controllers. They could be used to monitor the guidance systems and the accuracy of the missile tests as well as the number of warheads carried by a missile, something that was regulated by the SALT I treaty. This is known as telemetry intelligence, or TELINT, and was of great significance to the American intelligence community. It could be used to ensure the Soviets were complying with their treaty obligations.[5]

The classified RC-135 missions were flown by pilots from Strategic Air Command out of a tiny remote island in the far west of the Aleutian Islands called Shemya. Each aircraft always had two navigators on board running separate navigation systems to ensure the aircraft did not enter Soviet airspace in error. When in position, they would normally fly figures of eight, recording the information they were assigned to gather. The photographic and computer data was then sent direct to the National Security Agency in Fort Meade, where signals intelligence gathered from all over the world was processed. The Cobra Ball missions were flown on average once every two or three days.

The RC-135s were only 'scrambled' when there was credible evidence of a launch. On the night of 31 August, the Norwegian intelligence service picked up signs of increased activity at a launch site in the far north-west of the Soviet Union near Murmansk. This was passed on to Fort Meade, who directed a satellite to photograph the launch site and decided that it looked as though the Soviets were about to test a new missile known as the PL-5. Shemya was immediately informed and a RC-135 laden with cameras and computers was airborne within a few minutes. It took up position off the east coast of the Kamchatka peninsula and started its routine of flying back and forth near to where it expected the missile to re-enter.

In these instances it was a case of everyone keenly observing everyone else. The Americans recorded details of the Soviet missile launches; the Soviets monitored the RC-135 flights. But if the American aircraft was on the edge of its radar coverage it would fly in and out of the Soviet radars. The operators would follow a blip on their screens, knowing it to be a RC-135 spy flight, and would then lose it briefly. Then it would fly back into their coverage and the blip would appear again until disappearing a few minutes later. On the night of 31 August it seems that the Soviets did not test-fire the PL-5, so after a few hours the RC-135 was recalled to its base. It passed out of Soviet radar coverage at about 1 a.m. and landed back in Shemya shortly after 2 a.m. Tokyo time.

While the RC-135 aircraft was still in its monitoring position that night, flight KAL 007, by now more than 150 miles off course from Romeo 20, flew into the same area, heading dangerously towards the Kamchatka peninsula. The Soviets later said they picked up the signal of a second aircraft at 12.51 a.m. The radar operators could well have seen the blip on their screen disappear and then reappear again. But this time, to their astonishment, after a few minutes as one blip turned back and disappeared, the other aircraft continued on into Soviet airspace directly towards Kamchatka. Moreover, it seemed to be heading towards Petropavlosk, where there was a major airfield and a naval port with a nuclear submarine base. This would have caused immediate alarm as it was breaking with the routine of these spying flights and entering a prohibited area of Soviet airspace. The whole region had been tense since the FleetEx 83 exercises in April, after which Andropov himself had ordered the Soviet defences to shoot-to-kill any intruder over Soviet territory.

Inside KAL 007 the passengers of course had no sense of the danger they were flying into. Many would have been watching the in-flight movie. In those days the film was projected on to screens that had been pulled down throughout the cabin. That night a little-known American movie called *Man, Woman and Child* was being shown. Others would have been sleeping in anticipation of a dawn arrival in Seoul.

At this point, if KAL 007 had been flying correctly down Romeo 20 it would have been passing the waypoint named NEEVA. It should have contacted Anchorage Air Traffic Control to report passing this point. It failed to do so. And, remarkably, Anchorage did not try to contact the aircraft to find out why it had not made a navigational report. Instead they contacted the sister flight KAL 015 which reported that all was well with 007. It seems incredible in retrospect that so many errors were made separately but simultaneously by air traffic control and on the flight deck without someone trying to sort out what was going on.

The nervous ground controllers of the Soviet Far East Air Defence Command now had evidence of an aircraft that seemed to have had some sort of rendezvous with an RC-135 entering one of their most sensitive military areas. They contacted local air traffic controllers to see if there were any other military or civilian flights in the area. But it was the middle of the night and no one was conducting exercises at this time. They later said they tried to contact the aircraft on emergency frequencies without success. There were clearly several minutes of panic among the air defence controllers as they watched the blip on their screens moving faster than RC-135s usually flew. The controllers knew that as well as national security, jobs and careers were at stake here. Officers who had failed to respond appropriately to previous violations had been demoted or discharged from the military. But still there was hesitation. Almost certainly the controllers in Kamchatka would have contacted the National Command Post of the Soviet Air Defence Force at Kalinin, not far from Moscow, and eventually, after more than half an hour, at 1.37 a.m., four Soviet fighter jets were scrambled. As they roared into the night sky, flight KAL 007 continued its journey, seemingly oblivious to the alarm it was causing. The Soviet jets gave pursuit but they never saw the airliner.[6] By the time they would have caught up with the Korean Air Lines jumbo, it had left Soviet territory and entered international airspace over the Sea of Okhotsk. For the interceptors, whatever they were looking for had got away.

We have no idea what was taking place on board the flight deck of KAL 007. The aircraft was well and truly lost but its crew did not acknowledge this or appear in any way concerned. After a few minutes over the Sea of Okhotsk, 007, which should have been passing the waystation of NIPPI, transferred from Anchorage to Tokyo Air Traffic Control. In a burst of messages it reported passing NIPPI even though the plane was 150 miles from it. We have to assume that the Soviets were intercepting such messages sent in the clear, but as they were in English there would have been a delay while they were translated. If the transcripts appeared in time they would probably have made the ground controllers believe that it was all part of the process of deception – in Russian known as *maskirovka*. This is how the Americans would disguise a spying mission.

Certainly the Russian military had nothing to be proud of so far. Their air defences had not proved to be efficient or fast responders and an unidentified aircraft that they believed was on an American reconnaissance mission had flown right over Kamchatka from east to west. Maybe they hoped that the strange blip on their screens would now disappear; that the mysterious intruder would turn south and, staying within international airspace, fly away. Their surprise and alarm must have been great when the aircraft did the opposite. It turned slightly to the north and was now heading directly towards Sakhalin island, another area of Soviet military bases and intense sensitivity.

At 2.44 a.m. the aircraft was picked up by Soviet radars on Sakhalin at Yuzhno-Sakhalinsk. It was still more than 200 miles from Sakhalin island but was approaching at the rate of 8 miles per minute. Twelve minutes later, a second force of Soviet fighter jets was scrambled from Sokol air base on Sakhalin. Within minutes three SU-15s and a MiG-23 were in the air racing to ascend to the height of the Korean airliner; supporting them were two more MiG-23s that would remain at a lower height as back-up. The next forty minutes were the crucial moments that would determine the fate of KAL 007 and the 269 passengers and crew on board.

The reason for the sudden turn to the north might have been that the flight engineer on KAL 007 had started to pro-gramme into his INS system the final waystations en route to Seoul. The INS by this point was probably totally out of joint. The captain's computer had throughout the flight most probably been 300 miles out of position. The other two had been reporting back what its unquestioning crew believed were indications that they were flying down Romeo 20. In the conversations with KAL 015 there was still no sense of alarm.

And all conversations were still with the co-pilot, Son Dong-hui. There was no word directly from Captain Chun. Maybe he was still in first class with his colleagues.

The move to the right was interpreted by the Soviet radar controllers as clear evidence that this was a military flight as it seemed to direct the intruder on to a course between two fighter stations on Sakhalin. Both stations would have been defended by batteries of SAM missiles and the mysterious aircraft seemed to be trying to avoid these. At about this point the Soviet Air Defence regional command at Kharbarovsk on the mainland was alerted. The deputy commander was woken up and informed of the situation. He had to decide what to do next.

It was the middle of the night in the remote north-west Pacific but the eyes and ears of several military listening stations were wide awake. Over the following days a mass of detailed information would be released about what happened during the next few minutes. At Misawa in north-east Japan there was a huge American electronic listening station that acted as a focal point for the collection of intelligence across the west Pacific. It monitored signals not just within the Soviet Union but also in China and North Korea. Here naval, aviation and military teams gathered masses of information, processed it and forwarded it to the Pentagon, to the separate forces' intelligence agencies and to the National Security Agency. The operators sitting in rows wearing headphones at their electronic eavesdropping equipment were able not just to see when Soviet radars were turned on but to monitor and record what these radars were seeing. They could also observe Soviet communications between regional command bases and their headquarters in Moscow. They were known as 'snap-ons' as the observers could see when the scrambled link was snapped on but could not then follow the encoded conversation. An increase in this level of traffic was nearly always a sign that something was up.

There was also a listening station at Wakkanai on the bleak far north of Hokkaido, Japan's northernmost island. This was only 27 miles from the southernmost tip of Sakhalin. Here too there was a Japanese radar station and electronic listening post. But Japan had a long-established commitment to avoid military involvement and was eager not to get drawn into Cold War politics. Alongside the Japanese establishment at Wakkanai was a top secret American installation where thirty of the country's most experienced signals specialists listened in to Soviet signals traffic from their Far East Air Defence Command. In August 1983 this installation was very new and so secret that many top Japanese government officials did not even know of its existence. All of these stations had the ability to record the signals they picked up, and they began to tune in to events that were unfolding in the skies over Kamchatka and Sakhalin.[7]

The lead pilot of the SU-15s that had been scrambled to track down the mysterious intruder was a highly experienced senior officer in the Soviet Air Force by the name of Major Gennady Ossipovich.[8] He was the deputy commander of what the Soviets called a 'regiment' (in the West, a 'wing') of squadrons and headed up the night shift on duty on 31 August at Sokol airfield just north of a large naval base on Sakhalin. For several months, Ossipovich recalled later, his regiment had been scrambled almost daily as various American aircraft were identified in the Sea of Okhotsk approaching Sakhalin. These were either Rivet Joint operations, which had been going on for years, or Cobra Ball missions, but both sets of flights always stayed outside the Soviet borders. More recently there were the PSYOPS flights that came right up to and occasionally entered Soviet airspace before speeding away. Ossipovich and his crews were exhausted from being scrambled for so many interceptions that came to nothing.

However, on this occasion, once he was airborne Ossipovich was told to check his armaments by firing his guns. This was a very rare order and he was surprised. When he asked what was happening his ground controller told him there was an intruder about 20 miles from the border. He was then directed to a position about 40 miles behind the Korean jet, too far away to see it. After a few minutes he was told it had turned right. 'Surely to the left, not to the right?' he asked, assuming the aircraft would be trying to escape Soviet territory rather than turn towards it. A few seconds later he received confirmation that the aircraft had turned to the right and he was instructed to close up to a distance of 20 miles. This he did. He was told to lock his anti-aircraft missiles on to the target. He did as instructed. As he closed in he could just pick out the shape of an aircraft, and reported at 3.12 a.m. that he could see the aircraft visually and on his radar: 'I see it. I'm locked on to the target.'

By this point, the deputy commander who had been woken up in the regional command centre at Kharbarovsk decided he had to get authorisation from Moscow before ordering the shooting down of an aircraft, even if it was an American spy plane flying through prohibited Soviet airspace. The Far East Air Defence Command was going through a reorganisation and the ground controllers had been left without a secure link and had to cross to another building to place a call. Here the Kharbarovsk deputy commander tried to contact Marshal Alexandr Kardunov, commander-in-chief of the Soviet Air Force and a Deputy Defence Minister. The American listening stations monitored the call as he made contact with Air Defence Headquarters in Moscow, and they could hear as he was put on hold. It was just after 10 p.m. in Moscow. The call was then scrambled and became a 'snap-on' so they could not tell whether he got through or, if he did, what orders he was given. The American electronic listening stations then picked up a set of 'snap-ons' as the Soviet air defences suddenly woke up and went into overdrive. Kalinin and Moscow sent signals to Kharbarovsk, Kharbarovsk sent messages to the air base at Sokol airfield, but who said what to whom remains unknown. The Moscow controllers probably reminded the local commanders about the standard rules of engagement in which an intruder had to be visually identified, given a warning, and ordered to land at the nearest airfield.

At this point, at 3.17 a.m. in the night sky above Sakhalin island, KAL 007 appears to have speeded up and made another change of direction. It could have been that the INS system on board was trying to catch up with the newly programmed coordinates and to correct its path. But as far as the watching Soviets were concerned this was clear evidence that the intruder was trying to take some sort of evasive action. Ossipovich, 20 miles behind and with his missiles readied, interpreted the aircraft's movements as a manoeuvre to get away from him. But instead of being told to fire he was now ordered to approach the aircraft and try to force it to land. In accordance with his training, Ossipovich would have been flying below the target aircraft so as not to be seen. He reported that he could see its navigation lights flashing. He then moved closer, and although he could not see the logo on the tail fin he could see a row of windows on the side of the aircraft. The windows would have been dark as the screens would have been down to allow passengers to sleep. The outline of a Boeing 747 jumbo was quite different to that of a Boeing 707, from which the RC-135 was adapted. But both had four engines below the wings and Ossipovich had never been trained in the identification of B-747s. He was absolutely sure that this must be some kind of spy plane disguised as a civilian airliner or a large cargo plane. He simply did not believe that a civil aircraft with all its modern navigation technology could possibly be so far off course.

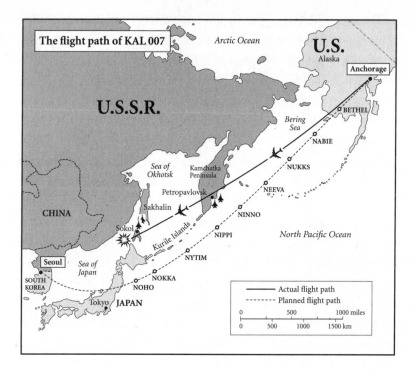

The flight path of KAL 007

According to the international rules of the air, Ossipovich tried to attract the attention of the intruder's crew by flashing his lights, then by waggling his wings. When neither of these tactics worked he was ordered to fire across the front of the aircraft to alert it. Having 'intercepted' an aircraft, he was then supposed to lead it down, and all aircraft had to follow an interceptor to the nearest airfield. Ossipovich's SU-15 was not armed with tracer, which would have glowed yellow or red in the dark, but with cannon. When cannon-fire left his aircraft it would have glowed for a fraction of a second but then would have been difficult to see in the darkness. But the sound of the SU-15's guns firing should have been clearly audible. 'Yolki palki!' exclaimed Ossipovich when he was ordered to fire in advance of the intruder. This could be translated as 'What the hell?' or something more crude like 'Holy shit!'. In thirteen years of monitoring American flights he had never been asked to do this before.

The crew on the flight deck were clearly not looking out for signs from other aircraft nearby. At 3.20 a.m., Tokyo Air Traffic Control gave KAL 007 approval to climb to a pre-agreed new height of 35,000 feet where the air was thinner and the aircraft used less fuel. It seems that at the exact time that Ossipovich was trying to warn the intruder with cannon-fire, the crew were concentrating on ascending to this new height.

The next few minutes remain very confused. The Soviet ground controllers were having difficulty following the intruder even though it had been within Soviet airspace for several minutes, and communication with the fighter planes was getting tense as the situation neared its climax. In the air, Ossipovich reported that the airliner had slowed down, presumably as it had begun to climb, and he had shot up alongside it. 'I'm abeam of the target,' he reported with some annoyance, meaning that he was below and alongside KAL 007. Just about at this exact moment, at 3.23 a.m., co-pilot Son Dong-hui reported to Tokyo that he had reached the new altitude of 35,000 feet. Meanwhile, Ossipovich slowed up to fall in again on the airliner's tail, and at 3.25 a.m. he was back in a position to fire his missiles.

About one minute later Ossipovich was ordered by his ground controller to fire. He launched two air-to-air AA-3 missiles. Each contained a warhead of about 40kg (88lb) of high explosives. One was a heat-seeking missile that would have been attracted to the Boeing 747's engines, and it exploded in the left wing, starting a fire. The second missile was radar-controlled and hit the rear of the aircraft, immediately causing the lights to fail and the passenger cabin to depressurise. Ossipovich reported back to his controller, 'The target is destroyed.' By this he meant that his missiles had connected and he had been able to see the explosions, which he described as being bright red. Now running low on fuel, Ossipovich peeled off and returned to his base.

However, even the last minutes of flight KAL 007 remain a mystery. About half a minute after Ossipovich's missiles had hit, co-pilot Son called Tokyo Air Traffic Control. He gave no Mayday signal but the controllers had difficulty hearing his message, which was shouted on the radio with indistinguishable sounds in the background. He made no mention of being hit by missiles. The message was recorded as 'Radio . . . Korean Air Zero Zero Seven . . . All engines . . . Rapid decompressions . . . Descending to one zero [10,000 feet – the standard height at which passengers can breathe without pressurisation or oxygen masks] . . . Delta . . . ' These were the last words heard from the crew of the stricken airliner.

It seems that an announcement was made on board in Korean, Japanese and English: 'We are making an emergency descent. Fasten your seat belts. Put on your oxygen masks.'[9] But it is impossible to imagine what was happening inside the cabin after the missiles hit. The quiet, sleepy calm of a long-haul night flight would have suddenly turned into terrifying chaos. The outside air temperature at 35,000 feet was minus 50°C. As the rear of the aircraft was hit, the sudden inrush of freezing air and the loss of oxygen would have generated a thick mist in the cabin. Many passengers might have rapidly frozen to death. Others, including children and babies and anyone who did not have a seat belt on, could well have been thrown around in the cabin. Some might have been sucked out of the gaping hole in the rear of the aircraft. Some of those further forward who put on the emergency oxygen masks and who were wrapped in blankets might have survived for a few dreadful minutes in blackness as the plane rapidly fell earthwards.

It was another nine minutes before the jumbo disappeared from radar screens and crashed into the sea. It was 365 miles off course when it was shot down, but only a few minutes from leaving Soviet territory and entering international airspace. Some fishermen on a Japanese boat, illegally fishing in the waters to the south-west of Sakhalin island where the sea was rich with squid and shellfish, reported hearing a boom and a flash in the sky above them. Then, some ten minutes later, they heard the roar of a plane passing low overhead. It was still dark and there was thick cloud cover. The engines seemed to cough and scream. Then, coming into vision, the aircraft passed near the terrified fishermen who saw it hit the sea and explode.[10] It was the end of KAL 007 and anyone on board who had survived the terrifying descent.

At Tokyo Air Traffic Control there was confusion and concern. Flight KAL 007 had made a strange call about decompression and was not responding to further requests to report back. After ninety minutes of hesitating about the lack of contact, at 5 a.m. Tokyo time an alert was put out about a missing and overdue airliner in the north Pacific. The Japanese military were asked to mount a search and rescue mission. This took a couple of hours to organise and then the search began at the point on Romeo 20 where the air traffic controllers assumed the aircraft had been, hundreds of miles from where it had actually come down. At the Wakkanai listening post the American signals specialists working through the night had followed the whole episode, listening in to the dialogue between the Soviet ground controllers and the SU-15 pilot Ossipovich. They had seen the aircraft drop to a height of 1000 feet before it fell off their radar. But they were as puzzled as the Soviets as to what this aircraft was, who it belonged to, and what on earth it was doing crossing the prohibited areas of Kamchatka, the Sea of Okhotsk and Sakhalin island.

When the confusion was sorted out over the next few days, the Cold War would become several degrees hotter.

10

Outcry

The first reports of a missing airliner in the Pacific came in to the United States during the evening of Wednesday 31 August.[1] The President was on holiday at Rancho del Cielo, his ranch near Santa Barbara in the Californian mountains. Both he and Nancy were looking forward to the Labor Day long weekend. Most of the senior White House staff were also on holiday at various points around the US. Only Ed Meese and the President's Press Secretary, Larry Speakes, were with Reagan. William Casey, the director of the CIA, was in Washington, as was George Shultz who, because it was so quiet with the President away and Congress in recess, had invited close friends from California to come and stay for a couple of days. The first Shultz heard about the incident was when he was called at 6.30 the following morning with news that a Korean airliner had disappeared over Soviet territory and had probably been shot down by the Soviets. He immediately realised the enormity of the situation. He was annoyed he had not been woken earlier. His limousine was soon waiting for him outside his home and he set off for the State Department. For Shultz, it would be the beginning of a frantic day that would reignite the administration's hostility towards the Soviet Union.[2]

By this time it was seventeen hours since Gennady Ossipovich in his SU-15 had been ordered to shoot down flight
KAL 007 over Sakhalin. Although the Secretary of State had
not been alerted until the Thursday morning, America's security agencies had been hard at work during the night. At just
after 3 a.m. local time at Misawa, Japan, an alert radio analyst
picked up traffic between a Soviet fighter pilot and his base
controller. She called her supervising officer over and they
could see that there had been a 'border violation' in Soviet
airspace, but could make little sense of what was happening.
Meanwhile, the specialists at the ultra-secret SIGINT operation further north at Wakkanai were recording the principal
sequence of events in real time and picked up the report by a
Soviet fighter pilot that he had fired his missiles. They even
heard the sound of live firing in the background. The larger
Japanese station at Wakkanai had also been recording signals
but the morning shift had not yet arrived to start their analysis.
The first question the analysts asked was if this was all part of
a Soviet exercise or if the Soviets had shot down an American
reconnaissance plane. But it was soon confirmed that the RC-
135 flying the Cobra Ball mission that night had landed safely
back at Shemya well over an hour before the shootdown.[3]

At 5.30 a.m. Tokyo time, the Japanese Transport Ministry
finally reported that flight KAL 007 was missing en route to
Seoul. Over the next couple of hours US intelligence officers
at Wakkanai tried to put together the information they had: a
report of a Soviet fighter pilot firing his missiles in what still
might have been an exercise over Sakhalin; reports of many
'snap-ons' between Moscow and the Far East Air Defence
Command; confirmation that no American aircraft were
missing; and news reports of a missing airliner. The question
remained, how could a civil airliner have been so far off course
over prohibited Soviet territory? Finally, as more and more
officers began to listen to the recordings, the penny dropped.

They had no secure link with the main centre at Misawa so they told them what they had heard over an open telephone line, reporting, 'Roger, we have an LMF [live missile firing].' At Misawa this message caused pandemonium. Everyone started charging about trying to listen to the recordings. The senior officer had to call his team to order. At just after 8 a.m. Tokyo time the Misawa watch officer filed a Critical Intelligence report, known as a CRITIC, to the NSA data collection centre at Fort Meade, reporting that Soviet air activity over Sakhalin might be linked to the downed airliner. It was logged at 7.10 p.m. Washington time. Within minutes the signal was put out on the top secret US government communications network, a sort of early secure intranet that encompassed the White House, the State Department, the Pentagon, the CIA, and other key security agencies. At first it was decided that as this related to a civilian airliner it was not a matter of national security. But the alarm bell had been metaphorically sounded.[4]

At the State Department, news of the missing airliner was itself causing concern. The flight had started in New York. There would be many Americans on the aircraft. It was soon realised that a right-wing American Congressman was on board. Some began to ask if the whole thing was some form of bizarre assassination plot against Larry McDonald. Lawrence Eagleburger, the Under Secretary of State, was informed. The director of Soviet affairs who had dealt with the April crisis over the mock attack on a Soviet base on the Kurile islands was called back to his office. Richard Burt, his boss, was at dinner with his fiancée and was called four times at the restaurant before later in the evening he returned to the State Department. But they decided not to wake up the Secretary of State until the situation was clearer.

On the other side of the world, anxious relatives were gathering at Kimpo airport in Seoul unclear about what had happened to flight KAL 007. Korean Air Lines had no information but after a couple of hours put out a statement that they believed the plane had been forced down and had landed on Sakhalin island. It was a ghastly twist, giving the relatives of those on board the stricken jumbo false hope. There was no word at all from Moscow about the incident.

Meanwhile, back in Misawa, American intelligence officers struggled to listen to and translate the poor-quality recording that had arrived. An officer at Wakkanai was instructed to rush to the Japanese recording station alongside the small American base and ask if they could borrow their better-quality recordings. After a ceremonial cup of green tea, the tapes were handed over and the officer rushed them to a plane to get them to Misawa. There, officials were completely stunned when they translated the message from the fighter pilot: 'The target is destroyed.' They passed this and further details through another set of CRITIC messages, and in Washington alarm bells rang more loudly. By the early hours of the morning (Washington time), the various intelligence agencies, including the CIA and the Defence Intelligence Agency (DIA), had concluded that the most likely probability was that the Soviets had shot down a civil airliner. There was shock and horror among the officials working through the night. When the message from the pilot that he was 'abeam' of the aircraft was translated it was thought that he must have been able to see that it was a civilian airliner but he was still ordered to shoot it down. Among the night staff at the Pentagon there was talk of scrambling a squadron of F-16 jets and sending them to Japan to stand by. This never in the end took place, which was just as well, as their very presence might have been enough to provoke a confrontation.[5]

The US Air Force had its own staff who prepared an intelligence briefing every night for their chiefs to digest at a daily 8.30 a.m. meeting. The ambitious Air Force Intelligence chief, Major General James Pfautz, pushed his team to stick their necks out in these briefings. Rapidly assembling as much information as they could and using the air force reports from their radar stations in the Aleutians, they prepared slides of a map of the possible route of KAL 007 as it drifted off course. They also showed how its path crossed that of the Cobra Ball RC-135 that was flying that night. They realised that to carry out an interception the SU-15 was likely to have been flying below the airliner, from where it would have been ideally placed to attack because it could not be seen, but from where it would have had only a limited view of the Boeing 747. They concluded that the Soviet air defences had got confused and mistaken the Korean airliner for the American reconnaissance plane. After failing to shoot it down over Kamchatka they had finally intercepted it over Sakhalin in what was a tragic error. The incident revealed a massive failure of the Soviet air defences and their command and control systems. It was a huge blunder by the Soviets, but definitely not an act of intended brutality. When the briefing was presented to the senior air staff, the air force generals were persuaded that the shootdown was a horrible accident and not intentional. General O'Malley, the air force chief, decided to take the briefing book complete with slides and maps to a meeting of the Joint Chiefs of Staff to be held that morning. Everyone felt this interpretation of events was the most likely. Pfautz felt he had a 'best seller' on his hands.[6]

The view in Air Force Intelligence that the shootdown was an accident was, however, completely out of line with the reaction of almost everyone else that night. For most government officials it seemed clear that the shootdown epitomised the Soviet neglect for human life and a willingness to adopt a 'shoot first and ask questions later' approach. How could any competent air force fail to identify a large civilian jumbo jet, believe it to be an enemy plane and shoot it down with the loss of so many innocent human lives? And even if the Soviets had thought the aircraft was an American spy plane, that did not condone their shooting it down simply because it was inside their airspace. That would potentially have been an even more serious matter. During the night the sense of moral outrage built up like water behind a dam, waiting to burst forth when the floodgates were opened.

When George Shultz arrived in his office at 7.45 a.m., his staff were unanimous that the tragedy exposed the Soviets at their most brutal, uncaring worst. He was shown the initial transcripts of the communications with the fighter pilot over Sakhalin and told that these unquestionably proved that the Soviets knew this was a civilian airliner but had still gone ahead and shot it down. Officials at the State Department were not aware that American intelligence bosses in Japan and in the US were still grappling to interpret these recordings and to understand what the pilot had seen and how the ground controllers had read the situation. Shultz was deeply shocked and saw an opportunity to prove to the world that the Soviet Union really was an evil empire. He spoke with Reagan in California who agreed that he should make a public announcement to get the facts out as quickly as possible. There then followed a brief but intense debate 'about how the United States would treat this disaster'. What was said that morning would characterise the American response to the crisis.[7] Several advisers suggested he should hint at a military retaliation of some sort. Instead, Shultz decided simply to lay out the facts as clearly as he could at this early stage. The big question was, should they reveal the top secret recordings they had? Intelligence agencies are always reluctant to reveal their sources, particularly as in this case the recordings had been made at a facility in Wakkanai that the Japanese government had never formally approved. Shultz asked Eagleburger to put pressure on the CIA, telling them that the stakes were so high they must agree to reveal their secret intelligence.[8]

At 10.45 a.m. Washington time on Thursday 1 September, twenty hours after KAL 007 had been shot down, Shultz gave an urgent press conference in the State Department that was covered by all the television networks. Shultz was not an emotional man, but this morning his quiet rage was obvious. He ended his brief statement about what it was believed had happened with the words 'The United States reacts with revulsion to this attack. Loss of life appears to be heavy. We can see no excuse whatsoever for this appalling act.' In answering questions from correspondents he revealed that the intelligence gatherers had recordings of all the conversations with the pilot and that it was clear the Soviets had knowingly shot down a civil airliner. He said they had tracked it for two and a half hours. There was no mention of an American reconnaissance plane in the vicinity. Nor of the fact that the Soviets kept losing the aircraft from their radar screens.

George Shultz at his press conference in the State Department, 1 September 1983. He claimed to know what had happened to KAL 007 but there was still intense debate within the US intelligence community.

Bettmann/Getty Images

The experienced Washington correspondents were blown away by what they heard. Speculation immediately began about why the Soviets had shot the plane down, and some journalists drew the conclusion that it must have been a premeditated act. A short while later, the President's Press Secretary, Larry Speakes, in California, revealed that the recordings came from a Japanese listening station. In Japan, some of those in the electronic intelligence-gathering community were shocked not only that their top secret SIGINT was being publicly debated on television but also that politicians were drawing untrue conclusions from it. 'How can the son-of-a-bitch do this?' asked one officer after seeing the Shultz press conference on television. 'He's making political and corrupt use of intelligence.'[9]

A wave of revulsion swept over America and much of the rest of the world. To many people, the facts of the case as reported seemed to speak for themselves, confirming their worst fears about the Soviet Union and proving that what President Reagan had been saying for years was true. The Soviets ran an evil empire and seemed to have little regard for human life, having callously shot down a civilian airliner with terrible loss of innocent lives. Senior Congressmen joined the chorus of Soviet bashers. Senator Patrick Leahy of the Senate Intelligence Committee declared for the cameras, 'If that's not cold-blooded outrageous murder, I don't know what is.' This seemed to be backed up by the lack of response from Moscow. For several days there were denials that the plane had crashed or that they had shot it down, but this made the Soviets look even more guilty. It was a propaganda disaster for the Kremlin and a further sign that the aged leadership had no grasp on how to handle a crisis that erupted suddenly and was making headlines around the world. Their knee-jerk response was to say nothing and deny everything. It seemed to many people around the world that the Americans knew more about what was going on in Soviet Far East airspace that night than the Soviets.

Reagan spoke with Shultz after watching his press conference on television. He was pleased and told him, 'We should keep on top of the story.' The President was genuinely appalled by what had happened but saw it as a way of keeping up the pressure on the USSR. He believed that his people had caught the Soviets red-handed with unmistakable proof of an act of barbarism. He felt he could ride out the next few days in California as he did not need to lead this crisis. But during the course of the day, as the story got bigger and bigger, the pressure built. Eventually the President was persuaded to return to Washington, which he did the following morning. At the naval air base in California as he was about to board Air Force One he remarked to waiting reporters, 'Our first emotions are anger, disbelief, and profound sadness ... What can we think of a regime that so broadly trumpets its vision of peace and global disarmament and yet so callously and quickly commits a terrorist act to sacrifice the lives of innocent human beings? ... What can be the scope of legitimate and mutual discourse with a state whose values permit such atrocities? And what are we to make of a regime which establishes one set of standards for itself and another for the rest of humankind?'[10] It was his first public comment on the shooting down of KAL 007, and it was his most outspoken attack yet on the Soviets, whom he was now comparing to terrorists. But how would he respond when he got back to Washington? Many saw the President as a shoot-from-the-hip leader who would use any excuse to attack the Soviet Union. Would the destruction of the Korean airliner provide the opportunity for some form of military action against the Soviets?

Reagan's tone set the bar for public outrage in the United States. Television news programmes were full of descriptions of the 'despicable' and 'barbarous' act. When Congressional leaders were briefed on the story they were played a recording of edited extracts of the words spoken by Ossipovich in his SU-15 to the ground controllers (their words had not been intercepted). Translations were handed out. They were suitably shocked and told the waiting reporters as much. Public opinion across America was quick to condemn the Soviet action as the brutal outburst of a cruel regime. The *New York Times* accused the Soviets of being guilty of 'cold blooded, mass murder'.[11]

But behind the scenes in the American intelligence community a very different understanding of events was taking root. The Air Force Intelligence briefing had explained some of the complexities of the situation in its initial overnight analysis, pointing out the confusion in the minds of the Soviet controllers about whether or not they were following a RC-135 spy plane and the fact that they had repeatedly lost track of the aircraft and then picked up what they believed was evidence of it entering, then leaving, then entering Soviet airspace. This report had now been lost in the overwhelming wave of animosity washing towards the Soviets. But in the President's Daily Brief prepared by the CIA for 2 September, the analysts concluded once again that throughout most of the incident the Soviets thought they were tracking a US reconnaissance mission. They noted that the fighter pilot had never positively identified the aircraft as a civilian airliner. With the blinds on the windows down at night, there would have been no internal lights showing. William Casey, not known for being soft on the Soviets, made this clear to Reagan at a National Security Council meeting. He told him that although there had been no American aircraft in the area of the actual shootdown, 'That is not to say that confusion between the US reconnaissance plane and the KAL plane could not have developed as the Cobra Ball plane departed and the Korean airliner approached the area north-east of the Kamchatka peninsula.' This version of events soon became the standard explanation among CIA and DIA analysts.[12] However, this was not what the President wanted to hear and he ignored their arguments.

The intelligence analysts also briefed Shultz about the likely confusion. But like the President, Shultz believed that 'a case of "mistaken identity" was not remotely possible'. He was utterly convinced that even at night it was impossible to mistake a jumbo jet for a military aircraft. He was puzzled by the response of the intelligence community and later wrote, 'That the CIA was advancing such a theory made no sense and raised my suspicions.'[13] Shultz wanted to score as many points against the Soviets as possible. Both he and Reagan took the same line. They did not want to escalate the situation with any serious retaliation or military confrontation. Unlike the Carter administration's response to the invasion of Afghanistan, they did not want to impose major economic sanctions. Negotiations on reducing intermediate-range nuclear forces were about to start up again in Geneva. Shultz had a prearranged meeting coming up the following week with Soviet Foreign Minister Andrei Gromyko, in Madrid. Some in the administration, like Caspar Weinberger, argued that this should not go ahead, that it should be cancelled in protest. But Reagan and Shultz wanted the talking to carry on. It was agreed that the meeting would take place and that Shultz would demand an explanation from Gromyko.

Yuri Andropov was at home on the morning of 1 September when he was called and told that an American warplane had been shot down over Sakhalin. He knew the rules of engagement and that the plane would only have been shot down if it had ignored warnings and a signal ordering it to land on Soviet territory. Later that day at the Kremlin, Defence

Secretary Dmitri Ustinov told Andropov that it was not an American aircraft but a South Korean airliner that had been shot down, and that enquiries into what had happened were taking place. Andropov was exhausted by the strain of the last few months. He was feeling weak and not at all well. He explained to Ustinov that he was ill and was heading off for a few days' holiday in the Crimea. Referring to what was clearly going to be a major crisis, he told Ustinov, 'As for the plane, you sort it out.'[14]

Anatoly Dobrynin was on holiday and was called in to the Kremlin that day by Andropov and ordered to return to Washington to handle the American side of the emergency. When Dobrynin met Andropov he found him looking 'haggard and worried'. The Soviet leader told his ambassador, 'Our military made a gross blunder by shooting down the airliner and it probably will take us a long time to get out of this mess.' He called the generals 'blockheads' and said they did not 'care a bit for grand questions of politics'. After all his efforts at improving relations with America he claimed they had 'made a mess of the whole thing'. Dobrynin later wrote that Andropov was ready to admit the mistake publicly but Ustinov persuaded him out of it. Before leaving Moscow, Dobrynin visited the Defence Ministry for a briefing. He found Ustinov scolding the generals from the Far East. A new radar system had been under construction that would cover the whole area from Kamchatka across the Sea of Okhotsk to Sakhalin, but it had not been completed. The previous night, of the six major control stations in the area, only two had been functioning correctly. It was a shocking reminder of the weak command and control system of the Soviet Air Force. Dobrynin was told that the old radar networks had lost the airliner as it passed through a hole between the forbidden zones and that the 'edgy' controllers had mistaken it for an American spy plane that had been in the area. Because 'their silhouettes were identical', they had shot it down. Dobrynin was not impressed but left for Washington to stand up for his country.[15]

The Politburo met in Moscow the following day, Friday 2 September. In Andropov's absence, his deputy Konstantin Chernenko chaired the meeting, which was dominated by the powerful figure of Ustinov. He wanted nothing more than to defend the Soviet Air Force and the Far East Air Defence Command. He was determined that the incident must not be used to discredit the Soviet military in any way, and that it was his duty to stand up for the military forces with their glorious history going back to the victory over fascism in 1945. This made him overlook failings, and he became blind to any technical deficiencies or command and control blunders that were apparent that night. Ustinov told his colleagues, 'I can assure the Politburo that our pilots acted in complete conformity with the requirements of their military duty.' He went on, 'in this situation their actions were perfectly justified because in accordance with international regulations the aircraft was issued with several notices to land at our airfield'. The minutes of the meeting show that everyone around the table agreed with Ustinov. Stung as they were by the vitriolic reaction in Washington, no questions were asked of the Defence Minister, and neither was there any probing of what the Far East Air Defence Command had done. Instead there was unanimous agreement that standard procedures had been followed, that this was a provocation by an American spy plane, and that the consequences had been appropriate. It was agreed that there was no need to be defensive in their public statements. There was absolutely no sign of remorse or any desire to apologise for the loss of life. Given the sense of horror that had swept around the world in response to the shootdown, the attitude of the Politburo was yet another reminder of how out of touch the elderly men of the Kremlin had become.[16]

The Soviet news agency Tass issued a statement claiming that the intruder had flown into Soviet airspace without clearance and had no navigation lights showing. It had failed to respond to all the warnings. Furthermore, Tass hinted that the flight had been some sort of provocation: 'There is reason to believe that those who organised this provocation had deliberately desired a further aggravation of the international situation [and were] striving to smear the Soviet Union, to show hostility to it and to cast aspersions on the Soviet peace-loving policy.' There was no apology for the loss of life in the tragedy, and this would continue to be the Soviet line. *Pravda*, the official state newspaper, concluded that 'the crude violation of the Soviet state border by the South Korean plane and its deep penetration into the Soviet Union's airspace was a deliberate, pre-planned action pursuing far-reaching political and military aims'.[17]

For Reagan, the Soviet action fitted perfectly with his view of the Soviet Union. In a national television address on Monday 5 September he described the shootdown as the 'Korean Airline Massacre', as 'a monstrous wrong', and spoke of the Soviets committing a 'crime against humanity'. He admitted that there had been a RC-135 in the air that night but utterly dismissed any idea that the Korean airliner could have been mistaken for it. He told the American people, 'make no mistake about it, this attack was not just against ourselves or the Republic of Korea. This was the Soviet Union against the world and the moral precepts which guide human relations among people everywhere. It was an act of barbarism, born of a society which wantonly disregards individual rights and the value of human life and seeks constantly to expand and dominate other nations.'[18] Reagan's words continued his rhetorical offensive against the USSR which he had launched earlier in the year. But now he was calling on the whole world to condemn the 'evil empire'.

The following day, the hard-line US representative to the United Nations Jeane Kirkpatrick presented a special meeting of the Security Council with a short video using the words of Ossipovich in the SU-15 subtitled in English. The Japanese government of Prime Minister Yasuhiro Nakasone had been deeply embarrassed by the whole incident and the revelation of the existence of an ultra-secret US SIGINT base on the northern tip of Japan. But as a good ally, Nakasone had agreed to support the US in making their recordings public. After showing the video, Kirkpatrick went directly on to the offensive, asking, 'If pilot error was responsible for this tragic mistake, why has the Soviet government not said so? Why has it lied and why is it complementing the murderous attack on KAL 007 with a lying attack on the United States for provocation and aggression?' The US was turning the Security Council into a global court of justice and had found the Soviet Union guilty of a systematic 'indifference to human life'.[19]

This attack finally prompted the Kremlin into life. None other than the Chief of the General Staff, Marshal Nikolai Ogarkov, led a two-hour press conference in Moscow on 9 September complete with maps, charts and his own recording. It was televised live in the US by the new Cable News Network (CNN). Ogarkov proved to be an articulate spokesman for the Soviet position. He insisted that the Soviet air defences were certain that the intruder was an American reconnaissance plane. He claimed, incorrectly, that the two planes had flown alongside each other off the north-east coast of Kamchatka. By directing a pointer at giant maps he showed the route of the intruder over Kamchatka and then Sakhalin. Ogarkov claimed that 'It has been proved irrefutably that the intrusion of the South Korean airlines plane into Soviet airspace was a deliberately, thoroughly planned intelligence operation. It was directed from certain centres in the territory of the United States and Japan.'[20]

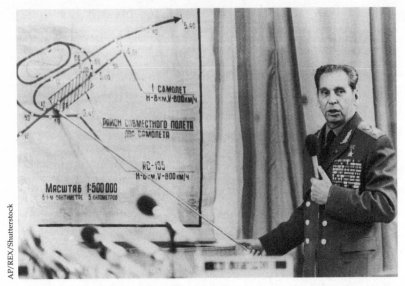

Marshal Nikolai Ogarkov gives the Soviet version of what happened to
KAL 007 at his press conference, 9 September 1983,
complete with charts and pointer.

Ogarkov also played a new part of the audio tape of the
SU-15 pilot's dialogue with his controller. In this Ossipovich
said he had fired cannon bursts across the bows of the airliner.
This caused some embarrassment in the US where this section
of the tape had not been released. It showed that accusations
that the jumbo jet had not been given any warning were
not true. This recording was genuine, and in the Japanese-
American recording had been obscured by static. The Soviet
military played another new recording as well. Again it was
difficult to hear and understand, but the pilot appeared to
say that the intruding plane was flying without its navigation
lights flashing. This was a complete fabrication. Ossipovich
later related how a senior officer had come out to his air base
on Sakhalin and ordered him to record these words. When
he read the required script the officer held an electric shaver

near to the microphone which made a background noise similar to the one in the real cockpit recordings. But this one was a fake.[21] Both sides were going to extraordinary lengths to prove their side of the case with what they claimed was 'irrefutable evidence'.

Shultz went ahead with his meeting with Gromyko in Madrid. Not surprisingly, it was unfriendly and confrontational. Gromyko maintained the Soviet position that the plane was on a spying mission. Shultz insisted that it had been callously shot down even though it was known to be a civil airliner. In the ensuing exchange, Gromyko lost his legendary cool at one point and threw his glasses on the table, nearly breaking them. He later said that it was the tensest meeting he had ever had in his experience with fourteen US Secretaries of State.[22] Later in the month, the governors of New York and New Jersey unilaterally banned Gromyko's aircraft from landing for his annual visit to the opening of the United Nations General Assembly. This was a violation of US guarantees that it would never prevent an official from a member state coming to New York to attend meetings at the UN. The use of a military airfield was offered but turned down. Gromyko stayed away.

Within the United States the public and political interpretation of what had happened that night continued to be totally out of line with the secret intelligence assessments. Although many Americans were genuinely outraged by the shooting down of an unarmed civilian airliner, others began to ask if the government had been totally open about the incident. And before long, the questions being asked by the intelligence community had leaked out into some of the papers. Among America's NATO allies, although condemnation of the Soviet Union was harsh, few governments were prepared to implement major sanctions.

Three weeks after the incident, William Casey decided that

there had been enough discussion of top secret intelligence and sources. It was time to stop the debate about where the US got its intelligence from and what it revealed. He decreed that 'it is now time to circle the wagons and stop talking'.[23] But the Reagan administration would never be able to completely let drop the greatest propaganda victory it had ever scored over the Soviet Union.

On 28 September, Andropov released his first public statement on the shootdown and its aftermath. He maintained the Soviet line that the Korean airliner was on some sort of spying mission masterminded by Washington. He described it as 'an example of extreme adventurism in politics' and accused Reagan's administration of 'imperial ambitions'. Referring to Ogarkov's account of the flight, Andropov insisted that 'The guilt of its organisers, no matter how hard they might dodge and what false versions they might put forward, has been proved.' Turning his focus on to Reagan, Andropov went on: 'One must say bluntly it is an unattractive sight when, with a view to smearing the Soviet people, leaders of such a country as the United States resort to what almost amounts to obscenities alternating with hypocritical preaching about morality and humanism.' Andropov then called on the long sweep of history and said, 'During the six-and-a-half decades of its existence, the Soviet state has successfully endured many trials, including the crucial one [i.e. the Second World War]. Those who encroached on the integrity of our state, its independence and our system found themselves on the garbage heap of history. It is high time that everybody to whom this applies understands that we shall be able to ensure the security of our country and the security of our friends and allies under any circumstances.' He summed up the current state of relations thus: 'If anyone had any illusions about the possibility of an evolution for the better in the policy of the present American administration, recent events have dispelled them completely.' In the version of his statement published in *Pravda*, the word *completely* was emphasised.[24] It was absolutely clear that in the eyes of the Kremlin, relations with America were at an all-time low, and that they believed the hostile administration of Ronald Reagan capable of almost anything.

The top-secret history of the NSA written in 1999 summed up the intelligence community's verdict on the KAL 007 incident. It noted that 'The Soviet concern for border security had escalated to paranoid intensity by August of 1983. The Reagan administration's campaign of psychological warfare and border probing had been bringing up the temperature for two years. Soviet tempers boiled over in April of 1983 as a result of the US naval exercise in the Sea of Okhotsk. By Soviet accounts, the US Navy flew bombing runs on April 4 that penetrated deeply into Soviet airspace in the militarily sensitive Kuril Chain area, and led to an Andropov-issued shoot-to-kill order.' The report concluded that 'the White House pounced on the shoot down and squeezed it dry of propaganda value. It was one of those opportunities that come but once in a lifetime ... It was the Reagan people who insisted that the Soviets could not have mistaken a 747 for a 707. That was their value judgement. It was wrong, but not so wide of the mark that one can impute anything more sinister than righteous wrath. It was the height of the Second Cold War.'[25]

In the end, what this tragic incident illustrates is how a series of minor mistakes can rapidly escalate out of control. The extraordinary failures on the flight deck of KAL 007 led a civilian airliner 365 miles off course over one of the most militarily sensitive areas on the face of the Earth. The already tense and anxious state of mind of the Soviet defence commanders after the PSYOPS operations conducted against them four months earlier encouraged them to misread a situation catastrophically. Despite the conclusions of the intelligence community in Washington, to the politicians the incident immediately played into their preconceived notions – that the Soviets were less human than Americans and operated on a different moral code. They could believe that the Soviets would knowingly shoot down a civilian aircraft and then not express regret or remorse. In Moscow, the Soviet leadership were equally convinced that this was some form of deliberate provocation, an attempt to gather evidence about Soviet defensive systems that had been planned and designed by the US leadership. So the entire episode, beginning with the mis-programming of an airliner's navigation system, ended up bringing the world close to nuclear conflict, with the President of the United States abusing the Soviet leader in the most outspoken way and the Kremlin fighting back with talk of defending Mother Russia from American aggression. It had been an astonishing sequence of events in what was already a year of remarkable confrontation.

Reagan himself later summed up the situation: 'If anything, the KAL incident demonstrated how close the world had come to the precipice and how much we need nuclear arms control. If, as some people speculated, the Soviet pilots simply mistook the airliner for a military plane, what kind of imagination did it take to think of a Soviet military man with his finger close to a nuclear push button making an even more tragic mistake? If mistakes could be made by a fighter pilot, what about a similar miscalculation by the commander of a missile launch crew?'[26]

And this was by no means the last example in 1983 of how the failure of technical systems or the miscalculation by one superpower of what the other was up to would bring the world to the brink of nuclear war.

11

False Alerts

The person charged with informing the President of any security crisis is his National Security Advisor. This includes waking him up at night if an emergency arises. Zbigniew Brzezinski was President Carter's National Security Advisor from 1977 to 1981. At 3 a.m. on 9 November 1979, Brzezinski was telephoned at home by his military assistant, William Odom, who told him that he had just heard on his communications net that 220 Soviet missiles had been launched against the United States. Brzezinski knew that the President's reaction time was between three and seven minutes, but as the alert had not been verified he decided to wait a minute before calling the White House. He told Odom to put Strategic Air Command on stand-by. A few seconds later, Odom called again. He now said that NORAD had reported that 2200 missiles had been launched. Brzezinski rang off, got out of bed, took a deep breath, and was just about to place his call to the sleeping President and suggest a full-scale retaliation against the Soviet Union when Odom called for a third time. This time he reported that other warning systems had not picked up the launch of any missiles. Sitting alone at home, in the middle of the night, Brzezinski had not even woken his wife. He assumed everyone would be dead within half an hour. But the whole thing was a false alarm. Someone had started to run a tape from a military exercise in one of the computer systems in NORAD at Cheyenne Mountain. This had temporarily muddled the early warning system. When it was sorted out a few minutes later, Brzezinski went back to bed. It's difficult to imagine that he got much sleep for the rest of that night.[1]

False alarms were frighteningly common throughout the Cold War period. There were accidents, technical failures, computer malfunctions and human errors galore. Looking back, it is nothing short of a miracle that nuclear war did not break out because of an accident or misunderstanding. Of the various mishaps involving nuclear weapons, several were truly frightening. In July 1957, while practising touch-and-go landings at RAF Lakenheath near Cambridge, an American B-47 bomber crashed at the end of the runway into a bunker housing three nuclear bombs which was engulfed in a gigantic fireball. Blazing jet fuel threatened to set off the TNT in the trigger mechanisms of the weapons. Fortunately fire fighters put out the flames and prevented East Anglia from being turned into a nuclear wasteland.[2]

In January 1961, a B-52 bomber flying over North Carolina split apart in mid-air. Its two 24-megaton thermonuclear bombs fell to earth. One of them was quickly recovered; the other landed in waterlogged farmland and has never been found. When the recovered bomb was examined it was discovered that five of its six safety devices, designed to prevent an accidental explosion, had failed. That last remaining safety control was the only thing that had saved North Carolina from oblivion.

On 17 January 1966, a B-52 bomber was on a routine mission out of Seymour Johnson Air Force Base in North Carolina armed with four thermonuclear bombs. It was part of Operation Chrome Dome. Since the late 1950s, twelve B-52 bombers of Strategic Air Command had been constantly airborne, 24/7, flying around the perimeters of the Soviet Union. In the event of an alert and the launch of the 'go-codes', the B-52s would fly into Soviet airspace to bomb their pre-assigned targets. This particular B-52's mission was to fly across the Atlantic, over the Mediterranean, and patrol the USSR's western borders before turning around and returning home. The long flight required two mid-air refuellings from a KC-135 tanker aircraft flying out of Spain, always a dangerous operation as the slightest change of wind speed or miscalculation could bring disaster. But they were a feature of all Chrome Dome missions and most crews regarded them as purely routine. At 10.30 that morning, on its second mid-air refuelling at 31,000 feet, the B-52 approached the KC-135 too fast and collided with it, causing a tremendous mid-air explosion. All four crew members of the KC-135 and three of the seven on board the B-52 died. The four nuclear bombs dropped to earth. Three of them landed close to the Spanish fishing village of Palomares, near Almeria. One landed without incident. The detonators in two of the other bombs ignited on impact, releasing a small nuclear cloud that drifted in the wind and contaminated about a square mile of Spanish territory with radioactive plutonium. The fourth landed in the sea.

A huge naval hunt involving more than twenty US Navy vessels with 150 divers was launched to find the bomb that had dropped into the sea. It was two and a half months before a submersible found it: it had fallen down an uncharted and very rare canyon in the floor of the Mediterranean to a depth of 2550 feet. This made the recovery of the bomb a tricky procedure and it took another three weeks to bring it to the surface. The Spanish government complained bitterly about contamination of a popular tourist resort so the US authorities organised a clean-up and removed contaminated soil, which was shipped back to the US. The Pentagon insisted there was no lasting damage. In the end the US ambassador to Spain went swimming at beaches near the supposedly infected areas watched by dozens of press and television crews to demonstrate that all was safe. Legal arguments about compensation between Spain and the United States dragged on for more than fifty years. After this Palomares incident and another B-52 accident over Thule in Greenland that again led to radioactive contamination, there were protests from several governments against the US Air Force overflying their territories with aircraft armed with nuclear weapons. This led to the abandonment of Operation Chrome Dome.[3]

Equally alarming were several post-Cold War revelations about the failures of the complex systems that were designed to respond to a nuclear attack and trigger retaliation. All such systems were constructed to include the notion of redundancy: if one element was taken out or went down, there would be a back-up in place; if one radar or early warning computer system was incapacitated, another would be available. But all these systems relied on human operators and were consequently never fail-safe. Even during the Cuban missile crisis, when one might imagine that everyone would have been super-cautious, errors occurred. At this time every military installation was put under special guard in case saboteurs tried to infiltrate bases and disable weapons systems. At the height of the crisis, in the middle of the night of 25 October 1962, an air force sentry on patrol at an air base at Duluth, Minnesota spotted an intruder climbing over the perimeter fence. He fired at the figure and rushed off to sound the alarm for sabotage. This set off a series of synchronised alarms at related air bases. But at Volk Field Air Base in Wisconsin, the wrong alert was triggered. A siren went off signalling that nuclear war had actually begun. Pilots scrambled to their planes armed with nuclear weapons. Just as they were lining up to take off, the base commander recognised the error and ordered a car to drive into the middle of the runway to flash its lights and abort the take-offs. The Top Guns taxied back to their hangars. Back at Duluth it was discovered that the intruder had been a grizzly bear.

But 27 October, known later as the 'Black Saturday' of the Cuban missile crisis, was the day when both sides felt that nuclear confrontation looked almost certain. That morning, radar operators at Moorestown, New Jersey were carrying out a regular check of their computer systems and inserted a software test tape that simulated a missile attack from the Caribbean. The test tape was intended to activate an alert and then, once the procedures had been checked, abort it. However, at the exact moment the tape was inserted, the radars picked up a satellite that crossed the horizon from the direction of Cuba. According to the command post log, the computers and their operators 'became confused' as to what was real and what was part of the exercise. They reacted as though a Soviet missile had been launched. Moorestown informed NORAD that a missile had been fired. Instantly they calculated its trajectory, predicting its target as Tampa in Florida. Strategic Air Command was alerted and the National Military Command Center at the Pentagon was told of the missile launch. Luckily, before the President was informed that the US was under attack and could give the order to retaliate, the radar operators at Moorestown realised what had happened and other radar stations reported that the 'missile' was a friendly satellite. There must have been one hell of a sigh of relief when on the most tense day of the Cold War to date it was realised that this was an exercise that had gone wrong and not the opening of a nuclear exchange. But no system could be created to cope with such an incredible coincidence as this – a test tape running at a radar base at the very second a satellite is picked up on the screen in the same spot as on the exercise.

False alarms or failures on the Soviet side were never reported during the Cold War. But we now know of one incident that had a significant effect on the unfolding events of 1983, at Serpukhov-15, a highly secure compound about 80 miles south of Moscow. No unauthorised visitors were allowed anywhere near the place. At the heart of this high-tech site was the principal Soviet early missile attack warning station. This was the newest and most sophisticated electronic warning station in the Soviet Union, equivalent to NORAD in the US.

All radars are limited in their range by the curvature of the Earth. The beams sent out go in a straight line from the point of the radar transmitter, so as the Earth drops away over the horizon, the beams head out into space. To get around this, during the 1970s the US had launched a range of satellites that were constantly in orbit above the planet enabling them to see, as it were, over the horizon, beyond the range of what even the most powerful radar could pick up. The American satellites were particularly focused on the areas where the Soviets were known to have their missile silos, giant underground bunkers where three or four intercontinental ballistic missiles would be located, stored vertically below ground, standing ready for launch. In the event of the order to fire the missiles, the hatch of the silo would open and the ICBMs would be fired into space, following a pre-assigned trajectory to their target. The orbiting satellites were programmed to search continuously for signs of missile launch and would provide the first warning of an enemy attack.

Although the Soviets had launched the first ever orbiting satellite, Sputnik, in 1957, their technology had fallen well behind that of the US. In the early 1980s Soviet engineers sought to catch up with the Americans, and computer scientists rushed to complete their own satellite early warning observation network, known as Oko or 'Eye'. This was a network of satellites that monitored the principal locations of the American

Minuteman ballistic missile silos situated in the Midwest of the USA. The scientists were pushed by the political and military leaders to get Oko into operation well before all the glitches and problems had been ironed out. They were told it was a matter of urgent national defence and no delay was allowed; problems could be rectified after the system had become operational. In late 1982 the new system was installed at Serpukhov-15. In its early days it was linked to five satellites orbiting the USA, each using infrared sensors to detect the flare of a rocket. Alongside this, the satellites contained optical telescopes that sent back computerised images of the ground. Each satellite was continuously sending data that the supercomputer at Serpukhov-15 would analyse, seeking to identify any signs of a missile launch. An American Minuteman missile launched from the Midwest would take around thirty-five minutes to reach its target in the Soviet Union travelling at about four miles per second. Serpukhov-15 could provide around twelve minutes' additional warning time of an attack over the radars stationed along the northern fringes of the Soviet Union. These extra minutes would be vital in giving the leadership time in which to respond appropriately; and to get to a shelter.[4]

At 7 p.m. on Monday, 26 September 1983, Lieutenant-Colonel Stanislav Petrov arrived at the compound's command centre having been asked at the last minute to take over a shift as another officer had reported in ill. At the centre he spent an hour talking with colleagues whose shift was finishing, receiving the latest reports and updates from them. Then Petrov ordered his team of twelve specialist officers to salute the Soviet flag and take up their positions in the control room. He sat in a large and comfortable reclining chair on the first floor overlooking the main floor of the station where the rest of the officers sat, signifying his importance as commander. Alongside him an assistant operated a switchboard which connected him to the Soviet military command centre. On the far wall in front of both floors was a huge map of the Earth, visible to everyone. The North Pole was at the centre of the map. North America was above this, spreading out in a giant arc across the top of the map. The Soviet Union was below, in the bottom half of the map. At exactly 8 p.m. Petrov signed the logbook accepting that he now held responsibility for what took place. His twelve-hour shift had begun.[5]

Petrov was forty-four years old, short and rather slight, with the look of a mildly eccentric boffin. He had served in the military for twenty-six years. He was now Deputy Chief of the Department of Military Algorithms. He had been primarily trained as a computer engineer to handle some of the complex formulae that were needed to operate advanced military computers. On most days at Serpukhov-15 he worked on sorting out glitches and developing new software. He was proud of the demanding technical work he did and he enjoyed the difficult challenges he faced. But, like other senior officers, once a month he was asked to take on a shift at the command centre to keep his hand in and to see the work from the operational side.

The shift began routinely enough. Over the next few hours the boundary between night and day, the dawn line, slowly passed across the United States. The satellite known as No. 5 was passing through the highest point of its orbit at nearly 20,000 miles above the Earth. It was the most sensitive of the satellites and it was sending back a continuous stream of data, more than usual, Petrov thought to himself. At 10 p.m. Petrov and his communications assistant took a short break for tea and sandwiches while remaining the whole time in their control room.

Suddenly, at fifteen minutes after midnight the quiet seriousness of the shift was abruptly interrupted as a loud klaxon rang out in the control room in a continuous run of very loud bursts. And on a large monitor in the control room a message in huge red letters against a white background flashed up announcing, in Russian, 'Launch ... Launch ... Launch'.

Petrov was stunned. The klaxon continued its deafening bleating and the words continued to flash on the screen. He glanced down at the main floor below him. All the operators and analysts were standing up and staring at him, wondering what to do. Petrov noticed that the alarm seemed to be coming from the point where the dawn line was passing and the satellites went from an infrared analysis to an optical analysis of the launch sites. The analysts following the optical images had to sit in a darkened area as their eyes would only become attuned to the images after at least an hour. Petrov urgently called on all of his team to report back. No one had seen any signs of a missile launch. There were lots of white marks on the optical images from the satellite but none of them looked like the flare from a rocket. Petrov quickly took the decision that this must be a false alarm. Later he admitted that he was not sure if he had made the right decision at the time. Nonetheless, he used his communication system to report to the military command centre that he had a false alarm. He instructed his team to turn off the equipment and after a few seconds to turn it back on again.

When the system came back on, Petrov was still on the phone to the military command centre. They could overhear everything going on in the background. Within seconds the klaxon came back on and the launch message flashed up on the screens again. This time it signified that a second missile launch had been spotted. Again Petrov followed his instincts and reported a false alarm. The system was disabled a second time. A few seconds later it came back on and the penetrating sound of the klaxon started up once more. This time the message changed to 'Missile Attack ... Missile Attack ... Missile Attack'. This told Petrov and everyone else that at least three missile launches had been picked up.

Petrov later admitted to feeling 'terrified'. He suddenly felt hot and very sweaty, 'as though I was sitting in a hot frying pan', he remembered. He could not feel his legs at all and felt dizzy as though temporarily paralysed. The interpreters of the optical satellite images continued to report that they could see no sign of a launch. But the computer analysts insisted there was no computer malfunction. Faced with this conflicting advice, Petrov held on. He knew that the alarm was already being passed up the system. The Chief of the General Staff, Marshal Ogarkov, and Minister of Defence Ustinov had been told that incoming missiles had been picked up at Serpukhov-15. He thought that possibly even Andropov would have been alerted by now. They would all be thinking about how to respond. Those in charge of organising a nuclear retaliation would have been preparing to receive their orders. Targets would be in the process of being sent out. Everyone would be looking to him. Was the alert a false alarm, or was it a genuine missile attack?

Still shaking with fear, Petrov remembered his military training. They had always been told that a nuclear war would start with the launch of a massive pre-emptive missile strike against the Soviet Union. Why would the Americans launch only a few missiles? he wondered. But he had to face the possibility of some sort of foul-up in the American launch systems. What if someone had gone mad and launched his nuclear missiles? he asked himself. But he and the other specialists at Serpukhov-15 knew that the Americans had double locks on all their ICBMs and that it was impossible for a rogue individual to launch a nuclear warhead. He knew that they were supposed to be protected against an accidental launch. 'On the other hand it is 1983 and our relations with the United States are very tense,' he reminded himself.

Over the next couple of minutes two more launches were picked up by the satellite. As far as he could think at all rationally under the pressure, Petrov continued to tell himself that his system was failing. He had been involved in its installation. He had helped to write the operating instructions for the command centre controller. He did not have the confidence that some of the other officers had in it.

After a few more minutes the commander-in-chief at Serpukhov-15 and the chief engineer arrived at the command centre. By this point all the senior officers were beginning to realise that if the missiles were for real they would by now have been picked up by other tracking stations. The Soviets had some tracking devices near the North Pole that would detect the passing of missiles. Also, although Petrov knew nothing of this, there were undercover agents in the American Midwest who would have reported back had any missiles been launched. They were all silent. As the senior officers gathered around him, and as Moscow continued to clamour for information, it became clear that this was indeed a false alarm. Petrov had been right. His conviction that a nuclear war would not start like this and his lack of confidence in the early warning system he controlled had been totally justified.

Later examination revealed that No. 5 satellite's infrared sensors had picked up the reflection of the sun on freak high-altitude clouds during the autumn equinox. The super-computer at Serpukhov-15 had confused this with the flare of a rocket. It was extremely fortunate that on this particular night Petrov happened to be in charge. He knew the limitations of a system he had helped to install. But the incident brought about the end of his career. He was put on a charge for not keeping a full written log of events that night. This would have been impossible to do as he had a telephone in one hand and a microphone in the other to communicate with his staff as the panic engulfed the command centre. But this was a pretext. Petrov had not followed protocols and sounded the alarm, even though had he done so it might have led to nuclear war. The following year he was discharged from the Soviet military. Petrov felt this was totally unfair, that he was being personally blamed for the failure of the satellite surveillance and computer systems. He found himself out of work with his pension massively cut back. No one wanted his technical skills, which had once been at the very peak of Soviet military expertise.

The September 1983 incident was kept top secret during the Soviet era, but after the collapse of the Soviet Union in the mid-nineties the story came out. By the time the first journalists got to Petrov he was living a wretched life in a ghastly tower block in a Moscow suburb. But on the black and white television set in his tiny apartment there was a small statue of a globe resting inside an open hand which Petrov proudly pointed out to visitors. It was inscribed with a few words from Kofi Annan, the Secretary General of the United Nations: 'To Stanislav Petrov, The Man Who Saved the World'.

By the autumn of 1983, the two superpowers possessed about 18,400 nuclear warheads. They were on the tips of giant intercontinental missiles held in silos spread right across North America and the Soviet Union. Submarines carrying nuclear missiles crossed every ocean, and heavy bombers fully armed with nuclear bombs were constantly on stand-by. In addition there were smaller tactical nuclear weapons lined up for use in a conventional war along every front line of the Cold War. The leaders on each side knew that they would have only minutes of warning in the event of the other side launching a nuclear missile strike. And both the Kremlin and the White House knew that systems could go wrong. The Americans, however, believed their technology was unquestionably superior. They had confidence in it, and in the training of those who used it, despite the many false alarms and technical mistakes over the decades. The Soviets, in contrast, were anxious about their shortcomings. They had been humiliated in April during the US naval exercises in the Sea of Okhotsk. Their command and control systems were so flawed that they had failed to distinguish between a civilian jumbo jet and a military reconnaissance plane at the end of August. And in late September their most advanced early warning system had mistaken reflections on high-altitude clouds for a nuclear missile launch. All this made Andropov feel even more apprehensive, and extremely vulnerable. He knew he could not afford to miss the next alert.

12

Truck Bomb

In the summer of 1982, Ronald Reagan had decided at last that the United States must intervene in the ongoing crisis in Lebanon. It had taken some time for him to be persuaded, and he would later bitterly regret his decision. Reagan saw the Middle East as 'an adders' nest of problems', not just because of repeated conflicts between Arabs and Zionists but also because of an alarming rise in radical Islamic fundamentalism. This had already wrenched away a close American ally in the region, Iran, after the Revolution that brought about the departure of the Shah and the takeover of the state by the fundamentalist cleric Ayatollah Khomeini. It also threatened Egypt after the assassination of Anwar Sadat because of his agreement to a peace treaty with Israel.[1] During the early months of 1982 all these tensions seemed to bubble to the surface in Lebanon, a state with its own fragile balance between Arabs and Christians that had been shattered by civil war a decade earlier and was now further unbalanced by the existence of a militant Palestinian community in the south of the country.

There had been a large community of Palestinians in Lebanon since tens of thousands had fled there after their expulsion from the new state of Israel in 1948 – an event memorialised in Palestinian culture as the *Nakba*, or 'Catastrophe'. For two decades the Palestinian cause had supposedly been taken up by the leaders of the Arab states. But after the humiliating military defeat in the Six Day War in June 1967, the Palestinians felt betrayed by their Arab brothers. The Palestine Liberation Organisation (PLO) emerged as the radical Palestinian voice, led by the charismatic and media-conscious Yasser Arafat. Through a series of violent acts of terrorism culminating in the massacre of Israeli athletes at the Munich Olympic Games in 1972, the militant factions of the PLO put the Palestinian cause before the world. After being evicted from Jordan, the PLO shifted their base to Lebanon. Here, in the western half of the nation's capital, Beirut, and across the southern part of the country, the PLO developed what amounted to a state within a state, organising schools, hospitals and social welfare. The Palestinians used their military bases in south Lebanon to fire across the border into Israel. The Israelis responded with several military incursions into south Lebanon, and a UN peacekeeping force (UNIFIL) had been placed along the Lebanese border. But when nothing seemed to stop the PLO militants, Israel's hard-line Prime Minister Menachem Begin decided enough was enough. Begin had been leader of the extreme Zionist group known as the Irgun at the end of the British Mandate and throughout his life had been prepared to use violence to achieve his ends.

On 6 June 1982, Begin and his highly aggressive Defence Minister Ariel Sharon ordered a full-scale invasion of the south of Lebanon. The UN peacekeepers could do no more than note the registration numbers of the Israeli tanks that poured across the border. Begin initially spoke about clearing Palestinian 'terrorists' out of a 25-mile buffer zone in southern Lebanon, but the Israel Defense Forces (IDF) did not stop there and in four days were within sight of Beirut. Israel's real objective was the total destruction of the PLO and its leadership.[2] Moreover, Israeli jets now attacked Syrian anti-aircraft missile sites in the Beqaa Valley to the north of Beirut and threatened to widen the conflict into a major Middle Eastern war.

By this time the Israeli-Palestinian conflict had already been absorbed into Cold War rivalry. The United States gave enormous military and economic aid to Israel. Every American President since Harry Truman had supported the nation. Reagan wrote, 'I've believed many things in my life, but no conviction I've ever held has been stronger than my belief that the United States must ensure the survival of Israel.'[3] The Zionist lobby in the States was immensely effective in denouncing any criticism of Israel among politicians and the media. On the other side, the Soviet Union gave military support to some of the Arab regimes like Libya, but most especially to Syria and its dictator Hafez al-Assad. The Soviets equipped the Syrian Air Force with MiG fighter jets and the army with their latest T-72 tanks. Also, PLO fighters were schooled at the Balashika training camp to the east of Moscow and were equipped with Soviet weapons to attack Israel.[4] A war in the Middle East risked flaring up into a confrontation between the US and the Soviet Union, as had happened during the October War (also known as the Yom Kippur War) of 1973 when the US put its nuclear arsenal on to DEFCON (Defense Readiness Condition) 3 – the only time since the Cuban missile crisis that American forces had been on this state of alert, just two levels away from actually seeking authorisation for the use of nuclear weapons. Within days of the Israeli invasion of Lebanon, the Kremlin sent a message to Reagan on the hotline accusing the US of complicity in the Israeli assault, claiming 'the Israeli invasion is a previously planned operation, whose preparations the US must have known about'. Reagan responded by saying the US did not support Israeli action in Lebanon, and the claim that Washington had prior knowledge of the invasion was 'totally without foundation'. He then accused the Soviet Union of having its share of responsibility for the crisis by failing to use its influence on Syria and the PLO to help stabilise the situation.[5]

On 9 June, the Israeli Air Force flying F-15 and F-16 American-built jets entered into a massive confrontation with the Syrian Air Force flying their Soviet-supplied MiG fighters. It was a classic Cold War 'proxy' engagement in which American and Soviet technology fought directly through military operations by their client states. The result was a total triumph for Israel: the Syrian Air Force was smashed, the Israelis later claiming to have shot down or destroyed 102 MiGs.[6] This success gave the White House and the Pentagon little cause for celebration, however. As the IDF closed in on Beirut they shelled and bombed the city repeatedly, trying to flush out the remaining PLO fighters. In addition they cut off water and electricity supplies to the west of the city. Reagan looked on in genuine horror as images came out of Beirut showing dreadful civilian casualties, including children and babies, as a result of the Israeli bombardment.

The State Department negotiator on the ground, Philip Habib, was highly experienced in Middle Eastern politics but was soon exasperated by Israeli aggression during the siege of Beirut. Every time he believed he had built up the basis for a compromise agreement, the Israelis began shelling civilian areas of the city. The first day of August became known as 'Black Sunday' as the IDF resumed its assault on Beirut when Israeli tanks moved into the southern suburbs and destroyed a Middle East Airlines Boeing 707 on the tarmac at the airport. After a brief respite, intense Israeli shelling of Beirut resumed again on 12 August. Habib called Shultz in despair, telling him, 'The city is being destroyed and America is being blamed for it. It's all going up in smoke! Tell Begin to stop or else!' Reagan put in a call to Begin but the Israeli Prime Minister was in a Cabinet meeting and the President had to wait. When they spoke, Reagan was angry. He recorded in his diary that he told Begin the shelling had to stop 'or our entire future relationship was endangered'. Reagan specifically used the word 'holocaust' to describe what was happening to the civilians of Beirut, knowing the word would be offensive to Begin. He told him that 'the symbol of this war was becoming a picture of a seven-month-old baby with its arms blown off'. Begin reluctantly called off the bombardment but was deeply upset by Reagan's attitude and use of language.[7]

The exact numbers killed in Beirut will never be known for certain. An international commission of inquiry later calculated that about 20,000 people died in Lebanon during the war and more than 100,000 were made homeless. The commission quoted many doctors in Beirut hospitals who said that for every fighter they treated there were four civilians, and concluded that of all casualties, 80 per cent were civilians.[8] The IDF had also suffered relatively high losses with 340 dead and 2200 wounded.

Eventually an agreement was reached. A Multinational Force was sent temporarily to Lebanon. Reagan agreed to include US Marines against the wishes of the Pentagon. The Marines went in along with French and Italian troops. The PLO forces left Lebanon for Tunisia in a blaze of publicity, hoping to turn a military defeat into a moral victory. Habib then tried to negotiate the withdrawal of both Israeli and Syrian forces from the country. After two weeks, with the PLO out of Lebanon, the Multinational Force withdrew, but as they left chaos returned. The Lebanese President-Elect, Bashir Gemayel, was killed in a huge car bomb explosion. No one knew who planted the device. The Lebanese Christians blamed the Palestinians. The Palestinians blamed Israel. Others thought it was an inside job. The following day, IDF units occupied the whole of West Beirut, finally completing their assault on the city that had begun three months before, claiming they were doing this to maintain law and order. On 16 and 17 September, Israeli troops allowed Christian Phalangist militiamen to enter the Palestinian refugee camps of Sabra and Shatila in the south-west of the city to 'cleanse' the camps of terrorists. Instead the Phalangists carried out a massacre. Nearly 2000 men, women and children were killed. Israeli soldiers looked on and did nothing to stop the slaughter. They even fired flares throughout the night to light up the camps and refused to allow civilians carrying white flags to leave.[9] Around the world there was revulsion at the pictures of piles of corpses, some being shoved by bulldozer into mass graves. These images especially hit home in Israel where they had a particular resonance.[10] A later Israeli inquiry condemned the nation's forces and its leadership, prompting the resignation of Sharon as Defence Minister.[11]

Uncredited/AP/REX/Shutterstock

US Marines arrive in Beirut as part of the Multinational Force, coming ashore from landing craft, Iwo Jima-style, in a show of force. Reagan would later say this led to a desperate low point for him.

Two days after the massacre, Reagan told the National Security Council, 'We should go for broke ... No more half-way measures.'[12] The Multinational Force was sent back in to Lebanon, this time consisting of US Marines, the French Foreign Legion, the elite Italian Bersaglieri regiment and British Paratroopers.[13] Their role was not clearly defined. America called on Israel to withdraw from Lebanon and put pressure on moderate Arab regimes like Saudi Arabia to demand Syria withdraw as well. Before many weeks had passed, US Marines came under fire from Syrian-backed paramilitaries. As Americans began to be killed in action, Reagan met with or spoke to the parents of every casualty. They all wanted to know, what had their son died for in Lebanon? Reagan remained reso-lute: America had to use its power and authority to try to settle the deeply held animosities in the region.

On 18 April 1983 a car bomb was detonated at the US embassy in Beirut, killing sixty-three people including sev-enteen Americans. A few days later, President Reagan and Secretary Shultz attended a memorial service at Andrews Air Force Base outside Washington. Reagan was in tears as he gripped the hands of the mourning families, 'too choked up to speak'.[14] In Lebanon, the US military responded by shelling paramilitary positions in the hills above Beirut from the heavy guns of the USS *New Jersey*, a Second World War battleship now moored off the coast. But violence only led to further violence.

On Sunday 23 October, Ronald and Nancy Reagan were enjoying a golfing weekend at the Augusta National Golf Course with George Shultz, Secretary of the Treasury Don Regan, US Senator Nicholas Brady and their wives. Reagan had not played golf for some time and 'didn't have high hopes' for his performance on the links. At 2.30 in the morning the President was awoken by a call from his new National Security Advisor, Bud McFarlane, and was told that a suicide bomber had just driven a truckload of explosives into the barracks of the US Marines at Beirut airport and detonated them. At least a hundred Marines had been killed. Reagan and his staff flew back to Washington that morning for a series of urgent National Security Council briefings in the White House Situation Room. The news got worse. By the time the rescue workers had finished sifting through the rubble of the Marines' barracks the final count had risen to 241 dead. It was the biggest body count of American soldiers since the Vietnam War and the largest loss of life of US Marines since Iwo Jima in 1945. Only a few minutes after the attack another suicide bomber detonated a bomb that killed fifty-eight French soldiers of the Multinational Force. It was discovered that these bombings and that of the US embassy earlier in the year had been the work of a new radical Islamic group in Lebanon, funded by Iran and supported by Syria to resist Israel and its principal backer, the United States. The new group was called Hezbollah, and its Shi'ite holy war would add another ghastly dimension to the ongoing conflict in Lebanon.

From the first reports of this tragic episode there was criticism of local US commanders in Beirut who had not given sufficient regard to the safety of their troops. Despite the attack six months before on the US embassy there was little protection of the Marines' compound and a truck driver had been able to drive into the heart of it and explode a massive 12,000lb device. Around the world, US military installations were put on to high alert. Ugly concrete bollards started to appear outside US Army bases, airfields and naval shipyards. The same thing happened outside government buildings across Washington, including the White House. Without hesitation the US military increased its alert status and prepared to defend itself from potential suicide bombers. They had no choice. It was a painful chapter in US history that was felt particularly by the President himself.

Over the same golfing weekend in late October, a request had come in from the Organisation of Eastern Caribbean States for the United States to intervene militarily against the tiny island of Grenada, which had been on the US watch-list ever since its Marxist Prime Minister, Maurice Bishop, had invited Cuban workers in to help lengthen the main runway of the island's airfield. This looked to its neighbours as though the island government was preparing to receive Soviet military transports in order to become a Soviet base in the Caribbean. In mid-October, Bishop was killed and replaced in a coup by an ultra-leftist group. Jamaica, Barbados, St Vincent, St Lucia, Dominica and Antigua now asked the US to step in and remove the regime. There were 740 American medical students on the island and Washington feared that they would be taken hostage if something was not done quickly.

In strictest secrecy, a military invasion of the island was planned. Reagan feared that if news of a prospective mission leaked out not only would the lives of the American students be put in danger, but figures in Congress would oppose the intervention, calling it 'another Vietnam' in which the US would be dragged into an ever-worsening scenario in the Caribbean. There was also the awkward issue that Grenada was a part of the British Commonwealth, and only the year before Margaret Thatcher's government had launched a military campaign to recapture another set of islands that had been invaded, the Falklands. Reagan and his team decided to go ahead without informing London of their plans, fearing there would be leaks.

At dawn on Tuesday 25 October, US Rangers and Marines landed on Grenada. Although the Cubans on the island resisted, they were no match for the military might of a global superpower. In a few days the island was safely in US hands. American officials found more Cubans than they had expected and discovered what was claimed to be clear evidence that the island's leaders intended Grenada to become a third Soviet bastion in the region after Cuba and Nicaragua. The takeover of Grenada was the first occasion on which American military power had rolled back a Soviet ally, and Reagan received much praise for standing up to Soviet aggression.[15] But there were accusations around the world that the invasion had been launched on totally trumped-up grounds, maybe even as a way of reasserting US might after the humiliation in Beirut. It was also later discovered that the plan to lengthen the runway was no more sinister than an attempt to make the airfield usable by the latest generation of large civil airliners as a way to boost tourism on the island.

Margaret Thatcher was enraged by this military assault on Commonwealth territory. Her anger was fuelled by frustration that the British government had not even been consulted about it. The British Foreign Secretary, Sir Geoffrey Howe, had announced in the House of Commons on 24 October that the new government in Grenada was no threat to British interests, that he was in the 'closest possible touch with the US and Caribbean governments' and had 'no reason to think that intervention is likely'.[16] But even as he said these words the invasion fleet was gathering. When Thatcher was made aware that Washington was preparing a military intervention she was at a dinner in London. She rushed back to Downing Street and telephoned the President on the hotline. He was called out of a meeting with Congressional leaders, and as she protested that this was not a wise course of action, Reagan could be heard struggling to get a word in during the tirade. He didn't like to tell her that the invasion was just about to start. Thatcher felt 'dismayed and let down by what had happened'. She later wrote that 'At best, the British government had been made to look impotent; at worst we looked deceitful.'[17] The Conservative government was still facing pressure to renegotiate the terms for the deployment of American Cruise missiles in Britain. The point was now forcefully made that if Britain was not consulted about military action against a member of the Commonwealth, was there any hope that the country would be involved in a decision to launch nuclear missiles from the UK?

A few days later, Reagan called Thatcher to apologise for any embarrassment he had caused. She was called out of a debate in the House of Commons on an emergency motion on the American action and was 'not in the sunniest of moods'. Expecting another verbal hand-bagging, Reagan hesitantly went through his prepared text. But the Prime Minister remained silent throughout. He was not used to a Thatcherite cold shoulder.

After the President had pleaded his case, Thatcher ended the conversation by failing to accept the apology, saying, 'It was very kind of you to have rung, Ron. I must return to this debate in the House. It's a bit tricky.'

Reagan responded with an attempt at friendly encouragement by telling her, 'Go get 'em! Eat 'em alive!'

'Goodbye,' said Thatcher, and rang off.[18]

It had been an extraordinary few days for Reagan and his Washington team. Despite Margaret Thatcher's disapproval, the swift victory in Grenada led Reagan to write, 'I probably never felt better during my presidency than I did that day.' There was a huge boost in support across the United States for the US military, beginning the turnaround from the hostility that had been felt since Vietnam. But if that action produced one of the 'highest of the high points' for the President, that same week had also produced 'the lowest of the low' with the attack on the US Marines base in Beirut. As Reagan later wrote, 'the sending of the marines to Beirut was the source of my greatest regret and my greatest sorrow as President'.[19]

13

Kremlin Paranoia

Throughout the summer of 1983, Yuri Andropov's health had been giving rise to growing concern. In desperate need of a break, the Soviet leader had left Moscow just as the Korean airliner crisis was about to erupt, looking gaunt and haggard. He went not to his normal holiday dacha at Kislovodsk in the North Caucasus, near to the region where he had grown up, but instead to a luxury villa kept aside for the leadership on the Crimean coast not far from Simferopol. With him went not only the key staff he needed to keep up with his vast workload but also an entire medical facility. Andropov was seriously unwell, suffering from a kidney problem that was made worse by his weak heart, and was finding it more and more difficult to walk, especially to go up stairs. Even to climb the few steps for the lift to his office at the Kremlin caused him difficulty, and he felt embarrassed if seen by others when his bodyguards helped him. He did not want people to know about his condition.

An American specialist, Professor Rubin, was called in and confirmed the diagnosis of the Soviet doctors that his kidneys were failing, and that he needed treatment with a dialysis machine. Such machines were rare in the Soviet Union at the time but the party leaders lacked for nothing: the latest technology was always available to them. So Andropov began the process of dialysis every few mornings: blood was removed from his arm, pumped through a machine that filtered out the waste products, and then returned, purified, back into his arm. But this was a process he found exhausting and draining. He could not hide the marks on his arms either, and soon both of them were covered in bandages from the wrist up. Painful sores began to appear on his body, and signs of general debility multiplied. However, the doctors were still encouraging about his prospects, and Andropov managed to keep up with his relentless workload. His son remembered that he still hoped he had several years left, to complete some of the reforms he had started.[1]

The health of the senior leadership of the Soviet Union had been of concern for some time and was not just the subject of much speculation by Kremlinologists looking in from the outside and trying to follow the ups and downs. In March 1983, the elderly members of the Politburo discussed in secret their own concerns about the effects on themselves of pressure of work. It was proposed that the working day be limited to nine-to-five and that members attend fewer evening engagements and receptions. It was also proposed that all Politburo members over the age of sixty-five should be allowed the opportunity to work from home for one day a week and that 'relaxation should take place on one's day off'. During the debate, the elderly and loyal Arvids Pelše declared that Andropov should strictly observe this regime, and went on record saying, 'you must take care and look after yourself, Yuri Vladimirovich'.[2]

Four weeks after he had left Moscow for the villa on the Black Sea, Andropov spoke out against the United States in an interview for *Pravda*, denouncing the 'militaristic course' of US policy. Two days after this interview appeared, on 30 September, Andropov went for a walk in a nearby park. He was only lightly dressed for the warm Crimean late summer. During the walk he became tired and sat down to take a rest on a granite bench in the shade. While there he became thoroughly chilled and soon started to shiver uncontrollably. The surgeon who had accompanied Andropov to the Crimea, Dr Yevgeny Chazov, was the Health Minister, a member of the Soviet Central Committee and chief of the Kremlin Clinic. He examined Andropov and found 'widespread inflammation, requiring surgical intervention'. A minor operation was carried out immediately and was a success, but Andropov's body was so drained of strength that the post-operative wound would not heal. The Soviet leader had taken a sudden turn for the worse. Chazov later wrote, 'His condition gradually worsened, his weakness increased, he again stopped trying to walk, but still the wound would not heal ... Andropov began to realise that he was not going to get any better.'[3]

Andropov spoke to his deputy Chernenko every day from his Crimean villa. He regularly conversed with Ustinov and Gromyko too. His protégé, Mikhail Gorbachev, telephoned Andropov on several occasions and after one call thought he seemed brighter. He hoped he was getting better.[4] After his exhausting medical procedures in the morning, Andropov liked nothing more than to sit on the veranda of his villa overlooking the Black Sea, reading the mountain of literature that was sent to him daily. All the most important papers from the Politburo and the Central Committee were despatched to him. Often he would in return dictate papers or memoranda for the Politburo. His staff would find statistics for him or search out papers or background briefings. He was determined to continue working, still hoping that he could throw off the ill health that was plaguing him.

No one knows what went through Andropov's mind during the months of September and October 1983 as he contemplated the many problems facing the Soviet Union, but almost

certainly his already paranoid outlook was affected to some
degree by the frustration and weakness he felt in himself and
the failings of his own body. He was of course keenly aware
of Operation RYaN and the indicators that the KGB were looking out for. Everything going on in Washington seemed to be
pointing in the same direction. Firstly there were those vicious
tirades unleashed by Secretary Shultz and the President himself after the shooting down of the Korean airliner. Although
Andropov feared that the Soviet air defenders had made a
huge blunder, he soon took up the military line that the airliner had been on some sort of CIA-sponsored intelligence
mission, had made a rendezvous with the RC-135 military
surveillance plane, and had for some reason continued on
its course through Soviet airspace and across its sensitive
Far Eastern defences. He began to wonder if the aggression
expressed by Reagan to the American people was a warming-
up exercise in some way preparing them for the justification
of a pre-emptive nuclear strike against the USSR. For sure,
Andropov would have repeatedly pondered this question.

At the root of all the tensions in 1983 were Reagan's claims
that the Soviet Union was an 'evil empire'. Again, Andropov
saw this as the President's way of preparing Americans for a
military strike. Then there was SDI and the American attempt
to overthrow the policy of nuclear deterrence that had kept
the peace for nearly forty years. Was the US trying to undermine decades of Soviet defence expenditure on building up a
vast nuclear arsenal? And at the heart of all Soviet fears was
the deployment of the Pershing II and Cruise Missiles, both
of which were to be rolled out in Britain, West Germany and
Italy in the final months of the year. Then, American missiles
would be only six minutes' flying time from the Kremlin.
Would these missiles be picked up by the faltering Soviet early
warning system that had only recently shown up its failings?
And even if they were picked up as they approached their

targets, would there be time to launch a retaliation? Perhaps the Americans were now calculating that they could entirely destroy the Soviet leadership before there was an opportunity to hit back. It was this fear of an attempt to decapitate the leadership with a limited nuclear attack on Moscow that most frightened the men of the Kremlin. Had Reagan convinced himself that he could fight and win a nuclear war by striking out of the blue? It would have been strange if these questions were not raised by the Kremlin leadership, and in Andropov's fevered brain they could well have grown rapidly into alarming daytime fears and terrifying nightmares.

Then, in late October, the KGB reported that the situation had suddenly grown dramatically worse. The Hezbollah attack on the US Marines on the 23rd of that month was widely reported in the Soviet Union. But now the KGB picked up that every US military facility around the world had gone on to a heightened state of alert. Was this a necessary outcome of the very specific attack on the Marines in Lebanon, or was it simply an excuse to close off military installations in every continent as the US prepared to launch its nuclear forces? The KGB, always keen to please its political bosses, noted that another major indicator of Operation RYaN had been met – the mobilisation of US armed forces around the world.

Within days, another sign KGB operatives were looking out for that they believed would signify an imminent nuclear attack also became evident. On 24 and 25 October, Soviet listening stations picked up increased communications traffic between London and Washington – a key RYaN indicator. For some reason they did not link this to the invasion of Grenada and the British government's outrage at US military action against an independent Commonwealth country. While Thatcher and the Foreign Office were registering their disapproval with American policy-makers and protesting against the lack of consultation, the KGB grew more anxious. On the big Perspex board in the KGB Centre in the Lubyanka, another cross was made with a marker pen. The board was rapidly filling up.

In the Soviet embassy in London, telegrams from the Centre arrived more and more frequently calling on KGB officers to go all-out looking for signs of preparations for war. Reading these instructions, Oleg Gordievsky felt disbelief at what he was being asked to do. But he continued to pass on these extraordinary orders to his MI6 minder, John Scarlett, and they were soon processed up the system.

Sir Geoffrey Howe had been made Foreign Secretary in June 1983, just after the General Election in which Margaret Thatcher won a landslide victory. One evening not long after his appointment, while he was still getting his feet under the table, the deputy secretary with responsibility for intelligence and security matters requested a meeting with him. He asked to see him alone, without his principal private secretary present, which was extremely rare. The Foreign Secretary was given a double envelope of papers and asked to read them there and then, not to make any notes, and then to return the envelopes to his waiting intelligence official. Howe was astonished to find that the material came from a mole run by British intelligence in the KGB residency in London. He was not told his name but was given a codename. Every few days he was shown more reports in the same secretive way. Howe was fascinated by what he read and later wrote that the reports built up a 'very powerful impression in my mind' that 'the Soviet leadership really did believe the bulk of their propaganda. They did have a genuine fear that "the West" was plotting their overthrow – and might, just might, go to any lengths to achieve it.'[5] Prime Minister Margaret Thatcher was the only other government member who also knew of these reports coming in through MI6. She later recalled, 'We had entered a dangerous phase.'[6]

In Washington, there was also concern about Soviet reactions. On Saturday mornings, Shultz regularly held breakfast seminars on Soviet affairs at the State Department attended by experts from across the administration. Robert Gates, deputy director at the CIA, was asked to one of these in late September 1983 and was invited to summarise his thoughts in writing. On the 27th he sent his report to Shultz in which he noted that since the halcyon days of détente 'the trend in the relationship [between the US and the USSR] was generally downhill'. He realised that on every occasion when there had been an opportunity to reverse that downhill trend 'there had been some action in Washington, Moscow or the Third World that had killed the opening'. Gates concluded that the tone of the relationship between the two superpowers was as 'pervasively bleak' as at any time since the death of Stalin thirty years before. He stressed that the problem was 'how to get through the next year without a further dangerous increase in tensions', and ended with a warning: 'It will take considerable skill and luck just to keep things from getting worse during the next year.'[7] It was indeed a bleak note of alarm from a senior American official. But Gates could not have imagined how right he was.

Towards the end of October, Andropov prepared to return from his Crimean villa to Moscow. Despite his illness and daily kidney treatments, he never seems to have considered stepping down or handing over the burdens of office to a younger man. That was not the Kremlin way. Once in power, a leader was expected to remain in control for the rest of his life. Even if Brezhnev had shown this up to be a charade by his all-too-evident incapacity, Andropov would carry on to the bitter end.

So Andropov continued to dictate policy papers and instructions to the Politburo. His speech-writers sent out statements to be delivered by representatives in his place. That October, Andropov proposed that China be brought into the campaign against the deployment of Pershing and Cruise missiles. This would not only add clout to the protests taking place in Europe but, Andropov argued, it would help to improve Sino-Soviet relations. At about the same time, he signed a memorandum on the Middle East calling for a more cautious policy towards Syria and its other clients to ensure that the Soviet Union did not become directly involved in the continuing violence in Lebanon. When he proposed modest reforms to the procedures for the forthcoming elections to the Supreme Soviet, sham elections where only one party was represented in the ballot, Chernenko and Gorbachev used the new proposals to try to break the bureaucratic inertia that held up almost any attempt at genuine reform. To the outside world, the leadership was very much presenting a face of 'business as usual'.

The Soviet people were not, of course, told about the illness of their leader. Although Andropov had not appeared in public for some time they were told he was on an extended vacation, and now the press reported that temporary problems kept him from participating in public events. To party apparatchiks and representatives of delegations from around the socialist world who expected to see him at meetings he sent messages saying, 'Dear Comrades, for temporary reasons, to my great regret, I am unable to take part in this meeting.' But usually a specially written speech was delivered on his behalf. Even many in the *nomenklatura* did not know the details of his condition. 'The General Secretary is getting better,' they were told. 'He will soon be giving a report at the next plenum' (or wherever it might be). As the celebrations of the sixty-sixth anniversary of the great October Revolution approached, Andropov looked anxiously at the programme, for the long event involved hours of standing about on the balcony overlooking Red Square. He knew he would not be up to it. A week before the anniversary word was put out that Andropov had a 'slight cold' and would not be attending ceremonies that year.[8]

It was all, of course, a massive deceit. The Soviet people may or may not have believed that their leader was still at the helm, steering the ship of state through troubled waters. Rumours flourished about the state of his health but the media kept to the line and there was no public discussion on the matter. In reality, the always paranoid leader was bedridden, filled with worries and concerns, and being misled by those he listened to about the actions and responses of their number one enemy, the United States. And now the last and most agonising phase was fast approaching that would bring the world to the brink of nuclear catastrophe.

14

Able Archer 83

In early November 1983, at the peak of the heightened level of tension between the Soviet Union and the West, NATO began an exercise by the name of Able Archer 83. Able Archer was an annual war game known as a Command Post Exercise. It did not involve sending troops out into the field. It did not require the deployment of tanks or armoured vehicles to their battle stations. Rather it was a communications game in which NATO's Allied Command Europe (ACE) could practise and refine their signals communications along with the command-and-control procedures to be used in the event of war with the Warsaw Pact nations. A group of exercise planners drafted a scenario in which a political crisis erupted in Europe and eventually escalated into a military conflict between Warsaw Pact and NATO forces. In Europe, the forces of the Warsaw Pact vastly outnumbered those of NATO in terms of soldiers, tanks, artillery and so on. In addition, they seemed well trained and highly motivated. The Soviet Union as a whole in the mid-1980s controlled one of the most formidable military machines ever assembled. There were more than 200 military divisions grouped in four main theatres of operation. They possessed more than 54,000 battle tanks and over 4500 helicopters. The Soviet Army,

Navy and Air Force could draw on five million active service personnel.[1] And behind all this, the Soviets possessed 11,000 nuclear warheads all pre-assigned to targets in the United States and western Europe. Only a part of this mighty force was lined up against NATO in Europe, but Able Archer was intended to test out the procedures for responding to a military assault from the East.

Able Archer 83 was itself part of a bigger group of NATO exercises that were taking place in the autumn of 1983, under the umbrella name Autumn Forge 83. These exercises took place in countries from Norway to Turkey and some of them did involve the movement of troops and matériel. For instance, an exercise known as Reforger 83 began in mid-September and included a momentous 'show of resolve' in the face of a Soviet invasion of western Europe, airlifting 19,000 troops and 1500 tons of cargo from the United States to Europe to rehearse the real-time process of providing military reinforcements in a time of crisis. One hundred and seventy aircraft took part in the airlift. Atlantic Lion 83 involved thousands of American, Dutch, German, British and Canadian troops as well as tanks and armoured vehicles.[2] Able Archer 83 came after these exercises and was intended to focus on one principal issue: a request by NATO commanders to deploy nuclear weapons as the final resort in a full-scale war with the Soviet Union and its Warsaw Pact allies that they felt they were losing. Able Archer 83, in essence, was a rehearsal for the release of NATO's nuclear weapons.

The Able Archer war game was played out deep inside the bunker known as the 'nuclear vault' located alongside the Supreme Headquarters, Allied Powers Europe (SHAPE) at Mons, about 30 miles south-west of Brussels. Signallers went out into the countryside, mostly into the woods of West Germany, and according to the prepared script sent in messages to Mons reporting on the war that was supposedly taking place. Soviet intelligence routinely monitored such exercises, but in 1983, Autumn Forge and Able Archer sparked such alarm in Moscow that they nearly engulfed the world in a nuclear Armageddon. As a top secret US report for the President later concluded, Able Archer 83 'may have inadvertently placed our relations with the Soviet Union on a hair trigger'.[3]

The war gamers invented a lively but credible scenario for Able Archer 83. In the elaborate run-up to war (according to the script), in February of that year, prompted by a sense that the socialist bloc was losing power and influence due to the aggressive stance of the Western alliance, there has been a dramatic change of leadership in Moscow. Following this coup, a hard-line Kremlin leadership takes over and launches a new offensive against the West. In March, they send military supplies to Iran in its continuing war with Iraq. Military aid is also sent to Syria and South Yemen. The following month the Gulf States, feeling threatened by the growing Soviet involvement in their region, seek US military aid and the US Navy increases its presence in the Gulf. In May and June the tension spreads from the Middle East to Europe. There is increasing unrest in eastern Europe as the Soviet Union fails to keep its promises of economic aid to its satellites. However, under instructions from Moscow, the Warsaw Pact nations carry out a series of training exercises and stockpile military supplies across eastern Europe. Factories in the Soviet Union go on to round-the-clock production to build up military provisions. Then in August, protests in Yugoslavia caused by their financial difficulties lead that nation to drop out of the Soviet bloc altogether and to seek economic and military assistance from the West. In the Kremlin this seems to threaten a complete break-up of the Soviet-dominated Eastern bloc. In response, during September the Warsaw Pact begins a full mobilisation of its armed forces. In October, these forces invade Yugoslavia to regain it for the socialist bloc. This leads to a major crisis in East–West relations. At the end of the month the Soviets invade Finland and, the following day, Norway, to open up the Atlantic for their fleet. Meanwhile Soviet air and naval forces begin a massive attack against NATO bases. In southern Europe, Soviet troops invade Greece while its navy launches strikes in the Adriatic and the Mediterranean. On 4 November, Warsaw Pact forces use their overwhelming superiority in numbers and matériel to attack West Germany through the Fulda Gap. Soviet tanks and armour soon overpower NATO forces and rapidly begin to spread across the north German plain.[4]

At this point in the scenario, Able Archer 83 began in real time. Those taking part in the war game in the bunker in Mons were faced with a massive assault against NATO forces and with air strikes against NATO bases from the Mediterranean to the Baltic. Regular reports started to come in to the bunker from various NATO command headquarters in Kolsas in Norway, Naples in Italy, and from other stations across western Europe, all according to the script. Teletype messages were sent from one NATO communication centre to another reporting on the escalating crisis. These were printed up on yellow lined paper and rushed in by courier from the communications centre to the war staff playing the game. In 1983 war gamers did not sit at computer screens but gathered around a huge table in the centre of the vault. On the wall was a giant map of Europe with markers indicating the current position of NATO and Warsaw Pact forces. In many ways it looked more like World War Two than World War Three. Around the side of the bunker were the various teams, intelligence, support, logistics, who would constantly update the war staff with the latest situation reports on the operational status of NATO air, ground and naval forces.

On the second day, as the war gamers geared up for their response, the scenario they were presented with took a sudden and terrible turn for the worse. In order to speed their advance, the Warsaw Pact forces launched chemical weapons against their NATO adversaries. Within twenty-four hours the NATO war gamers decided they had no alternative but to respond in kind and called for permission to employ reserves of their own chemical weapons and launch them against the Soviet-led invasion forces. At this point of the game, some of the US Air Force players were instructed to evacuate to an alternative NATO base near Birkenfeld in West Germany and to put on helmets, gas masks and chemical protection suits for several hours.[5] It must have been extremely uncomfortable for them.

The war game was intended to be as realistic as possible, and this involved putting the players under considerable pressure by constantly feeding in new and unexpected developments in the unfolding scenario. Colonel Spike Callender was in the directing staff for Able Archer 83 and he recalled, 'There's always an ever-changing situation and you would have to be continually adapting just like you'd expect to in any combat.' Sometimes commanders were fed with conflicting reports and they would have to decide how to interpret contradictory assessments. Callender explained, 'In the fog of war not everything will be consistent and a commander could be faced with two different reports that could be entirely different.'[6]

All of those taking part in Able Archer 83 knew that it was an exercise but played along as though it were real. Eugene Gay was the Nuclear Operations Officer in the NATO war staff in 1983. Sitting at his desk in the bunker he was receiving updates every few minutes. His desk rapidly filled with pieces of yellow paper. He recalled the exercise as very intense with factors constantly being fed in that altered the operational plan he had to prepare. At the time there was no access to an integrated database, so he had to draw together a lot of information about NATO's nuclear capability, in line with the scenario. He remembered, 'My job was to prepare a nuclear execution plan.' As the exercise reached its climax there was barely time to reflect on the enormity of the game they were playing. 'Our job was to be professional planners and to understand how to use the nuclear weapons. But we were obviously concerned that one day a real crisis would reach the point where nuclear weapons might have to be used.'[7]

Meanwhile, across the real Eastern bloc, in a series of listening stations, Soviet radio operators followed the Able Archer war game with increasing concern. Each radio signal sent out was preceded by the message 'Exercise . . . exercise . . . exercise'. The Soviets picked up on this but grew doubtful about whether this was in fact simply a game. In Moscow they began to ask if it was all a case of *maskirovka*, or deception. The Soviet military commanders knew that the Warsaw Pact had its own contingency plans to attack the West under the cover of military exercises. This would deceive NATO into thinking that there was no real threat. They now began to believe that the radio messages they were picking up from Able Archer 83 were a mirror image of their own plans. Maybe this had started out as a war game, but was it in reality intended to disguise plans to launch an actual assault on the Soviet Union?

Panic began to spread at the KGB Centre in Moscow, still obsessed with Operation RYaN and finding evidence of an imminent attack by the West. Increasingly frantic messages went out from the Centre to KGB residencies. And agents around Europe and the world remained only too keen to feed their bosses in Moscow with what they wanted to hear. This helped to sustain the vicious circle of intelligence in which field agents reported not what they believed but what they knew they were expected to observe. So reports were sent back confirming the state of alert at US military bases around the world. They noted different and unusual patterns of officer movements, and that some bases were practising an hour of radio silence each day. The heightened state of alert was the consequence of the dreadful Beirut bombing as each military installation increased its external defences and rehearsed its own internal security measures, but to a paranoid KGB hierarchy this looked like the countdown to nuclear war.

On Sunday 6 November, the KGB Centre sent out to its London residency and it seems to all its residencies in western Europe and North America, an urgent message. For the first time the Centre also revealed the timetable for a likely first strike by the West. The KGB telegram read: 'It can be assumed that the period of time from the moment when the preliminary decision [for a nuclear attack] is taken, up to the order to deliver the strike will be of very short duration, possibly 7–10 days.' During that brief period before the outbreak of nuclear war, 'preparations for the surprise attack would necessarily be reflected in the work pattern of those involved'. All agents were given a checklist of likely indicators that the countdown to a surprise nuclear attack had begun. In London this included the names of key individuals who might be involved in consultations with the US leadership before a first strike. They all had to be watched. Also on the list to keep under the closest observation were key Ministry of Defence installations; underground command post bunkers where national and local leaders would head in anticipation of a nuclear exchange; NATO offices in Britain where there would be increased and perhaps frenetic activity; and British and American nuclear air bases, nuclear submarine bases, ammunition depots and communication and intelligence centres. Agents were instructed to look out for 'unusual activity' at all of these sites. It was also assumed that there would be unfamiliar comings and goings at Downing Street and a noticeable increase in the numbers of soldiers and armed police on the streets. Agents were also told to report back on preparations for the evacuation of the 'political, economic and military elite' of the United States who were living in Britain, while it was anticipated that US embassy and CIA staff were likely to remain behind in embassy bunkers.[8] To those, like the ever-paranoid Vladimir Kryuchkov, at the KGB Centre in Moscow, receiving alarming reports from NATO during Able Archer 83, all these instructions seemed logical and necessary. If the Western powers were about to launch a nuclear strike against the Soviet Union some of these indicators would predict how and hopefully when a war was about to begin. This would give the Kremlin just enough time to respond.

Among those sitting in embassies in Western cities there was no sense of alarm and of course no awareness of what was going on in an obscure war game in Belgium. Life generally carried on as normal. Millions of people travelled to work and took their children to school every morning. The television and news media gave no messages of warning, nor did they broadcast any instructions for how to prepare for an approaching holocaust. In a city like London, the pubs, clubs and restaurants were full every evening as workers enjoyed a night on the town. Had they known about it, the RYaN operation would have seemed absurd and meaningless.

On Monday 7 November, at the SHAPE bunker at Mons where Able Archer was being played out, the imagined crisis continued to worsen. On the north European plain, to the south of Hanover, reports came in that German I Corps and British I Corps were taking massive casualties. Warsaw Pact forces were also advancing through Turkey and Greece. The NATO players running the war game decided they were losing the conventional war. They had to escalate the conflict, so the levels of DEFCON were counted down. So far during the Cold War the DEFCON level had never gone above 3, and it had only reached this level during the worst moments of the Cuban missile crisis and towards the end of the October War in the Middle East in 1973. Now the war gamers counted to DEFCON 2, defined as 'The Next Step to Nuclear War, with armed forces ready to deploy within six hours'. Then they passed to DEFCON 1. This was the stage at which they called for the use of nuclear weapons.[9] Initially just a few tactical nuclear missiles were fired at the advancing Warsaw Pact troops. Some targeted Soviet tank regiments, others targeted units assembling in East Germany, Czechoslovakia and Romania. However, this failed to stop the onslaught, and the Warsaw Pact responded with strikes against several NATO headquarters. In the imagined scenario these attacks wiped out the commander of NATO forces in central Europe located in the south-east of the Netherlands, and also took out the US Air Force command base at Ramstein in West Germany, the Northern Army Group headquarters at Mönchengladbach and the Central Army Group headquarters at Heidelberg, also in West Germany, as well as NATO command posts in Norway and Italy.[10]

On Tuesday 8 November, the war gamers at Allied Command Europe in NATO decided to request from their political masters authorisation for a massive nuclear strike against the Warsaw Pact. Based on various assessments coming in from NATO stations across Europe, the planners started to calculate how many megatons of nuclear weapons would be needed, how they would be carried and where they would be directed. This time they would request permission to attack a whole range of targets inside the Soviet Union including air bases, missile launch sites, and communication and political centres. This would be a full nuclear strike against the Soviet Union.

All of this was being followed keenly at the Soviet listening posts. But at this point, to the amazement of the Soviet signals experts, NATO did what it had never done before and changed the codes it was using, and had used in every previous version of Able Archer. A new code was introduced for the most sensitive part of the operation – the request to use nuclear weapons. To the anxious Soviet officers listening in, this could only have one meaning: Able Archer had moved from being a regular exercise to the real thing. The Western powers were indeed about to launch a huge nuclear first strike against the Soviet Union and its allies.

In the initial draft of Able Archer, at this moment leading politicians of the Western alliance were to play a cameo role in the exercise. The request from NATO to employ nuclear weapons was to be processed to the National Security Council and the Pentagon in Washington. The President then had to play his part and authorise the use of nuclear weapons. In London, it was Margaret Thatcher in Downing Street, along with her Secretary of State for Defence, Michael Heseltine, who were to sanction the use of British nuclear weapons in response to the NATO request.[11] In previous years this had been part of the point of the war game, that the politicians as well as the NATO leaders should be aware of what would happen and the role they needed to play in the event of a real crisis. However, just before Able Archer 83, Reagan's National Security Advisor Bud McFarlane calculated that the international situation was too tense and there were too many demands on the President's time, so the war game need not go this far. 'If you go to the point of having the Principals, the decision-makers, actually involved the question is raised, is this an exercise or are we not facing a possible attack?' The President understood this, and that 'however misguided Soviet perceptions might be we shouldn't add to them by having the Principals involved, and so he declined to participate'.[12] Instead, on the morning of 8 November, after a short NSC meeting to discuss a possible strike against Hezbollah targets in Lebanon, President Reagan and the First Lady waved to the waiting television cameras and stepped on board Air Force One to depart for a short tour of Japan and the Far East.

In Washington, however, the Joint Chiefs of Staff were playing their part in the NATO war game. There was a small group within the JCS who performed the role of the political leadership and approved the request from NATO to use nuclear weapons. In London, too, the lead politicians had decided to follow the example of Washington and not participate in this year's Able Archer. Instead there was a response cell inside the Ministry of Defence in Whitehall who were acting out the part of the British political establishment. They too responded positively when requested to authorise the use of the British nuclear deterrent.[13]

At NATO communications centres across western Europe, Able Archer was reaching its climax. One NATO officer based in Norway spent twelve hours each day pretending to live through the crisis being acted out. He later wrote, 'As the exercise progressed over a few days we began to settle into our routines and have conversations about the exercise and what we were seeing. Eventually we began doing the what if questions ... "What if the Soviets actually think we're going to launch nuclear weapons and we're disguising it as an exercise?" "What if they launch against us?" "What if, what if, what if ..." It was a pretty crazy time.'[14]

By now the Soviet intelligence and military establishment was seriously rattled. The fact that the President was very publicly leaving Washington did not lessen the sense of crisis in Moscow. It was well known that on board Air Force One were all the communication systems and codes necessary to launch nuclear weapons. The President did not have to be at his desk in the Oval Office to start a nuclear war. Inadvertently, Able Archer had convinced the Kremlin that a war was about to break out. At the KGB Centre in Moscow, where paranoia was never far below the surface, there was panic. But the big question was, how would the elderly Soviet leaders who controlled the massive Soviet nuclear arsenal respond?

15

Combat Alert

In November 1983 there was, 20 miles to the west of Moscow, nestling among the tall silver birch trees of the vast Kuntsevo forest, a heavily guarded structure surrounded by a 10-foot-high concrete wall. The building was known variously as the Kremlin Hospital or the Kuntsevo Clinic. It was a medical foundation reserved for senior Communist Party members, and its comforts were in line with what the party elite would expect. Every client at the hospital had his own private suite. All patients enjoyed full-time nursing care and had access to the best doctors in the Soviet Union. And only a quarter of a mile away, near to the exclusive suburb where Stalin had his dacha in the 1930s, was the renowned Cardiology Research Centre, the best heart hospital in the country. Here, top cardiologist Yevgeny Chazov was director, the doctor who had been with Andropov in the Crimea and who was personally in charge of the health care of the leaders of the Soviet Union.

It was essential that the Soviet people and the wider world did not know who was being treated at the Kuntsevo Clinic. That was why on the road out to it from Moscow there were security men posted at quarter-mile intervals monitoring who was coming and going, watching for journalists, foreigners and other unwelcome visitors. Changes in the highest ranks of government were a sensitive subject in the Soviet Union and no leader wanted it known that he was undergoing medical treatment. It was thought to convey a sign of weakness. Moreover, it was believed that internationally it could cause uncertainty and become a risk to national security. If the Western powers knew the General Secretary was unwell they might choose the moment to attack. Bulletins and statements continued to be issued from the Kremlin in the name of Yuri Andropov, even if he was never seen in public.

At the end of October, when Andropov returned to Moscow from his extended stay in the Crimea, he had not gone back to his office in the Kremlin. He was no longer capable of operating out of a conventional workplace. Instead he had gone straight into the Kuntsevo Clinic where he became a full-time resident. Much of the first floor of the well-equipped clinic was given over to the Soviet leader and to the support staff he needed around him. In a large and airy set of rooms, the General Secretary of the Communist Party of the Soviet Union began to carry out his daily work. Andropov's face had become unnaturally pale and drawn. His voice had grown hoarse. Normally he was a cheerful and lively figure who would get up and greet every visitor with an outstretched hand, but that autumn he never rose from behind the working table set up in his room in the clinic. To all those close to him it was clear that he was growing frailer by the day.

Among the leadership, inevitably, a process of jockeying for power began. For those who saw themselves as a potential future leader of the Soviet Union, the day-to-day health of Andropov was of vital concern. For the factions who wanted to keep out one candidate or push forward another, too, knowing the state of the delicate health of their present leader was essential. Initially there were whisperings in corridors. Then the rumour began to spread around the Kremlin: 'Andropov has had it'. It was a bit like the court of a medieval king, where courtiers waiting for their sovereign to die knew that this would trigger a challenge for the succession. But still nothing about Andropov's dire condition was known outside the small ruling clique. The official word from the Kremlin was that the Soviet leader was still on an extended holiday in the Crimea.

Members of the Politburo travelled out to the Kuntsevo Clinic in their Zil limousines for meetings at Andropov's bedside so that he could continue with his duties as head of government. These vehicles were always allowed to drive at speed along the road to Kuntsevo, preceded and followed by escorts from the security services. One of those who visited regularly was Politburo member Mikhail Gorbachev, who was genuinely fond of his mentor and who wrote of these bedside encounters, 'whenever the doctors permitted it I went to the hospital. In fact everyone had been visiting him – some less often, others more frequently; some to support him, others to check on his condition once more.' So the suffering induced by his illness was aggravated by another worry: Andropov knew what was going on around his bedside. Or, as Gorbachev put it, 'he sensed the intrigue'.[1]

Of the ministers and officials who drove out to the clinic for those bedside meetings, Andropov clearly had his favourites. Defence Minister Dmitri Ustinov was one of his closest friends and mainstays. His support had been decisive in Andropov becoming General Secretary on the death of Brezhnev. Another of those regularly making the short drive out to Kuntsevo was Marshal Nikolai Ogarkov, the Chief of the General Staff, the nation's number one soldier who had distinguished himself in his press conference on the shooting down of the Korean airliner by claiming the aircraft's mission was a CIA plot. Both were hard-liners who were deeply suspicious of the West, particularly of the United States and its hawkish administration. These Soviet leaders were proud men. Despite talk of the decay and economic decline of the

Soviet state in the West, the men who led the USSR rightly felt that they were in command of a great superpower and a vast military machine. They had been deeply offended by the hostile accusations of recent months. They did not like to be insulted, especially by their arch enemy. In Washington, Robert Gates was one of the few Soviet watchers who believed that his government's open hostility was counterproductive. He later remarked, 'I think the Soviet leaders in a strange sort of way were deeply offended and hurt. Anything that questioned their legitimacy, or the fact that they were civilised people, really got under their skin.'[2]

Towards the end of the first week of November, Andropov and his closest colleagues in the intelligence and military establishment had become desperately worried. Operation RYaN had ticked nearly all the boxes. Andropov said in an interview in *Pravda*, 'It is time they [the US] stopped devising one option after another in the search for the best ways of unleashing nuclear war in the hope of winning it. Engaging in this is not just irresponsible, it is insane.'[3]

The growing alarm in the Kremlin was expressed to the Soviet people in many ways. There was a series of organised peace rallies and sponsored 'peace' classes in schools. There were closed briefings on the danger of war for party activists and military personnel. Civil defence measures were increased, including air raid drills that were held in factories across western Russia. There was a rather heavy-handed television film that depicted a warmongering America bent on world domination. Reagan was regularly described in the media as a 'reckless criminal'; he was even compared to Hitler. Stalin's famous speech from the autumn of 1941 to troops in Red Square about to go out and face the advancing German Army was invoked in radio broadcasts and quoted in newspapers. It's extremely difficult to assess the effect all this had on the ordinary Soviet citizen, many of whom were no doubt suitably sceptical of official 'messages'. But certainly some people seem to have been concerned. One Russian said in an interview to a Western journalist while in West Germany, 'We have been hearing a lot of rumours about the possibility of war in the near future. At political information meetings they are saying that the United States is getting ready to attack the Soviet Union, and that we should be prepared for an attack at any moment. From what I could see, those who believed these warnings significantly outnumbered those who didn't.'[4]

On 5 November, on the eve of the big celebration of the anniversary of the Russian Revolution, a speech by Politburo member Gregory Romanov gave another indication of the anxiety felt by the Soviet leadership. In addressing the Soviet people he declared that 'perhaps never before in the post-war decades has the atmosphere in the world been as tense as it is now'. He went on, 'Comrades, the international situation is at present white hot, thoroughly white hot.'[5] But it was about to get still hotter.

The Soviet military had already speeded up the response time of its nuclear forces. Missiles like the SS-20s had to be ready to come to full combat alert in less than eight hours (a few years earlier at least a day was needed). Aircraft had to be ready within thirty minutes. In the autumn of 1983 all military support for getting in the harvest was terminated. The last time this had happened was in 1968, prior to the invasion of Czechoslovakia. The transport aircraft that ferried troops around Russia and the Ukraine to help farmers were all called in for combat duties. In October, nuclear weapons had been transported from storage sites to delivery units by helicopter. Some nuclear missiles had been deployed to Czechoslovakia and East Germany.[6]

Moreover, by that autumn the Soviets had developed their own strategy of 'Launch Under Attack'. Knowing that time was so short to react during a nuclear assault, particularly with the Pershing IIs only minutes away from Moscow, the military recommended to the political leadership not to wait until the enemy's missiles had landed but to launch their own weapons as soon as evidence came in of a launch by the other side. It was only a very short step from this to launching simply on the fear that the other side were about to launch. This would significantly shift Soviet policy from one of retaliation to one of pre-emption. This never became formal policy but the military drew up a new set of targets for their heavy ICBMs based in silos hidden across the west of the Soviet Union, and these were reviewed every few months. Assuming that the US had already fired their missiles, they decided not to target the launch sites that would presumably be empty. According to Vitalii Tsygichko, an analyst working for the General Staff, the Soviet ballistic missiles were allocated targets 'such as airfields, ports and C3 [command, control and communication] facilities, and against the US political and economic infrastructure including transportation grids and fuel supply lines'. Such an attack would prove to be an 'annihilating retaliatory nuclear strike'.[7] This meant that Washington and many other major cities would be hit in the first wave of a Soviet nuclear assault.

In one form of logic, when time was crucial and every second counted, this made good sense. But it also made the possibility of miscalculation even greater. Only six weeks before, the Soviet early warning system had malfunctioned by interpreting reflections of the sun on clouds in the Midwest of the United States as a sign that missiles had been launched. On that occasion the cool head of Stanislav Petrov had defused the situation, but there was no guarantee that the officer on duty would respond in the same way to another early warning. The entire Soviet nuclear launch system was resting on a knife edge. Either man or machine could interpret a situation wrongly and the consequence would be nuclear war by miscalculation.

When on 8 November NATO changed its top secret codes during Able Archer 83, the Soviet leaders felt confident that this could no longer be a war game. Andropov and his close clique of regular military and intelligence visitors convinced themselves that the West was about to launch a first-strike nuclear attack on their country. Fearing that if they waited any longer it would be too late to respond, they put the entire Soviet nuclear arsenal on to the maximum state of combat alert. The paranoid Soviet leadership, headed up as it was by a man who was desperately ill in a clinic, now prepared to take the world to the brink. It was a critical moment in the Cold War.

Outside their cocoon, some comrades would not have believed that a Western nuclear strike was a possibility. Andrei Gromyko had been Foreign Secretary for an extraordinary twenty-six years and was one of the few in the Soviet leadership who knew the West and its leaders well. Had he been asked whether a first strike by the West was imminent there is no doubt he would have said 'No'. Gromyko was fully aware of the tensions with the US. Only a few weeks earlier he had had what he described as one of the worst meetings of his life with US Secretary of State George Shultz. But Gromyko would never have been persuaded that the US was about to launch its strategic nuclear missiles. When he visited the bedside at Kuntsevo he would have argued for caution and restraint. But was Andropov in a mood to listen? It was a small community around Andropov now. Oleg Kalugin, KGB bureau chief in Leningrad, summed up the atmosphere: 'Paranoia became a distinct feature of Soviet life, paranoia in the leadership ... It did not affect the Russian people in the sense they were busy making ends meet, but the Russian leadership was just struck by paranoia.'[8]

In the US only the President can authorise the use of nuclear weapons. The Americans use a system called the nuclear 'football' in which a top military aide who has gone through the most rigorous security vetting is never more than a few steps from the President, carrying a briefcase often hand-cuffed to his arm that contains the codes for launching nuclear weapons. Wherever the President goes, the 'football' is always nearby. The leather briefcase weighs about 18 kilograms and its contents are officially top secret. But it is thought to contain a seventy-five-page document called 'The Black Book' listing the options for a retaliatory attack; another book listing sites around the US where the President can be taken in the event of an emergency, including any attack on the United States (this was opened and used on 9/11); and a three-by-five-inch card listing the authentication codes, known as the Gold Codes, which are changed daily and link the President to the National Command Authority from where strategic nuclear missiles are launched. This has sometimes been called 'the button'. The case also contains a secure military satellite communication system. At any time there are five White House military aides, one of whom always accompanies the President – even waiting a polite distance away when he's in the lavatory.

The Soviets had their own equivalent system called the 'cheggets'. Not so much detail is known about this, other than that it worked on the same principles as the American 'football' – effectively it was the nuclear button containing the launch codes to communicate to the Soviet military. In the Soviet Union in 1983, three men could give the order to launch nuclear weapons. They were the leader, Andropov; the Defence Minister, Ustinov; and the Chief of the General Staff, Ogarkov. This system was intended to foil a first strike whose intention might be to decapitate the leadership and leave no one with clear authority to order a retaliation.

As Able Archer 83 moved towards its climax on the evening of Tuesday 8 November there was a lot of to-ing and fro-ing to the Kuntsevo Clinic. The mood on the first floor was particularly tense. Doctors and nurses noticed a lot of military men in their bright starched uniforms visiting the hospital. We now know how nervous the leadership became when either Andropov or Ustinov, or, most likely, both of them together, put the entire Soviet nuclear arsenal with its 11,000 warheads on to maximum combat alert.

There were several layers to the Soviet nuclear forces. Firstly there were the huge missile silos, scattered across western Russia and the Ukraine, where giant SS-19 intercontinental ballistic missiles were located. Each one was a beast standing at 27 metres tall and weighing over 100 tons, with a range of 10,000 kilometres (well over 6000 miles). In the early 1980s, every SS-19 was armed with six separate MIRV warheads. Each warhead had the destructive capacity of roughly forty Hiroshima bombs. When a silo was on stand-by, each missile was fully fuelled and every warhead pre-assigned a target in the United States or Western Europe – a military installation, a command centre or a city.

There were always two officers in command of a bunker. If the order to launch came through, the senior officer had to break a seal and open the safe, which contained an envelope. On opening the envelope the operators would find two keys. Both men had to insert their keys and turn them at the same time in special lock devices in order to launch the missiles from their silo. Officers for this highly responsible work had to be specially selected, and were constantly assessed medically and psychologically so as to ensure they would carry out their orders to the letter in the knowledge that this would almost certainly mean their total destruction in a retaliatory strike, along with the death of their families. The two men were on duty for six hours on and six hours off during a twenty-four-hour period in a confined space 50 metres (164 feet) below ground in the heart of the bunker, so they also had to be psychologically compatible with each other. The whole process from the instruction to launch, from receiving orders to the missiles taking off, was about two minutes. At times the officers were ordered to prepare to launch their missiles but were not told whether this was an exercise or the real thing. It was not unknown for even these specially selected and trained men to tremble and hesitate when it came to launching their missiles. But only once had an officer been unable to turn his key.

Captain Viktor Tkachenko was in charge of one of these missile silos. He remembered early November 1983 as a period of great tension.[9] Political officers had briefed Tkachenko and his team on the NATO exercises that were taking place and had warned them that this might not in fact be an exercise but cover for a first-strike assault on the Soviet Union. Tkachenko recalled very clearly one particular shift. He remembered it precisely because it was at the time of the national holiday to mark the anniversary of the Bolshevik Revolution of 1917 – a holiday that was held on 7 or 8 November each year. 'We had always been told that war would begin on the eve of some holiday, when people were out celebrating, when people were relaxed,' Tkachenko recalled. On the 8th he had dinner with his wife and two young sons, who lived nearby on the base, and then said goodbye, knowing that he would have to miss the celebrations as he was on combat duty. Then he departed and descended to his bunker command post.

'When we reached the command bunker that night we received a special order,' he recalled. 'We were told to immediately go to raised combat alert.' Very unusually there was a third man present that night. This man explained that as they were now on heightened alert he was there to ensure there was no breakdown in communication with Moscow. Almost certainly he was a KGB officer, there to make sure that if the order came to fire their missiles it was acted on immediately.

Tkachenko later recalled that he would have gone ahead and launched without hesitation if ordered: 'I was fully ready to do it then.' That was his duty. The nation would be relying on him. He felt confident that he would only ever be asked to fire his missiles in retaliation, if the Soviet Union was itself coming under nuclear attack. 'We were ready for the Third World War but only if it had been started by the Americans,' he said.

The Soviet arsenal of medium-range nuclear missiles was also put on a similar state of heightened alert. The principal weapon in this category was the SS-20 or Pioneer missile. It was far smaller than the SS-19, at 16.5 metres (54 feet) tall and weighing 37 tons, with a shorter range of up to 5000 kilometres, or just over 3000 miles. The SS-20 could carry up to three MIRV warheads, each with the destructive yield of about ten Hiroshima bombs. Its key distinguishing feature was that it could be launched from mobile launchers spread out across the countryside. In normal times, only about 10 per cent of all SS-20s were in the field on manoeuvres. However, in early November 1983, at least 50 per cent of the total SS-20 force was mobilised and each missile was ordered to take up its top secret field station. This deployment involved hiding the missiles up to 150 kilometres (nearly 100 miles) from their bases. The transporters were able to travel over all forms of rough terrain, including swamps and mountain roads. They could cross rivers and could even deploy in forests. When in position they were covered with camouflage nets to prevent them from being spotted by spy satellites overhead. These nets were also radio absorbent to prevent them being located from the radio signals emitted. From receiving the order to launch, it would take between two and three minutes to clear the nets and bring the missiles into their vertical launching positions. As in the silos, each group of missiles needed two officers with special keys to activate a launch.

The GRU (Soviet military intelligence) kept the commanders fully informed about the Able Archer exercise. General-Colonel Ivan Yesin was a SS-20 Rocket Forces commander based in their general headquarters. He remembered receiving daily reports on the progress of the NATO war game. 'It was a time of peak tension,' he said. 'We had to stay extra vigilant so as not to overlook the moment when a nuclear strike might have been delivered against the Soviet Union.'[10] Yesin recalled that when it came to responding to an attack, every second counted. 'The greatest fear of the Soviet missile men [was] that too much time would be wasted in making the decision to launch, the political decision ... that the General Secretary would take too long to think about what to do.' Knowing the capabilities of the new Pershing missiles, there was precious little time for decision-making. Yesin recalled how at the time of the Revolution holiday on 8 November, 'during the climax of the NATO exercise our state of alert was increased. The commanders of missile forces were told to stay in their bunkers full time in constant radio communication ... They were on the most heightened state of alert waiting for the orders to launch.' Yesin and his team were in constant radio contact with Marshal Ogarkov, who on the 8th had descended to the principal military command bunker outside Moscow from where he had the authority to launch nuclear weapons should the General Secretary be killed in a first strike.

The Soviet Navy was commanded by the formidable and aggressive Admiral Georgi Gorshikov who had been commander-in-chief since the mid-1950s. He had turned the Soviet Navy from a third-rate force that had played virtually no role in World War Two into a mighty fleet that matched the US Navy in nearly all its ships and firepower. In the event of imminent war, the Northern Fleet based at Severomorsk near Murmansk would deploy to the Barents Sea. But the greatest nuclear threat to the West came from the submarine fleet.

In the mid-1980s there were two principal classes of nuclear weapon-carrying submarines in the Soviet Navy. The Delta class was nuclear-powered and each sub carried twelve SS-N-8 missiles with an immense range of up to 7800 kilometres (4800 miles), although the SS-N-8's accuracy was not good. Most of these missiles were not targeted on specific sites such as airfields or military bases but more generally on US cities, which were well within the accuracy of their targeting systems. The other class was the immense Typhoon submarine, which caused a great stir when Western intelligence became aware of it in the early 1980s. The Typhoons were among the largest submarines ever built at 25,000 tons with a length of 171 metres (560 feet). The crew enjoyed an unusual level of luxury for a Soviet ship with plenty of space and facilities that included both a swimming pool and a sauna. This was because the Typhoon was intended to spend most of its patrols sitting at the bottom of oceans for long periods of time – up to a year. It would sit out a nuclear exchange and only fire its twenty huge SS-N-20 missiles months after war had broken out in a final assault on enemy territory.[11]

Sergei Lokot was an assistant commander on a Delta-class submarine in the Northern Fleet. He too remembers the tension rising from September 1983 onwards, culminating in the Able Archer war scare. During the crisis his sub slipped out of port and took up its battle station sitting under the Arctic ice, where it was almost impossible for reconnaissance aircraft or satellites to find it. The submarine maintained constant communication with its base and was in a continuous state of combat alert. He recalls this period as 'The only time in my eighteen years of service on Northern Fleet submarines when I witnessed such a difficult situation.'[12] Despite the constant strain, Lokot maintains that he and his fellow submariners had always trained and prepared for being on combat alert and that this is what they expected to do in the event of a crisis. If the order came, the submarine would ascend to the surface, break through the ice and launch its nuclear missiles against its targets. Like the missile commanders, Lokot never questioned what his duty was. 'If we had received the order we would have launched the nuclear missiles,' he said. 'I can't imagine having any doubts about whether to do it or not.'

The Soviet strategic bombing force never had the equivalent role to that assigned to the US Air Force. The Soviets always relied more heavily on their missile capability. They feared that their bombers would always be vulnerable to a surprise American attack while the aircraft were still on the ground. The Soviet Air Force had almost been wiped out on the ground in the first hours of Hitler's invasion, Operation Barbarossa, in June 1941. The memory of this and the lack of preparedness of the air force still haunted the Soviets. But in 1982, as the tension with the US escalated, and in anticipation of the arrival of the Pershing II missiles in West Germany, the Soviet Air Force deployed some squadrons of their nuclear weapon-carrying bombers to East Germany. The Tupolev Tu-22M was a supersonic variable-wing strategic bomber codenamed by NATO 'Backfire'. Many Tupolev bombers were known for poor workmanship and for being difficult to fly, but that was not the case with the Tu-22M. Dramatic improvements had been made on the earlier models.

Colonel Maxim Devetyarov was a navigator on the Backfire who in 1982 took up a position at a bomber command headquarters in East Germany. He also remembers 1983 as 'a very tense time in the relations between the two superpowers'.[13] The air force, the General Staff and the Ministry of Defence carried out constant checks on airborne readiness and assessments of their preparations for war. During Able Archer, many bombers were kept on combat alert, fully fuelled and loaded with weapons, and crews on fifteen minutes' stand-by.

Several Soviet fighter squadrons were put on an even higher

level during Able Archer known as 'strip alert'. This meant that the fighters were fully fuelled and armed with their pilots and crews on board, their engines running, waiting at the end of the runway for the order to take off. They could be scrambled within seconds of receiving an alarm and their task was to keep the airspace clear of intruders by intercepting enemy aircraft. They also had the ability to make pre-emptive strikes against NATO nuclear delivery systems on the ground if it was thought they were about to launch missiles against the Soviet Union. During Able Archer, Soviet fighter squadrons in Czechoslovakia and East Germany were also put on strip alert. This was psychologically draining for the pilots and aircrews and they could only be kept in this state for between thirty minutes and one hour at a time; then a new squadron would roll out on strip alert. Fighter interceptors like the Su-24 and the MiG-23 did not carry nuclear weapons but were the most obvious sign of the Soviet war scare. US spy satellites picked up their presence at the end of runways during the days around 8 and 9 November.

Marshal Viktor Kulikov was the Soviet commander of the Warsaw Pact forces. Not long after the panic he gave a chilling warning in an article in a Soviet military magazine: 'When the United States and NATO play with fire, as they are now doing, theirs is not simply an irresponsible activity, but ... an extremely dangerous one ... the US-NATO military and political leadership must realise that whatever they create and whatever means they elaborate for unleashing an aggressive war and conducting combat operations, the Soviet Union and its Warsaw Pact allies will be capable of a fitting response.'[14]

The situation had reached its most dangerous point. If the Soviets, straining at the leash that November day in 1983, had launched their nuclear weapons, Armageddon would have followed. Tens of millions would have been killed directly by the impact of the missiles across western Europe and the

United States, from Verona to Vermont, from Newcastle to New York. This would have triggered the firing of the massive arsenal of US nuclear missiles in retaliation, from the huge silos in the Midwest and from submarines situated across the oceans of the world. US commanders had long talked of blasting the Soviet Union back into the Stone Age. Tens of millions of Soviet men, women and children would have perished. Hundreds of millions more around the world would have lost their lives as a consequence of the nuclear radiation that would be scattered across continents, carried by winds and rain, and countless millions more as a result of the starvation and chaos that would follow in what was called the 'nuclear winter'. It would not only have been the end of human civilisation but probably the end of most forms of life on Earth. Some people believe that only the cockroach and the scorpion would have survived.

16

Night

On the evening of Wednesday, 9 November 1983, everything came to a head. In their bunker in Mons, NATO commanders reached the most dramatic phase of their war game: they received the message that their request to launch 350 nuclear weapons against targets across the Soviet Union and the Eastern bloc had been given approval by their respective political leaderships. It would take just a few hours to confirm targets, check systems and to send the launch codes. But by this point, of course, several members of the Soviet leadership had already persuaded themselves that a nuclear attack from the West was imminent, that the mobilisation of nuclear forces was real and urgent. They knew that if incoming missiles were identified they would only have minutes to respond.

At his bedroom in the Kuntsevo Clinic, a military aide sat beside Andropov with the chegget, ready to send out the nuclear launch codes. Marshal Ogarkov, one of the other men authorised to launch nuclear weapons, settled into the central command bunker outside Moscow for the night. Officials can remember no other time when this happened. As NATO progressed through all the states of alert from normal readiness to General Alert, toadying KGB officers on the ground

eager to win favour in the Moscow Centre sent back alarm-
ist reports of the increasing readiness of NATO for nuclear
war. They reported on the increased level of alert at US
military stations and the fact that radio silence descended
across many NATO bases from 1800 to 1900 hours Moscow
time every night. This, along with the use of that new and
unknown code at the peak of Able Archer 83, convinced the
senior figures in the KGB, the GRU and the Kremlin that this
war game was different to all previous war games. Just as
they had plans to attack the West under the guise of military
exercises, so NATO was about to launch a pre-emptive strike
against the Soviet Union.[1]

That evening the KGB and the GRU sent out Top Secret and
Super Urgent 'Flash' telegrams to their residencies around the
world, telling their agents that the situation was now critical
and that the NATO exercise was in all likelihood preparation
for a sudden nuclear attack. They were instructed once again
to look out for any unusual signs of military activity, or any
of the many key indicators laid down by Operation RYaN,
and to report back as a matter of urgency.[2] Oleg Gordievsky,
the deputy head of the KGB residency in London, received
the Flash telegram and, knowing that life was carrying on as
normal all around him, thought the panic absurd. 'How can
we take such a task seriously?' he asked later.[3]

In addition to sending a rare Flash telegram to their residencies, a courier was urgently sent to contact the spy operated by
East Germany's foreign intelligence service, the HVA, at the
heart of NATO. Rainer Rupp, 'Topaz', was head of the Current
Intelligence Group, the nerve centre of intelligence gathering
in Brussels, and a man with the highest level of security
clearance within NATO. East Berlin wanted to ask urgently
on behalf of their KGB masters if a real nuclear attack was
imminent. Rupp had been alerted to Able Archer earlier in
the exercise by his bosses in East Berlin. He had been told to

'keep his eyes open' and report back.[4] However, in his group there was no discussion about Able Archer, which was being acted out within a completely different operational division of NATO. Most importantly, Rupp could see that there was absolutely no gearing up for war at NATO headquarters. The war game was just that and no more.

Earlier in 1983, Rupp had been given a small machine that looked like a simple electronic calculator. He was told that this was to be used for sending short messages in the case of an emergency. To operate it was very simple. Rupp would write down the short message he wanted to send. He would then code every letter as a number and punch these into the calculator device. The machine would then condense this and create a short audio signal out of it. When he played this signal it sounded like a short crackling sound or electronic bleep. Rupp was surprised when he received the machine and thought it was a bit extreme and rather unnecessary, but when during the summer he had his annual meeting with his courier, the professor from East Germany, he was told about the scale of the tension between East and West and the anxiety building in Moscow. He kept the machine at home because it looked like a calculator and would not have attracted any attention had his house been searched. It was there in case of an emergency.

When the courier contacted him on 9 November, Rupp was puzzled by the request. At NATO headquarters in Brussels it was just another day at the office. So he wrote a short message to the effect that everything was normal and 'there was no indication that NATO was preparing for war'. He coded it and inserted the numbers in the calculator device. That evening Rupp drove out of the centre of Brussels a few miles and stopped at a public telephone box. According to his instructions, he dialled the number he had been given and said a few words like 'Hello, how are you?' Then, holding the machine over the mouthpiece of the telephone, he pressed play and the short audio burst played out. At the other end the audio signal was received, decoded, and the message passed on.

From HVA headquarters in the Lichtenberg district of Berlin, the communication Rupp had sent was immediately passed on to the KGB Centre in Moscow. It was as though the Centre was getting a message direct from the command headquarters of NATO that nothing untoward was happening. But what effect did this message have? No doubt for some it would have been reassuring to receive. But it was simply from one agent out of many. No single source could be relied on. Maybe the asset had been turned and was passing on this news under duress. Maybe it was yet another example of *maskirovka* – deception. And even if NATO was quiet, this did not mean that in Washington the US military was not preparing to launch a nuclear first strike while NATO was playing its war game. A paranoid leadership could never trust one source that stood out against the rest. But almost certainly Rainer Rupp played a small part in helping to save the world from a nuclear holocaust.

At Ramstein Air Force Base in south-west Germany, the US Air Force had its European headquarters. It was one of the bases taking part in Able Archer 83. In those crucial days of heightened alert in Moscow, Lieutenant-General Leonard Perroots was Assistant Chief of Staff for Intelligence. He was a career air force officer who from the mid-1950s had chosen to go not into flying but into intelligence and had served at a number of bases across the United States. He rose rapidly up the ranks, and after service in Vietnam he returned to Washington as chief of the Current Intelligence and Briefing Branch, and as such briefed White House staff, Congressional committees and the Joint Chiefs of Staff on air force matters. In 1980 he was sent to Ramstein to run the European air force intelligence operation. Everything about his career suggested he was a thoroughly professional, reliable and conventional intelligence officer.

At the beginning of that second week of November, Perroots started to receive reports of increased Soviet air activity. There were at least thirty-six Soviet intelligence flights over the Baltic, the Barents Sea and the sea around Norway, many more than usual. These aircraft were almost certainly in the air to see if the US Navy was moving vessels forward in support of Able Archer. Then reports from spy satellites came in that nuclear bombers had been put on stand-by at airfields in Poland and East Germany. Further reports came in of fighter jets on strip alert in East Germany and Czechoslovakia. It was also reported that many SS-20s had deployed into the field, but their locations were not known. In all, this amounted to military reactions that were 'unparalleled in scale' with any other NATO exercise.[5]

But Perroots was not alarmed. He had received no intelligence briefings warning him that the Soviet leadership was anxious about Western preparations for war or that Able Archer 83 had prompted a serious panic. There was no heightened state of alert on the NATO side. So he decided to do 'nothing in the face of evidence that parts of the Soviet armed forces were moving to an unusual level of alert'. He later said that this was down to his 'gut instinct not informed guidance'. He simply could not imagine that the Soviets were mobilising their nuclear arsenal for an attack on the West. This seemed utterly inconceivable to Perroots, despite the general level of international tension. So he did not sound the alarm or raise the alert status of the US military. The Soviets might have interpreted a new US alert as clear evidence of the prelude to a nuclear attack and responded according to their Launch Under Attack doctrine. So, like Stanislav Petrov six weeks before, the world was lucky that Perroots stuck to

his 'gut instinct'. As a later report confirmed, 'it was his rec-
ommendation, made in ignorance, not to raise US readiness
in response – a fortuitous, if ill-informed, decision'.[6]

Back in the Kuntsevo Clinic, it was a long and tense night in
the first-floor suite of Yuri Andropov. All the senior members
of the Politburo and the leadership had vivid memories of the
Second World War. They knew the savage destruction that
war could bring. The Soviet Union had lost an estimated 27
million soldiers and citizens during that conflict. Thousands
of square miles of its territory had been occupied, and the
devastation caused by the Nazi invaders was almost unimag-
inable with thousands of townships and villages destroyed,
and tens of thousands of collective farms and factories left in
ruin. Without doubt Andropov in his clinic, Ogarkov deep
in the central military command bunker and Ustinov in the
Ministry of Defence did not want to push the nuclear button
unless they absolutely had to, and bring down on a new generation of their people an even worse catastrophe. Maybe this
is what made them hesitate. Perhaps the leaders were still
uncertain that Operation RYaN had got it right and that the
doom-mongers like Vladimir Kryuchkov were correct in their
predictions. Perhaps the news from Topaz that there were no
plans for war in NATO headquarters saved the day. Whatever
it was, they sat out that night, trembling, no doubt looking up
into the dark sky as though looking out to spot incoming missiles. But no alarm was received of enemy launches, and the
leaders refrained from launching their own nuclear weapons
in anticipation of an assault. Probably the most dangerous
moment of the Cold War passed. As dawn came up on another
day, the world had survived.

In Washington, London, Bonn and Paris there had been no
awareness of this panic. NATO officials carried on with their
routine exercise with no notion of the scare it had provoked

in Moscow. On the morning of 11 November, the Able Archer 83 war game came to an end. They had practised the release of nuclear weapons. That was it. The exercise did not follow on with what would have happened next. That was not the point of it. All the players emerged from their deep bunker at Mons into the light of day. It had been an intensive exercise with long twelve- to fourteen-hour shifts for several days. But they were in a good mood. In NATO terms it had gone well. No doubt many of them went and had a good breakfast. Some who had been working through the night probably went for a celebratory drink. Farewells were said. Backs were slapped. Departures made. Able Archer was over for another year. Spike Callender remembered that after a week of intense work he could now look forward to getting a good night's sleep. Like the rest of NATO he remained oblivious to the panic in Moscow. 'We felt that this exercise was no more provocative in 1983 than it would have been in 1981 or 1982,' he said later.[7]

CIA satellites had picked up evidence of nuclear bombers standing by and of fighters on strip alert in Czechoslovakia and East Germany, but few of the other signs of nuclear mobilisation. And of course it was impossible for satellites to pick up any insight into the state of paranoia in the Soviet leadership, the panic that had gripped several key intelligence, military and political leaders in the USSR. Robert Gates, then deputy director of the CIA and later Secretary of Defense for Presidents George W. Bush and Barack Obama, described this as an immense intelligence failure and summed it up terrifyingly when he said, 'We may have been at the brink of nuclear war and not even known it.'[8]

17

'Really Scary'

The intelligence failures in November 1983 had in fact been on a staggering scale. And the failings were on the part of both superpowers. Operation RYaN had persuaded an already paranoid KGB and political leadership to put Soviet nuclear forces on to a maximum state of alert. Intelligence officials had reported not what they believed was actually happening but what they thought their bosses wanted to hear. And the Soviet intelligence system lacked any effective analytical power. Everyone within the system went along with what they were told or were asked to prove. Neither agents working out of residencies nor senior officers at the KGB Centre in Moscow openly questioned or applied any critical rigour to the information in front of them. This had brought the world to the very brink of nuclear war.

On the other side, although the military and the CIA had detected elements of the mobilisation in the East, they had not understood its extent. Nor had they any insight into the minds of those giving the orders. Only later was it appreciated how severely rattled the Soviet leadership had become and how they had come to believe what no American could accept: that the United States would unleash a war by taking the initial step and launching a pre-emptive first strike. If a nation wants one thing from its intelligence service, it is to know what the other side is thinking and what they plan to do next – especially if they are about to launch nuclear weapons against you. In this the US intelligence establishment entirely failed. For years the question would be asked in the CIA, how had we missed such a dangerous moment?[1]

Immediately following the events of November 1983, the CIA and the NSA went through a period of denial. On 30 December that year the CIA responded to the evidence of the Warsaw Pact military alert during Able Archer with a report entitled 'Soviet Thinking on the Possibility of Armed Confrontation with the United States'. It concluded that 'Contrary to the impression conveyed by Soviet propaganda, Moscow does not appear to anticipate a near-term military confrontation with the United States.' The CIA directorate of intelligence decided that any attempt to play up the possibility of 'war danger' was simply a ploy to stop the deployment of Pershing II and Cruise missiles in western Europe and to deepen divisions within the Atlantic alliance, putting pressure on Washington for a more conciliatory line. It was all put down to part of a programme of Soviet disinformation to discredit the US and bolster opposition to the siting of American missiles in Europe.[2]

The US intelligence establishment remained adamant that there was nothing to be concerned about. In May 1984, analysts produced a Special National Intelligence Estimate entitled 'Implications of Recent Soviet Military-Political Activities'. The assessment was specifically set up to examine the Soviet reaction to Able Archer 83 and it noted the various military responses, including the placing of Soviet and East German aircraft on to a heightened state of readiness. It admitted that the 'elaborate Soviet reaction' was 'somewhat greater than usual [by comparison to previous Able Archer exercises]', but it still concluded decisively, 'We believe strongly that Soviet actions are not inspired by, and

Soviet leaders do not perceive, a genuine danger of imminent conflict or confrontation with the United States.' More
emphatically it affirmed that the Soviets did not fear 'an
imminent military clash'.[3]

The clearest hint at how dangerous the situation had in
reality become emerged from the most unlikely source. The
British double agent inside the KGB, Oleg Gordievsky, passed
on to John Scarlett of MI6 the sequence of messages from the
KGB Centre, even though he thought them absurd. When they
reached the desk of the Foreign Secretary, Geoffrey Howe realised their importance. He later wrote, 'Gordievsky left us in no
doubt of the extraordinary but genuine Russian fear of real-life
nuclear strike.' He and Margaret Thatcher were both impressed
and used every opportunity 'to warn allies and friends of the
genuineness of Soviet fears'. At the Commonwealth heads of
government conference in New Delhi later that month, less than
two weeks after the Able Archer 83 exercise had finished, there
was a discussion with the Tanzanian president Julius Nyerere
and others. Neither Thatcher nor Howe made any reference to
their secret sources but they found a receptive audience to the
idea of how fearful the Soviet Union had become in the face of
American aggression. The veteran African leader summed up
the situation by saying, 'When the weak are frightened, that
threatens no danger to the world. It is when the powerful are
threatened that the world feels extremely nervous, and rightly
so.' Nyerere then cited a Swahili proverb: 'When the elephants
fight, it is the grass that suffers.'

Listening in, the Prime Minister of Singapore, Lee Kuan
Yew, added, 'So too when the elephants make love!'

'I would prefer that,' replied Nyerere, 'for at least it would
enhance the prospects for peace.'[4]

Intelligence summaries from Gordievsky were regularly
passed on to US intelligence agencies but they failed to
change the Washington view that the Soviets were simply

playing a game by exaggerating the level of the war scare that November. In March 1984, the British ambassador to the United States, Oliver Wright, had a meeting with the Under Secretary for Political Affairs at the State Department, Lawrence Eagleburger, and tried hard to persuade him of the dangers American policy was provoking. He drew Eagleburger's attention to the British evidence that the Soviets had nearly gone to war some four months earlier. However, it seems that the ambassador's presentation was weak and that he was not fully briefed on the secret MI6 sources. Eagleburger refuted the British point of view completely and accused the Soviets of 'pursuing a massive propaganda campaign'. Others in the State Department were even more critical and believed the Foreign Office was overstating Soviet fears simply as a way to try to force the President to tone down his rhetoric.[5]

One person in Washington who *was* genuinely impressed with the British intelligence was Reagan's new National Security Advisor, Bud McFarlane. He had been in office for just a month when Able Archer 83 began. He later remembered, 'The Gordievsky debriefs were quite shocking to me in the sense that this extremely reliable source, an insider, was reporting genuine alarm in the Soviet leadership towards what they saw as American intentions.' He concluded that 'there was widespread fear, anxiety, alarm on the Soviet side about the United States' intentions of possibly launching a first strike'. McFarlane was convinced that Andrei Gromyko would have acted as a moderating influence in the Kremlin, knowing the West and its leaders as well as he did. He would have tried to persuade the rest of the leaders that with all the checks and balances in the US system, no President could go ahead and unilaterally launch a first nuclear strike. However, he had to conclude that the evidence from Gordievsky 'made it clear that there was no denying this fear on the Soviet side was real'.[6]

While much of the US intelligence establishment refused

to be concerned, it was McFarlane's concerns that got through to the President. It's not clear exactly when Reagan first heard about the Soviet panic during Able Archer. McFarlane later claimed that he discussed it with the President several times very soon after the war game was over, and while they were still on their tour of South Korea and Japan. According to McFarlane it was even discussed on Air Force One. McFarlane said the President responded with 'genuine anxiety' and disbelief that his own actions and speeches could have provoked the Soviets in such a way. 'It did bother him that they [the Soviets] could even take seriously the very idea [of a US first strike],' he recalled.[7]

Certainly the prospect of nuclear war was weighing heavily on Reagan's mind during the autumn of 1983. In October, the President had watched a preview of an expensive, high-profile movie ABC had produced for American peak-time television called *The Day After*. It imagines a scenario in which tensions between NATO and the Warsaw Pact countries in Europe escalate into a nuclear war between the United States and the Soviet Union. The film focuses on a group of families in Lawrence, Kansas – a typical town in middle America. After a nuclear exchange in Europe, the Soviets fire ICBMs at the United States, and the first air-burst missiles take out the electricity grid. Minutes later, a second salvo of missiles devastates the central states with giant ground-burst hits that generate mushroom clouds across America. The film graphically shows the massive destruction, death and chaos that would follow. After watching the preview, the President wrote in his diary, 'It is powerfully done – all $7mil worth. It's very effective and left me greatly depressed ... Whether it will be of help to the "anti-nukes" [peace protesters] or not, I can't say. My own reaction was one of our having to do all we can to have a deterrent & to see there is never a nuclear war.'[8]

Just three days after returning from his Far East Asian

tour, Reagan once again descended to the Situation Room in the White House basement for another briefing on the sequence of events that would follow in the event of a nuclear war. This again involved the implementation of the Single Integrated Operational Plan (SIOP). Defence Secretary Caspar Weinberger and the head of the Joint Chiefs, Admiral Vessey, were among those taking part. As in 1982, when he had gone through the last similar exercise and was stunned when all the red lights came up on the map of America signifying hits from nuclear missiles, Reagan found the experience 'most sobering'.[9] McFarlane, who was also present, remembers that Reagan disliked the whole thing and felt this was 'a kind of rational analysis in a very irrational context of Mutual Assured Destruction that he rejected'.[10]

On the same day, Reagan agreed with George Shultz to set up a small in-house group of experts on Soviet affairs to think about the possibility of forging new channels of communication with the Soviet leaders. Reagan confided to his diary, 'I think the Soviets are so defense minded, so paranoid about being attacked, that without being in any way soft on them we ought to tell them that no one here has any intention of doing anything like that. What the h—l have they got that anyone would want.'[11] These comments are revealing. The fact that Reagan felt the Soviet leaders were 'so paranoid about being attacked' certainly confirms that he had been given some sort of information about their reaction to Able Archer. The small group of senior diplomats met with Secretary Shultz and Vice President Bush over breakfast the following day to discuss policy towards the Soviet Union. Lawrence Eagleburger from the State Department pointed out that 'the Soviets could be dangerous when they are in trouble and there is uncertainty in their leadership'. He went on, 'We must keep that in mind and take steps to reduce the potential for miscalculation.'[12]

When the President met his ambassador to the Soviet Union, Arthur Hartman, early in 1984 he was still puzzled by the Soviet reaction. 'Do you think the Soviet leaders really fear us,' he asked the ambassador, 'or is all the huffing and puffing just part of their propaganda?'[13] It was a good question that got to the heart of the matter. Had the Kremlin leaders really panicked in November 1983 or was it all a matter of posturing to try to build up anti-American sentiment within the USSR and drive a wedge between the Western allies by making Reagan out to be a warmonger?

Definitive evidence of Reagan's reaction to the Soviet war scare came only a few months later, in June 1984, when CIA director William Casey circulated a memorandum to the President, the Vice President, the Secretaries of State and Defense, the National Security Advisor and the Joint Chiefs of Staff. Going against the CIA intelligence estimate of the previous month, Casey concluded that there were a 'rather stunning array of indicators [during Able Archer]' of an 'increasing aggressiveness in Soviet policy and activities'. When told of this, Reagan described events as 'really scary'.[14] Even if this was not entirely new to him, to read in stark terms about how edgy the Soviets had become astonished the President. Again, it was the fact that the Soviet leadership seemed to believe America would actually launch a first strike against them that so stunned Reagan. The entire American defence and intelligence establishment shared the long-held view that 'The US does not do Pearl Harbors'. The fact was, the Soviets thought they might. Reagan found it both 'astonishing and inexplicable that anyone could imagine such an intention'.[15]

That year the global situation was beginning to change. Andropov finally died from his kidney disease in February 1984. It was unclear whether the programme of reform he had started would die with him or be maintained by the next leader. To the surprise of most outside observers, the Politburo decided the succession should go to Konstantin Chernenko, aged seventy-two, who was almost as frail and ill as his predecessor. He had been a heavy smoker all his life and was now suffering from a lung disease that frequently left him breathless. Along with this he had a weak heart. He had been Brezhnev's favourite and his appointment indicated clearly that the Politburo, for now, wanted to keep power in the hands of the elderly elite who had clung on to it for the last few decades. Again Moscow was the scene of a major state funeral. Again many Western leaders, including the US Vice President, attended. This time Margaret Thatcher also decided to go. She had just returned from a successful visit to Hungary, the first time she had ever visited the Eastern bloc. Despite Soviet propaganda that scorned her as the 'Iron Lady', ordinary Hungarians had given her a tremendous welcome. In Moscow, like all the other world leaders, she had to stand in line and wait for two hours in the freezing winter cold of Red Square. It was a strange gathering. Standing not far from Thatcher was the unshaven PLO guerrilla leader, Yasser Arafat. She ensured that for the whole time they stood waiting she made no eye contact with the Palestinian leader.

Like Brezhnev's funeral only fifteen months before, the event provided an opportunity for Western leaders to size up the new Soviet head of state. Chernenko gave a short, breathless commemorative address in Red Square during which his emphysema was evident to most. He kept coughing throughout the speech and frequently stopped to wipe his brow. Afterwards, Bush had twenty-five minutes with him. Thatcher, surprisingly, spent forty minutes with him, but most of that time was given over to Chernenko reading out a long prepared text. He read it very slowly and stumbled frequently. Thatcher was 'unimpressed'. She felt that the cost of the expensive, thick, fur-lined Russian boots she had taken with her had not been a waste. She would probably need them again soon.[16]

It was election year in the United States. Disregarding his age (seventy-three), Reagan had decided to stand again. Despite the problems of recent years, with record deficits having been run up to fund his vast military rearmament, and the disastrous intervention in Lebanon, America was starting to feel good about itself. The economy was doing well and a new high-tech revolution was beginning to have an effect. The tone of his re-election campaign was resoundingly upbeat. One popular television commercial for Reagan called *Morning Again in America* showed an elderly man raising the Stars and Stripes one morning at a farmstead with young faces looking up in adoration. As the music reached its syrupy climax, a narrator said, 'It's morning again in America ... and under the leadership of President Reagan, our country is stronger and prouder and better. Why would you ever want to return to where we were less than four short years ago?'[17]

The fact was, Reagan did feel personally stronger than four years before in that he did not have to display his anticommunism so forcefully. And by this time his popularity rating had soared. In addition, he felt that America was economically and militarily strong again and had reversed the trend of the détente years that seemed to give the advantage to the Soviets. But he was also deeply concerned by the disturbing reports linked to Able Archer. If the Soviets really believed that he would trigger a nuclear war then what he feared most, the slide into some sort of accidental conflict, was a real possibility. He wrote that he had learned 'something surprising about the Russians. Many people at the top of the Soviet hierarchy were genuinely afraid of America and Americans ... many Soviet officials feared us not only as adversaries but as potential aggressors who might hurl nuclear weapons at them in a first strike.'[18] Gordievsky's revelations about the Soviet war scare the previous November had totally changed Reagan's outlook towards the Soviet Union. McFarlane later confirmed that 'Able Archer had a big influence on Reagan's thinking'.[19]

Reagan decided to modify his tone during the election campaign. Sometimes this has been put down to the growth in influence of moderates within the administration. But on issues like this, Reagan was his own man. He was passionately anti-communist and had been since the late 1940s. But he also believed in the biblical prophecy of Armageddon, which he interpreted as a belief that if humankind continued to make war with ever more powerful and destructive weapons then the day would come when there would be a nuclear holocaust. The events of November 1983 had made this horribly possible. He wanted to do what he could to ensure this would never happen, and decided he had to do more to achieve his ultimate goal of creating a world free of nuclear weapons. To do so, he would have to speak to the other side, get to know the Soviet leaders.

He kicked off his re-election campaign with a televised speech from the White House to the nation and to allies overseas about US–Soviet relations. He talked about returning to the negotiating table with the Soviets. 'Living in this nuclear age makes it imperative that we do talk,' he said in a guarded reference to the events of the previous November. He then returned to his old theme about ridding the world of its nuclear arsenals and concluded, 'As I've said before, my dream is to see the day when nuclear weapons will be banished from the face of the Earth.' He ended the speech with a vintage Reagan story that he had written and added himself. 'Just suppose with me for a moment that an Ivan and an Anya could find themselves, oh, say, in a waiting room, or sharing a shelter from the rain or a storm with a Jim and Sally, and there was no language barrier to keep them from getting acquainted. Would they then debate the differences between their respective governments? Or would they find themselves comparing notes about their children and what each other did for a living? Before they parted company, they would probably have touched on ambitions and hobbies and what they wanted for their children and problems of making ends meet ... Above all they would have proven that people don't make wars. People want to raise their children in a world without fear and without war ... If the Soviet Government wants peace, then there will be peace. Together we can strengthen peace, reduce the level of arms, and know in doing so that we have helped fulfil the hopes and dreams of those we represent and, indeed, of people everywhere. Let us begin now.'[20] When one White House staffer read this handwritten addition to the prepared speech he exclaimed, perhaps a little too loudly, 'Who wrote this shit?'[21] But the press and public immediately picked up on the change of tone. The President was moving on from the anti-communist crusader who called the Soviet Union an 'evil empire' that committed acts of 'terrorism'.

Not everything went swimmingly during the election campaign. On 11 August, Reagan was about to record his weekly radio address to the American public and was asked to do a quick voice-check. Not content to do a simple 'One-two, one-two', he joked, 'My fellow Americans, I'm pleased to tell you that today I've signed legislation that will outlaw Russia for ever. We begin bombing in five minutes.' Although supposedly off the record, it was picked up and recorded by the three radio networks and was later broadcast by NBC and ABC. No doubt the sound engineers at the White House, the intended audience for the President's aside, found it very funny. But the Kremlin was not at all amused and issued a statement calling it 'unprecedentedly hostile towards the USSR and dangerous to the cause of peace'. As a bizarre postscript to the incident, four days later an American listening station in the Pacific picked up a strange message to the Soviet Pacific Fleet announcing that 'war has begun with the United States of

America'. It was four hours before the message was cancelled. It was probably retaliation for Reagan's poor-taste joke.[22]

Reagan had great confidence in his ability to get on with everyone as an individual. He believed those who called him the 'Great Communicator'. He was confident that if he were put in a room with Konstantin Chernenko, all would come out well. For some time in the early months of 1984 he toyed with the idea of a summit meeting with the General Secretary. He wrote in his diary, 'I have a gut feeling we should do this . . . maybe they are scared of us and think we are a threat. I'd like to go face to face & explore this with them.'[23] In March he sent a seven-page letter to Chernenko in which he wrote, 'I fully appreciate the priority you attach to the security of the Soviet state, particularly in light of the enormous costs shouldered by your people in helping to defeat Nazi Germany.' He went on that the United States 'has no desire to threaten the security of the Soviet Union and its allies' and he suggested the 'development of better communications and procedures to avert miscalculations or misunderstandings that might lead to disaster during an international crisis' – a clear reference to the Able Archer war scare.[24]

But the time was not right. The Soviets were not keen on a meeting between their breathless and often confused leader and the lively, confident American commander-in-chief. And old-fashioned Soviet thinking still prevailed. That summer the Soviets found an excuse to organise a boycott of the Olympic Games being held in Los Angeles. They claimed they were concerned for the security of their athletes. In fact it was a tit-for-tat retaliation for the US-led boycott of the Moscow Games four years earlier. The inevitable result was that without competition from some of the great Eastern bloc athletes, the US won more medals than in any Olympics before, and this whipped up an orgy of patriotism, especially in the American television coverage of the Games.[25]

During the last months of 1984, the United States turned

inwards to focus on the presidential election. In August the National Intelligence Council had produced another security estimate. This report outlined as its 'central concern ... the possibility of major Soviet initiatives to influence the November election'. The Soviets had identified the Reagan administration as 'a more consistently hostile opponent of the USSR's interests and aspirations than it has faced in many years'. Fears grew that the Soviets would spread rumours and disinformation to try to discredit Reagan and make him look like an aggressive leader whose actions would put the people of America at grave risk. The November 1983 war scare was once again presented as 'hostile propaganda, which blames the United States for an increased danger of war' in order to 'excite opposition to Washington's policies' and to 'undercut the President's re-election prospects'.[26] In reality, the Soviet Union was too weak and leaderless to exert any real influence upon the outcome of the US election. But it certainly did not look like that in Washington. Just as in 2016 with Donald Trump's campaign, fears began to spread that the Soviets were trying to influence the outcome of an American presidential election.

Despite Reagan's change of tone during the campaign, a private poll in July had revealed that four out of ten Americans imagined a nuclear holocaust would annihilate mankind during their lifetime. But if he was still seen by some as a warmonger, far more Americans were won over by the improving economy and a sense of pride in growing national strength. Reagan was re-elected in November 1984 with a landslide majority in the Electoral College of 525 to 13 votes, although in the popular vote his lead was more modest, with 59 per cent against the Democrat candidate Walter Mondale's 41 per cent. Following the example of his *Morning Again* television ad, his strongest support tended to come from the young, who presumably thought he was providing them with a better future than the Democrats.[27]

*

Meanwhile, in Britain, Margaret Thatcher had convened a seminar of Soviet experts at Chequers, the Prime Minister's official country house in Buckinghamshire. She wanted to reassess her own policy towards the Soviet Union, and with the alarming reports coming in from Gordievsky she had concluded, just as Reagan had done, that building a dialogue with the Soviets was going to be essential. The question was, with whom? When Geoffrey Howe paid an official visit to Moscow in July 1984 he spent some time with both Chernenko and Gromyko and became thoroughly depressed. He found they 'displayed the old Soviet Union at its most unyielding'. The Soviets had walked out of the START talks in Geneva earlier that year in protest at the deployment of the Cruise and Pershing II missiles. It was clear that nothing could persuade them to return. Gromyko refused to discuss any issues about human rights and the treatment of dissidents in the Soviet Union and instead attacked Reagan. 'From the beginning,' he said, 'the American President has set out to destroy all that had been good and positive in US-Soviet relations.' Moreover, Howe found Chernenko 'bewildered and incoherent' for most of their meeting. His speech was often 'interrupted by stumblings (in order to breathe)' indicating at times 'a total lack of comprehension' of what was being discussed. He did, however, ask for one message to be sent to Washington. 'Tell Uncle Sam,' Chernenko told the British Foreign Secretary, 'to stop pointing his nuclear pistol at my forehead!'[28]

Foreign Office experts calculated that three men were likely successors to Chernenko: Viktor Grishin, in his seventies, another from the clique of old men who seemed eager to cling on to power; Grigory Romanov, in his sixties, the Secretary of the Party Central Committee, who had spoken about the situation being 'white hot' during Able Archer 83; and Mikhail Gorbachev, the youngest member of the Politburo, then in his fifties. When reports came in from Canadian Prime Minister

Pierre Trudeau that he had heard Gorbachev was tipped to succeed Chernenko, it was decided to invite him to Britain. Gorbachev was chairman of the Foreign Affairs Committee of the Supreme Soviet and he could be invited as leader of a parliamentary delegation without offending Gromyko. It was made clear to him that if he accepted he would be guaranteed a meeting with Margaret Thatcher. Gorbachev accepted almost immediately.

Now acting head of the KGB residency in London, Oleg Gordievsky was swamped with requests from Moscow for information that could be used to prepare Gorbachev for his visit. What would Mrs Thatcher be likely to talk about? What would Geoffrey Howe want to ask? What was the situation with regard to the coal miners' strike that was threatening to undermine the government? Although he had never met Gorbachev, Gordievsky got the strong impression that he was someone who wanted to know all about Britain, to be very well informed generally and to make an impact on his guests. Not only did Gordievsky pass on all the requests he received and his responses to his MI6 minders, but he also asked them for advice on what both Thatcher and Howe might want to discuss. To his amazement, he was shown a copy of Howe's briefing notes for his meeting with Gorbachev, which enabled Gordievsky to write a clear and specific note of advice. He pretended he had got this from his general contacts and from reading the British press.[29] The KGB Centre was impressed. But in reality it was a sign of how skilfully British intelligence were using their agent. They knew precisely what he was giving them and receiving in return. The Soviets got useful information but had no sense of where it had originally come from. And, of course, they had no idea that Gordievsky was simultaneously briefing the British about Gorbachev's requests.

Gorbachev arrived in Britain in mid-December 1984. With his distinctive facial birthmark and a pleasing, open smile, he made an instant impression on everyone he met, and on the British media. Unlike previous senior Soviet visitors he was fifty-three years old and looked youthful, vigorous and energetic. Those whom he met were delighted with his openness and willingness to discuss any issue. Unlike Gromyko, he did not try to avoid controversial subjects like human rights. And it was rare for wives to accompany Soviet leaders on such visits but Gorbachev brought his, and Raisa was equally impressive. She had studied philosophy and taught it at university level. She had a particular interest in British political thought and literature. She was bright, intelligent and forthcoming. She also dressed smartly and looked like a decidedly modern Western woman.

On the day after his arrival in London, Sunday 16 December, Gorbachev and his wife went to Chequers for lunch. What followed helped to change the course of history. Thatcher was accompanied by Howe, Heseltine and other senior ministers; Gorbachev was with Raisa, the Soviet ambassador and a small group of close advisers. The Prime Minister was particularly taken by the outfit Raisa was wearing, a well-tailored grey suit with a white stripe – 'just the sort I could have worn myself', Thatcher decided. While the main meeting was taking place, Raisa spent some time in the Chequers library and must have been a very unusual companion for the Prime Minister's spouse, Denis, with whom she tried to discuss some of the great British political theorists of the seventeenth century.

Over lunch, Thatcher and Gorbachev outlined the conventional positions of their governments. Thatcher argued that by injecting private enterprise into the Soviet system it would become more efficient and less centralised. Gorbachev explained indignantly that the system was not always centrally controlled and made a vigorous defence of how much fairer the socialist system was to its people. The Prime Minister concluded, 'Our systems are very different from each other. We each believe in our own, in our own alliances – and I'm not going to try to break yours up. So you leave ours alone as well. But we do have to find ways of living together on the same planet.' Gorbachev agreed heartily and joked that he had not come with instructions from the Politburo to convert Thatcher to communism.[30]

After lunch a smaller group convened in the sitting room over coffee. Thatcher relished the debate that followed as a free-ranging, combative but friendly argument between two confident leaders promoting their different systems. She was also extremely impressed with how well informed Gorbachev was about the West. At one point he quoted Lord Palmerston, saying, 'Britain has no permanent friends and no permanent enemies – only permanent interests.' He went on, 'It is up to us to identify the interests we have in common.' When they discussed arms control, Gorbachev said that unless measures were taken to reduce the numbers of nuclear weapons the danger of a misunderstanding or nuclear accident remained alarmingly possible. This was particularly relevant in the light of events the previous year. Gorbachev then quoted a Russian proverb, 'Once a year even an unloaded gun can go off' and made clear his distrust of President Reagan and his Star Wars initiative. The Prime Minister argued that Reagan could and should be trusted, but she sensed that Gorbachev wanted to prevent the Star Wars programme from progressing at almost any price and was trying to exploit divisions between Britain and America. Thatcher made it abundantly clear that Britain and America were the closest of allies and there was no question of dividing the two nations. She was equally frank in asserting that she did not believe in the President's dream of a nuclear-free world.[31]

As the afternoon wore on and the meeting overran by ninety minutes, Thatcher began to realise that she was talking to an entirely new type of Soviet official. Although Gorbachev frequently adopted the standard Marxist line, she quickly appreciated that the way he spoke, usually without notes and often with passion and sincerity, 'could not have been more different from the wooden ventriloquism of the average Soviet apparatchik'. She concluded, 'His line was no different from what I would have expected. His style was ... I found myself liking him.' Gorbachev had not come to negotiate but simply to present himself and the Soviet cause to the British leader.

At 6 p.m., he and Raisa and their entourage swept away from Chequers in a fleet of fast cars. The next day, the BBC's political editor John Cole asked Mrs Thatcher what she thought of the Soviet politician. 'I like Mr Gorbachev,' she replied simply. 'We can do business together.'[32]

In a meeting with Reagan a week later at Camp David, she passed on her views about Gorbachev to the President in person.

Mikhail Gorbachev with Margaret Thatcher after their meeting at Chequers, 16 December 1984. They got on well and Thatcher famously declared 'We can do business together'.

*

The Soviet leader, Konstantin Chernenko, had spent much of 1984 in and out of the Kuntsevo Clinic where Andropov had only recently been confined. As with his predecessor, Chernenko never seems to have considered standing down. His staff carried on issuing letters and instructions in his name even though a facsimile of his signature was now affixed to them. Again, the Soviet people were not told the truth about their leader, although many must have suspected it. In early 1985 his health declined even further and he developed chronic hepatitis and cirrhosis of the liver. On 10 March he went into a coma and died that afternoon of a combination of his emphysema and heart failure. It was a sad end to what had become a sad life.

Later that evening the members of the Politburo met. The two leading candidates for the succession were Gorbachev and Viktor Grishin. The latter's appointment would mark the continuation of power in the hands of the old men of the Kremlin. Before the meeting, in the room where members often met in advance, Andrei Gromyko offered Gorbachev a deal. He would give him his support if Gorbachev agreed to let him stand down as Foreign Minister and appointed him to the honorary position of head of the Supreme Soviet, effectively head of state. Gorbachev agreed. In the meeting that followed Gromyko made it clear he was backing the youngest member among them. At the critical moment when it came to nominating the person who would chair the funeral commission, always the candidate who would become the next General Secretary, there was a pause. The members fell into an embarrassed silence. After a few moments, Grishin spoke up. 'Why the hesitation about the chairman? Everything is clear. Let's appoint Mikhail Sergeyevich.' He must have realised that Gromyko siding with Gorbachev was decisive. Gorbachev, however, suggested postponing the decision until the following day.

After a hectic round of talks with other Politburo members, Gorbachev finally got home at 4 a.m. Raisa was still up waiting for him. They went out for a walk in their garden to discuss the situation. They never spoke about serious matters inside their home – 'one never knew', as he later wrote. Gorbachev later remembered precisely what he had said to his wife at the end of their long conversation. 'You see, I have come here [to Moscow] with hope and the belief that I shall be able to accomplish something, but so far there was not much I could have done. Therefore if I want to change something I would have to accept the nomination – if it is made, of course. *We can't go on living like this* [italics in Gorbachev's original].'[33]

As they finished talking the sun was coming up. A new dawn was rising. That afternoon at the Politburo meeting, Gromyko formally proposed Gorbachev as General Secretary. One by one every member of the Politburo spoke up in support of the proposal. The leadership was, as usual on such occasions, unanimous. It was nothing less than a revolution in the leadership of the Soviet Union. The old guard had finally handed power to a new generation. The next phase of the Cold War was about to play out.

18

Spy Wars

A month after Gorbachev's succession to the top job in Moscow, a middle-aged American with a thick moustache and large glasses entered the Soviet embassy in Washington. He went straight to the reception desk and handed an envelope to the duty officer. It was addressed for the personal attention of Stanislav Androsov, the KGB resident or head of station in Washington. After delivering the letter the American turned and left. His name was Aldrich Ames and he was a middle-ranking CIA officer who worked on the Soviet operations and counter-intelligence desk. One of his tasks was to track down KGB spies working in the United States, but he also had extensive knowledge of CIA operations in the Soviet Union. When Androsov opened the envelope that had been left for him he must have been stunned. Ames was offering to supply information to the KGB. As an indication of the intelligence he could pass on, he listed the names of a small number of Soviet citizens who had approached the CIA and offered their services. He also gave a clear indication that he knew remarkable details of CIA operations in eastern Europe and the Soviet Union. The intelligence he could supply would be like gold to the KGB. A CIA spy hunter was offering to turn into a double agent.

What distinguished Ames from most other double agents of the Cold War era was that he was not acting out of any ideological commitment. Most individuals who gave intelligence to the other side, from Kim Philby onwards, did so out of disillusionment with their country's political system or out of political conviction and support for the competing bloc. With Ames it was much more simple. He had just divorced his wife and thought that the alimony he had to pay would bankrupt him. Moreover, he had taken up with a Colombian woman named Rosario whom he had met in Mexico and she had expensive tastes and enjoyed lavish shopping sprees. Ames wanted to keep his new partner sweet, and in order to fund her lavish lifestyle he decided to earn some extra income by trading intelligence with the Soviets. In his letter to Androsov he asked for a payment of $50,000. He later admitted that the reasons for his treachery were 'personal, banal, and amounted really to greed and folly. It was as simple as that.'[1]

On 15 May 1985, Ames returned to the Soviet embassy in Washington. He was taken into a small sound-proofed room and told that the KGB had agreed to pay for information from him. A few days later a KGB officer passed to him $50,000 in crisp, new $100 bills. It was the beginning of what would become one of the greatest betrayals of US intelligence in the late twentieth century, extending even beyond the end of the Cold War. For a period of nine years, Ames supplied the Soviets and then the Russian Federation with a mass of details about CIA operations in eastern Europe and Russia. He named names and supplied technical details of US defence and security policies. He betrayed the identities of at least twenty-five agents spying for the US, mostly double agents within the KGB and the GRU who were supplying intelligence to Western agencies. As a consequence at least ten of them were arrested and executed. Another committed suicide. His treason has been described as the CIA's 'greatest counter-intelligence failure, and perhaps its greatest operational failure, during the last half of the Cold War'. It was claimed that he 'devastated CIA's human intelligence and counterintelligence effort against the Soviet Union'.[2] For eight years the CIA tried to find the source of the leaks but was reluctant to admit that they could be coming from a mole within their own ranks. They believed instead that the Soviets had broken some of their codes. Although Ames was living a lifestyle way beyond that of a middle-ranking CIA officer, with a grand house in Arlington, Virginia and a smart Jaguar car, he let it be known that Rosario, his Colombian girlfriend whom he married in late 1985, had inherited wealth and he was enjoying the benefits of this. When Ames was finally tracked down and arrested in 1994, he had been paid $2.7 million and had nearly $2 million more due to him.

The day after Ames received his first payment in Washington in May 1985, Oleg Gordievsky was in his office in the Soviet embassy in London when a cipher clerk came in and handed him a message. He was to return to Moscow immediately for an urgent meeting with Viktor Chebrikov, the chairman of the KGB, and Vladimir Kryuchkov, head of the First Chief Directorate. The news hit Gordievsky like a 'thunderbolt' and he felt sweat break out on his back. Had he been found out? He was now the KGB resident in London and had been in Moscow only a few months before, being briefed for his promotion. Why was he being called back to Moscow so soon? How could his bosses possibly have come to suspect him? He requested an urgent meeting with his MI6 minders. They were reassuring. He expected them to suggest that he immediately go into hiding and defect. Instead they were interested in what he could find out about the KGB master plan for Britain. Two days later, Gordievsky boarded a plane for Moscow.[3]

From the moment of his arrival, Gordievsky knew that the situation was bad. At the airport he was held up at passport control while the officer studied his documents for an inordinate amount of time and made a telephone call (he later found out that all passport officers had been told to report his arrival to the KGB). When he got to his flat he immediately knew that someone had been in as a third latch on the front door for which he had long lost the key was locked. Nothing was missing so he assumed the KGB had searched the property and probably bugged it. When he went to the KGB offices, his colleagues, who had always been very friendly, seemed distant, off-hand, and sometimes rude. He was kept waiting around for several days, all the while growing increasingly concerned about what was happening. The MI6 officials in London had given him some pep pills, and he started taking these regularly to calm his nerves.

After a few days, Viktor Grushko, an old colleague who was now deputy head of the First Chief Directorate, called for him one morning and drove him a few miles to a bungalow that was usually kept for KGB visitors to Moscow. When they were inside, two men in dark suits joined them, one in his late fifties and the other about ten years younger. Both were formal and unsmiling. They were General Golubev and Colonel Budanov of Directorate K (Counter Intelligence) but neither man was introduced to Gordievsky. There were two servants waiting on them who produced sandwiches for lunch, then a half-full bottle of the best Armenian brandy, known as a real delicacy. Everyone had a glass, but when it came to Gordievsky's turn the bottle had run out so the waiter went and got another one and poured his glass from this. As soon as he drank the glass of brandy Gordievsky felt 'a different man'. He did not pass out but felt a sensation of being someone else and found himself suddenly talking quickly. One part of his brain was telling him he must not lose control, while another part told him the effort might be impossible.[4]

The next thing he knew for sure was when he woke up in bed in one of the guest rooms the following morning. He had been drugged and while in a stupor had been interrogated. He felt dreadful and had a fierce headache. And of course he had no idea what he had said or if he had confessed to being a double agent. He felt 'more depressed than ever before' and kept thinking, '*They know*. I'm finished.' He later wrote, 'How they had found out I could not tell. But there was not the slightest doubt that they knew I was a British agent.' He was terrified.

The following day he went into the office and was called in by Grushko, who told him, 'We know very well you've been deceiving us for years. If only you knew what an unusual source we heard about you from!' However, he was told that Kryuchkov had decided he could remain in the KGB but not return to London. His family would be flown back to Moscow in a few days. He was told that he should take the holiday that was due to him and after this he would be allocated to a non-operational position. He found this encounter surreal. Many individuals had been drummed out of the KGB for all sorts of petty offences, like fiddling expenses or over scandals with women. Why would they allow a man who was thought to be an agent for a foreign power to remain within the service? Gordievsky concluded that perhaps they were not certain about him, or perhaps he had not confessed to being a British agent in his drugged state. Perhaps they wanted to monitor him and see if he would try to make contact with MI6. On the morning of his interrogation he had taken one of the pep pills given to him before he left London. It was possible that the pep pill had kept him from losing all consciousness of what was happening.

Slowly, over the next few days, memories of his interrogation started to come back to him. He remembered determinedly answering the questions they put to him. Why did he have copies of banned political books from the West in his flat? Because it was part of his job to know of these works, he answered. This conversation confirmed to him that his flat had been searched. Why was he proud that his daughter could recite the Lord's Prayer in English? Because in England this was quite normal. This question confirmed that his flat had been bugged as he had only confided this to his mother and sister around the kitchen table when they visited him. He remembered being told, 'You'd better confess. *Prinznaysya!* Confess!' But all he could remember was denying that he had anything to confess.

In fact, Gordievsky had not confessed to being a British agent. Had he done so he would almost certainly have been shot as a traitor. In Washington, Ames had handed over to the KGB a batch of documents that included direct references to Gordievsky. For a further payment, Ames had informed the KGB that Gordievsky and another senior Russian were handing over information to the West. But like all intelligence agencies, the KGB was reluctant to believe suggestions against one of its own. Kryuchkov and the KGB were suspicious of Gordievsky but did not yet have proof of his betrayal.

Gordievsky met his family when they arrived from London and told his wife that they would not be returning to Britain. He lied that this was because of various intrigues against him within the KGB. She was shattered. Gordievsky was sent to a luxurious KGB sanatorium on a wooded hill by a river 100 miles south of Moscow for his 'holiday'. There he quickly realised that he was being watched the whole time by other inmates. He decided that he had to get out of the Soviet Union. He felt he was under a suspended sentence of death. When his family visited him he said a tearful farewell to his wife and two daughters. Then, after his spell in the sanatorium, he returned to Moscow.

One of the other individuals Ames had supplied information about was Adolf Tolkachev. He was an engineer and a specialist in airborne radar working in one of the top Moscow aviation institutes. From 1979 he had passed on to the CIA an extraordinary mass of material about the Soviet aviation research and development programme including details of the design of Soviet fighter jets and radar systems, and hundreds of copies of circuit boards and blueprints photographed in his laboratory on miniature cameras. In April 1984 Tolkachev handed over to his CIA case officer in Moscow rolls of film containing ninety-six images of top secret documents and thirty-nine pages of handwritten notes. In October he handed over two miniature cameras containing photos of ninety pages of secret documents and twenty-two pages of handwritten notes. He often photographed the documents in the toilet of his research institute. He was one of the CIA's greatest assets in the first half of the 1980s and it is calculated that the details he supplied, particularly of Soviet aircraft, enabled the US government to save billions of dollars on their own research and development but still produce fighters that it was known could outperform their Soviet counterparts. Consequently, he became known as the 'Billion Dollar Spy'.

The regular handover of documents was made from Tolkachev's flat in a smart apartment block in Moscow where many of the aviation elite lived. On 13 June 1985, his CIA handler set out to make a routine exchange. He carried with him two plastic bags. One contained 125,000 roubles in bank notes (equivalent to $150,000) and five new miniature cameras each hidden within a key fob; the other bag contained books in which there were coded messages for Tolkachev with instructions and requests for particular intelligence the CIA wanted him to copy. There was a simple system in place by which if Tolkachev left open a small ventilation window above the main window in his flat then it was a sign that all was clear for the handover. The experienced CIA handler, Paul Stombaugh Jr, walked around the block and could not see any surveillance and noted that the small ventilation window was open. When he went to enter the apartment block he was jumped by about a dozen KGB personnel in military camouflage outfits. After Ames had named Tolkachev, the KGB had put his flat under surveillance and filmed or photographed his comings and goings. By the time of the handover, Tolkachev had already been arrested and taken away. Stombaugh was taken to the Lubyanka, the historic KGB headquarters and prison. There, everything in the two bags he was carrying was opened and examined. In one of the books was a request to photograph the documents in a place where there was more light as some of the secret photographs had been too underexposed to be legible. The money, the cameras hidden in fobs and the secret instructions proved two things to the KGB. Firstly, they had without doubt caught a traitor. Secondly, they now realised they could trust the evidence Ames was selling to them.[5]

On the evening of the disastrous failed handover in Moscow, in a restaurant in the smart suburb of Washington DC known as Georgetown, Ames handed to his KGB minder a bag containing probably 'the largest batch of sensitive documents and critical information ever turned over to the KGB in a single meeting'.[6] It included information about at least ten Soviets who were passing top-level intelligence to the CIA, the FBI or other Western agencies, among them Gordievsky and Tolkachev. The KGB now had proof of their activities. Tolkachev was kept in prison and interrogated for a little over a year. The KGB wanted to know exactly how his betrayal had come about and every detail of how he had supplied the Americans with aviation intelligence. He was finally executed for treason in September 1986.

In October 1985, Robert Hanssen, an FBI agent of some twelve years' standing, an analyst on Soviet affairs based in

New York, also made contact by letter with the KGB officer in Washington who was running Aldrich Ames, Viktor Cherkashin. Like Ames, Hanssen offered to sell information to the Russians, and this included naming names of KGB agents who were supplying intelligence to the US and other Western powers. As was the case with Ames, Hanssen's treachery carried on for many years and outlasted the Cold War. He loved the process of being a spy and continued the relatively simple task of depositing plastic bags packed with pages of information in pre-agreed 'dead drop' sites in various parks in Virginia for sixteen years. He did it all anonymously; the KGB were not even certain they knew his real name. Like Ames, he provided the names of dozens of agents to the KGB and its successor the SVR, and several arrests and executions followed. Like the CIA, the FBI found it difficult to accept that they had a double agent within their own ranks although for many years investigations were carried out to see if such a mole existed. At one point Hanssen himself was put in charge of an investigation into tracking down the mole, and unsurprisingly failed to identify himself.[7] The KGB now had two excellent sources in the two separate arms of the US security and intelligence establishment, the FBI and the CIA. It was an extraordinary coup for the Soviets that had come about in the most unusual way. Neither of them had been recruited by sharp-eyed, smooth-talking Soviet agents. Both men had simply contacted the KGB in Washington and offered to work with them for cash.

Valery Martynov was a lieutenant-colonel in the KGB who had worked at the Soviet embassy in Washington since 1980. He was allocated to Line X, the KGB operation to steal Western technology, including the computer systems to run the new oil pipeline that had been infected with malware. But from 1982 he too had become a double agent supplying information to the CIA. He had never handed over anything substantial but he was young and the CIA hoped he would grow into a more significant asset. He was another spy who had been named in the information handed over by Ames at the Georgetown restaurant, and also named by Hanssen. In November, Martynov was sent back to Moscow where KGB security officers were waiting for him. He was arrested on arrival, and there was even a KGB photographer on hand to record the moment. A year later he was executed in the traditional KGB way, with a single bullet to the back of his head. Other arrests and executions followed from the names supplied by Ames and Hanssen.

Gordievsky was unaware of any arrests or executions when he returned to Moscow from his 'holiday' in the KGB sanatorium. But he sensed that the KGB net was closing around him and had made up his own mind that he needed to get out as quickly as possible. He had agreed an escape plan with MI6 while still in London. The first stage of this was to sound the alarm that he was under severe suspicion. To do this he had to stand on a busy street corner in central Moscow at 7 p.m. under a particular lamp post. He was to be holding a plastic Safeway shopping bag and remain there for about six minutes on the edge of the pavement. Every evening at 7 p.m. from mid-May, when he returned to Moscow, an agent from the British embassy would pass by this spot and see if Gordievsky showed up. Gordievsky spent three hours getting to the rendezvous point, changing from bus to train, walking a few hundred metres, waiting in shops, and all the time trying to ensure he was not being followed. In Russian this technique was known as *proverka*; the Americans called it 'dry-cleaning'. But by the time he got to the central square, Gordievsky was extremely nervous. He felt very conspicuous standing on the pavement and was convinced that everyone passing by was looking at him. The agreement was that if the signal was picked up he would a few days later be met by a female British agent wearing grey and would pass her a message on the first floor of St Basil's cathedral in Red Square. When he arrived at St Basil's he was horrified to find that the first floor was closed for renovations. He waited around for twenty minutes but no woman wearing grey arrived. The first attempt to get out had clearly failed. Gordievsky was getting desperate.[8]

He spent an anxious and sleepless night, expecting that at any moment the secret police would break in, arrest him, and he would be taken off for a full interrogation. He decided that he had been too nervous at the rendezvous point and had not waited there long enough. The next day, Tuesday 16 July, he resolved to repeat the entire process. So once again he left his flat at 4 p.m. and went through the elaborate dry-cleaning procedure, getting on and off trains and buses, waiting in shops, visiting the apartment block where his sister lived and looking out from the window on the staircase. When he was certain that he was not being followed he went on to the main square and stood there on the edge of the pavement at exactly 7 p.m. with his Safeway bag. He was so anxious that he bought a packet of cigarettes to try to calm his nerves. It was a busy time, with official limousines regularly passing and commuters charging by on their way home. He waited and waited, growing more and more tense and feeling horribly conspicuous. The minutes went slowly by. No one seemed to fit the bill. Then, at last, Gordievsky spotted a very British-looking man carrying a dark green Harrods bag and eating a Mars bar – the arrangement was that the man from the embassy would be munching something. He passed by just a few yards from Gordievsky and they exchanged eye contact. Gordievsky stared at the man, 'shouting silently, "Yes! It's me! I need urgent help!"' He was sure that this time contact had been made. What he did not know was that the British agent, who had never met Gordievsky before, had recognised him from photos but had become suspicious because Gordievsky was smoking. He knew that he didn't smoke, and when he returned to the embassy there was a discussion about whether this was a signal that all was not well, or if it was some sort of trick. Nevertheless, the look in Gordievsky's eyes must have convinced the agent that the appeal was genuine, and urgent. It was decided to request permission to carry out the exfiltration plan and go to the next stage. This involved Gordievsky getting to an agreed rendezvous point near the Finnish border where British agents would attempt to smuggle him by car into Finland.

This now became a major operation for MI6, and although there was a detailed plan in place the risks were high, not only for Gordievsky, for whom capture would mean certain execution, but also for those trying to get him across the border. If caught, all they could do would be to claim that the body had been planted in their vehicle and that they knew nothing. But would they be believed? The team running Gordievsky within MI6 felt they needed authorisation to carry out such a risky operation. A few days after Gordievsky had given the signal at the crossroads in central Moscow, the Foreign Secretary, Sir Geoffrey Howe, was at his official country residence at Chevening in Kent. At the end of the day's work, two officials sought an urgent meeting. One was his security adviser from the Foreign Office, the other from MI6. They outlined the situation and confirmed the importance of Gordievsky to British intelligence. They explained how for some unknown reason the KGB had become suspicious of him, and requested formal permission to carry out the exfiltration plan. Howe listened carefully as the risks were laid out. Then he gave his approval for the operation to go ahead.[9]

Gordievsky, still in a state of extreme anxiety and paranoia, knew nothing of these discussions with the Foreign Secretary. All he knew was that under the original plan drawn up for his extraction he had to buy a train ticket to Leningrad in order to get to the agreed meeting place with the British agents. This also involved a complex game of losing those who were supposed to follow him. En route to the train station in Moscow he spotted a fat man following him and two young agents in a Lada car. But he managed to lose them all and buy his train ticket for the following Friday evening. He made several telephone calls to friends and arranged meetings for the next week, all of which he hoped would deceive the KGB listening in.

That Friday afternoon, 19 July, Gordievsky left his apartment block dressed simply in a track suit and carrying a carrier bag containing a few possessions. He had to pass the concierge who would have reported any suspicious activity. If she noticed him she probably thought he was going for one of his regular jogs around the city. He ran through some trees to a shopping precinct where he bought a cheap plastic hold-all in which to transfer his things. Dry-cleaning his way across Moscow, he eventually reached the railway station in good time for the 5.30 p.m. train to Leningrad. By now he was suspicious of everything, and when he found the station full of anti-riot police he was convinced they were looking for him until he realised they were there to police a major international youth festival that was taking place in Moscow that weekend. He realised that this could prove to be good news for him as the Finnish border would be busier than usual and the guards hopefully distracted by all the young Scandinavians heading for Moscow.

He arrived in Leningrad early in the morning of Saturday 20 July, looking unshaven and dishevelled. He had fallen from his bunk in the night and cut his forehead. Believing he would attract attention in his wretched state he hired a taxi to the Finland station and bought a ticket for Zelenogorsk, 90 kilometres (55 miles) north of Leningrad, towards the border. From there he took a local train to Terioki and a bus to Viborg.

He tried to make himself as anonymous as possible but people kept stopping him to engage in conversation. At one point on the bus a young and rather drunk couple asked him 'Where are you from?' in slurry voices, and 'Where are you going?' Gordievsky made up some fictitious answer and moved further down the bus.

At Viborg he found a café but did not stay long because he was certain that a group of KGB officers were there, probably looking out for defectors along the border. He left, and was relieved when they did not follow him. He got a lift to the remote spot that he recognised from photos as the place in the forest by a large rock where the rendezvous was to take place. He went and hid in the marshy undergrowth. It was summer, and in this environment there were mosquitoes everywhere. Gordievsky felt he was being eaten alive. At last he heard a vehicle approaching and jumped up, only to find it was a bus carrying wives to a nearby military base. He leaped back into the undergrowth – and the mosquitoes.

The rendezvous had been timed for 2.30 p.m., but nothing happened. Again the time passed horribly slowly. About twenty minutes later two cars drew up right next to the rock. Two men got out, and Gordievsky recognised one of them as the man with the Harrods bag from the Tuesday contact. He clambered out of the undergrowth and introduced himself. By now his nerves were in a dreadful state. They bundled him into the boot of the second car, which he was surprised to find was being driven by two British women. There was a flask of cold water, a sedative and an aluminium space-blanket to pull over himself in case the border guards used an infra-red heat detector on the car. The women put on a cassette of loud Western pop music and drove off towards the border.

Gordievsky found it horribly claustrophobic curled up in the boot of the car and he became hotter and hotter. At last, as the car came to a halt, he realised they had reached the border.

But at this crossing point there were five frontier barriers to pass through. The drivers kept the music playing to distract the guards as they slowly went through each checkpoint. It took more than half an hour. Gordievsky was sweating profusely and in his state of nervousness was finding it difficult to breathe. At the fifth checkpoint the car stopped and the music was turned off. He picked up the sound of Russian voices. He heard the border guards talking about the number of young Finns who were trying to cross the border to visit the international youth festival in Moscow. They complained about how many of them were drunk as they headed south. Then he heard dogs, obviously trained to search out anything mysterious, yapping around the car. He knew this could be fatal. What he did not know was that one of the women was feeding the Alsatians with potato crisps to divert their attention from the car. Eventually he felt the passengers get back into the car, the engine was turned on, the music started up again, and they moved forward. Was this it? Or were there further checkpoints and more hurdles to cross?

As they drove forward, the pop music stopped again. There was a pause. Gordievsky feared another border control. Then Sibelius's *Finlandia* started playing. He knew they had made it. They had crossed the border and were in Finland. They drove on for several miles, away from the border, then the car stopped. Gordievsky was at the end of his tether when the boot was opened but he looked up to see pine trees and blue skies. Looking in and smiling was none other than the face of his case officer, Joan, whom he had known in London. She had come to Finland to greet him. Gordievsky knew at once that his troubles were over, that the intense pressure of the last few weeks was behind him. His relief was immense.

In a meticulously planned but extremely daring operation, the British Secret Intelligence Service had successfully exfiltrated a double agent out of the Soviet Union. It was the only time during the entire Cold War that a KGB officer spying for the West was smuggled out. For decades, all the others who had been named by Kim Philby and other spies in the first half of the Cold War, or by Ames and Hanssen in the latter part, were arrested, and all senior KGB and GRU officers were shot. Gordievsky knew how fortunate he had been. He later admitted that he felt he was 'incredibly lucky'. He summed it up by saying, 'It's like having a second life.'[10] But there was a price to pay. Gordievsky had found freedom, but he had lost his family.

19

Pay-off

When Reagan was woken up in the middle of the night and told of the death of Chernenko, he turned to Nancy and supposedly said, 'How am I supposed to get anyplace with the Russians if they keep dying on me!'[1] But he had already heard from Margaret Thatcher in glowing terms about the man who was likely to succeed as General Secretary of the Communist Party of the Soviet Union. There are moments in history when unconnected events come together and seem to point in a single direction. Reagan's realignment in 1984 and early 1985 as a consequence of his fear of a nuclear war by misunderstanding after the Soviet war scare during Able Archer, the death of Chernenko, the appointment of Gorbachev – all these things created a new opportunity. But it would take time for that to become clear.

Some Western leaders recognised the epoch-making nature of Gorbachev's succession and were confident that his appointment would make for a break with the past. John Browne, a British MP who had met the Gorbachevs on their visit to London, even spoke of the charismatic Mikhail and Raisa as the new John and Jackie Kennedy on the world stage.[2] Reagan was more sceptical, and when it was suggested that he should go to Moscow to meet Gorbachev, he confided in his diary that even though he had been told Gorbachev was 'a different type than past Soviet leaders ... I'm too cynical to believe that'.[3] Despite this cynicism, he still sent an invitation to Gorbachev on his first day in office to talks in Washington. He wrote, 'history places on us a very heavy responsibility for maintaining and strengthening peace and I am convinced we have before us new opportunities to do so. I believe our differences can and must be resolved through discussion and negotiation.'[4]

Gorbachev took nearly two weeks to respond but wrote back positively about arranging a 'personal meeting between us ... to search for mutual understanding on the basis of equality'. But the letter included a serious rebuke about Reagan's aggressive public stance against the Soviet Union over previous years while continuing to make friendly overtures in private. He wrote that 'trust is an especially sensitive thing' that would not be enhanced 'if one were to talk as if in two languages: one, for private contacts, and the other, as they say, for the audience'. In a clear reference to the war scare of November 1983, Gorbachev asserted that it was their duty 'not to let things come to the outbreak of nuclear war which would inevitably have catastrophic consequences for both sides'. Gorbachev thanked the President for his invitation to Washington but left it open as to where such a meeting should take place.[5]

By the spring of 1985 a debate was raging in Washington over how to deal with the new Soviet leader. The Reagan administration was deeply divided in its attitude towards Gorbachev. Many were barely lukewarm. The CIA produced a paper for the President in June entitled 'Gorbachev, the New Broom'. This argued that he was the natural successor of Andropov and wanted to continue with the drive against corruption and alcoholism. He was presented as a leader overwhelmed with the challenges of domestic problems but that he was merely a reformer of the system, not a revolutionary

who would sweep it all away. In foreign affairs, the CIA predicted that Gorbachev would continue to support the war
in Afghanistan as well as its key Third World friends and
would seek to drive a wedge between the US and its allies.
William Casey wrote a cover note for the President that went
even further, noting that Gorbachev and his supporters 'are
not reformers and liberalizers either in Soviet domestic or
foreign policy'. He called for a revival of the agenda from
Reagan's first term of building up military strength, providing
leadership for the Western alliance, and increased ideological
opposition to the Soviet system.[6] The analysis showed how
woefully ill-informed the CIA were about new thinking and
changing attitudes in the Kremlin. According to the CIA,
Gorbachev would simply be more of the same with a little
more flair. They could not have been more wrong.

Officials in the State Department, on the other hand, were
far more enthusiastic about the opportunities offered by the
new Soviet leader. After his first meeting with him, George
Shultz told the press, 'Gorbachev is totally different from any
Soviet leader I've met.' He was genuinely impressed with
Gorbachev's quality of thought and with 'the intensity and the
intellectual energy of this new man on the scene'.[7] Shultz had
helped to persuade the Soviets to restart arms control talks in
Geneva. He saw this as a new beginning in relations with the
USSR. As the President began his second term, with a new
leader in the Kremlin, he was keen to seize the moment. If the
CIA took the glass-half-empty view of the Soviet leadership,
Shultz certainly took the glass-half-full approach.

Events once again intervened. Towards the end of March
1985 the shooting of an American army officer by a Soviet
sentry in a no-man's-land area of Berlin blew up into a major
incident. Major Arthur Nicholson was based at Potsdam but
had intruded into an area the Soviet military regarded as
closed. Without warning, it seems, a Soviet sentry opened fire

on him. The sentry would then not allow Nicholson's driver to come forward with medical help, and Nicholson died. As with the Korean airliner, the Soviets claimed the American major was on an espionage mission. The US claimed that Soviet forces in Berlin had prevented medical support from getting through to the wounded officer, who as a consequence bled to death. This, they argued, was another sign of the inhuman nature of the Soviet system. Defense Secretary Weinberger demanded the Soviets apologise. In Washington, hard-liners suggested the administration should break off all talks and diplomatic exchanges with the Soviets. But the momentum of international events was too important to be derailed, even by the shooting of an army major. Reagan overruled the objections of his hawkish Defense Secretary and planning for a summit resumed.[8]

Shultz went to Vienna for a high-level meeting with Gromyko in May. They talked together for six hours, going through a long agenda of issues. As he left, Shultz was told that Gromyko wanted a private word. In a corner of the grand room where they had spent the day in discussion, Gromyko whispered, 'What about the summit?'

'What about it?' Shultz replied.

'Gorbachev will not go to the United Nations [for the September opening of the General Assembly],' said Gromyko. 'November would be better. President Reagan would be welcome in Moscow.'

'It's your turn to come to Washington,' Shultz countered, as though arranging a dinner party between friends.

'Out of the question,' Gromyko exploded. 'It should be in Europe, in a third country.'

'I will communicate that to Washington,' said Shultz. 'Are you suggesting Geneva?'

'If you say Geneva, I'll have to say Helsinki,' growled Gromyko.[9]

With this remarkable off-the-record exchange, the initial steps were taken towards arranging the first summit between Reagan and Gorbachev.

At the beginning of July, formal agreement was reached that the two leaders would meet in Geneva in mid-November. The announcement in Moscow was combined with another piece of news: Gorbachev had honoured his deal with Gromyko, who was appointed to the ceremonial post of head of the Supreme Soviet after twenty-eight years as Foreign Minister. His replacement was the Georgian Eduard Shevardnadze. He had been the First Secretary of the Communist Party in Georgia but was almost completely unknown internationally. Like Gorbachev he was a reformer and had helped Georgia's economy grow while that of the rest of the Soviet Union stagnated. Like Gorbachev, too, he was in his fifties, and so would represent a new broom in Soviet foreign affairs. Shevardnadze and Gorbachev would form a close partnership and determine the shape of Soviet foreign policy for the next five years.

In Washington there was continuing uncertainty about the upcoming get-together of the leaders of the two superpowers. It would be the first such encounter since 1979, when Carter had met Brezhnev. But no one wanted to build up hopes that could not be met. And would the young, assertive, fast-thinking Soviet leader outmanoeuvre the elderly President? Gorbachev was impressing everyone with his mastery of detail; Reagan was known to be weak on detail. Bud McFarlane wanted to play the whole thing down and suggested calling it a 'meeting' rather than a 'summit'. Shultz wanted to take a more optimistic view of what could be achieved and told the President, 'I think we should take a much more positive and commanding attitude towards Geneva than is at present apparent to the public.' He knew that if Reagan was encouraged to be himself he would be 'self-confident and positive' and would be most likely to achieve his objectives.[10]

As the date of the summit in Geneva approached, it was clear that one of the core subjects that divided Reagan and Gorbachev was the President's Strategic Defence Initiative, his 'Star Wars' programme. Gorbachev was convinced that this merely took nuclear rivalry into space and would inevitably lead to the development of a new generation of space weapons to threaten the planet. He repeatedly stressed that if it went ahead Soviet scientists would simply counter anything America could come up with. Reagan, however, was constantly told that progress was being made by American scientists towards the goal of intercepting incoming missiles in space and was determined to hold on to his vision of a defensive shield for the United States. He knew that American scientists had an unbeatable lead over their Soviet equivalents and that this was an area where the US was definitely one up over their rivals. After a combative and confrontational pre-summit meeting with Gorbachev, Shultz reported that the Soviet leader was adamant that Reagan would have to cave in over SDI. Reagan responded, 'Well, this will be a case of an irresistible force meeting an immovable object.'[11]

Reagan's staff started to brief him. They studied every interview Gorbachev had given to Western journalists to try to predict the line he would take and attempted to fill the President with a mass of detail for every imagined response. Reagan grew tired of the briefings and wrote in his diary, 'I'm getting d—n sick of cramming like a school kid. Sometimes they tell me more than I need to know.'[12] Reagan preferred to talk with Presidents Nixon and Carter about their experience of negotiating with Soviet leaders. And he clearly grasped one vital idea: he appreciated that the Soviets wanted to be treated as equals and there was no way in which he and his team could talk down to them. In a pre-summit memorandum he wrote, 'Let there be no talk of winners and losers. Even if we think we won, to say so would set us back in view of their inherent inferiority complex.'[13] It was an astute comment, and it suggested that Reagan was beginning to grasp the mindset of the Soviet leaders.

Arms control was clearly going to be the core issue at the summit. But would it be possible to reach any agreement? Gorbachev suggested that he would consider a 50 per cent reduction in offensive strategic nuclear weapons but the terms were very favourable to the Soviet side. The reduction he proposed would include the US Pershing II and Cruise missiles because they could reach the Soviet Union, but not the SS-20 missiles because they could only reach western Europe and not the United States. It would include weapons on aircraft carriers and bombers, but the Soviets had only a few aircraft carriers and relatively few bombers. And, again, the reduction would only be approved if the US agreed to axe the Star Wars programme. This was going to be a non-starter for the Washington delegation.[14]

As the preparations neared their climax, a new sequence of bizarre events once again intervened. Vitaly Yurchenko was a general in the KGB, a specialist in counter-intelligence who ran a series of Soviet spies in the US and Canada. On 1 August he defected to the US while on a visit to Rome. Within days he was in Washington being debriefed by, among others, Aldrich Ames, who by now was supplying the KGB with masses of intelligence about CIA operations. Yurchenko revealed some extraordinary information to the CIA. Firstly, he told them that a CIA trainee was selling secrets to the KGB. And secondly, he disclosed that an employee of the National Security Agency had handed over details of the American operation to tap Soviet underwater cables in the Sea of Okhotsk – an operation that had consequently been discovered and compromised by the Soviets. Ames noted all these revelations and passed on details of them all to the KGB. The CIA were delighted with their coup. Director William Casey met Yurchenko and had dinner with him. He encouraged a leak to the press about the general's defection, despite an agreement to keep it secret. He clearly wanted to crow.

On 2 November, Yurchenko persuaded his CIA minder to take him for dinner to a restaurant in Georgetown. When they arrived, Yurchenko asked to go to the men's room. He slipped out of a rear window and managed to reach the Soviet embassy before the search party found him. There he announced he had in fact been kidnapped in Rome by the CIA and drugged in order to reveal information about KGB operations – a common KGB technique to extract confessions, as Oleg Gordievsky had discovered. He then flew back to Moscow.

The incident raised a series of questions that have never been fully answered. Was Yurchenko's defection some kind of elaborate deception planned by the KGB? Or, as is probably more likely, was it simply that he had grown tired and irritated with his treatment by the CIA? There were rumours that he had wanted to marry a Soviet woman living in Canada but she had turned him down. Perhaps at this point he had decided to return to Mother Russia and invented a story to cover up his defection. Either way, neither side came out of the incident well. The KGB lost, albeit temporarily, a senior figure. The CIA showed it could not keep hold of a major catch.

But, embarrassing though they were, not even spy scandals could throw the summit off course. In mid-November, US officials began two very different sets of preparations in Geneva. A White House team arrived to check out the location and prepare for the massive media presence in the city. More than 3000 journalists and television crews were expected to cover the summit, the biggest news story of the year.[15] The two leaders would meet at the Maison Fleur d'Eau, a luxury château on the banks of Lake Geneva. The

press were positioned where it was thought they would present Reagan in the most favourable light. They even planned
to put lights along the side of the lake to create a perfect
backdrop for the top news anchors who would be in Geneva
to present the nightly television news. A short distance from
the main villa there was a comfortable and scenic boathouse.
It was decided to light the log fire here so that at any point
Reagan could invite Gorbachev for a private chat. Working
for a very different purpose, a CIA team arrived in Geneva
and tried to organise a series of loud demonstrations against
Gorbachev's visit to make him feel uncomfortable in the city.
An exhibition was mounted revealing the Soviet Union's
secret role in undermining the regime in Cambodia. The
CIA knew that the thousands of newsmen and women from
around the world covering the summit would have plenty
of time on their hands and this was a perfect opportunity to
promote Soviet perfidy in the Third World. Nothing was to
be left to chance.[16]

In Moscow, Gorbachev was also preparing intensively for
the meeting. He and his closest aides studied all of Reagan
and Shultz's recent speeches. They went back over the lengthy
correspondence between the two leaders. The Politburo, the
Ministry of Foreign Affairs, the Defence Ministry and the KGB
were all consulted on substantive issues such as arms control
and nuclear disarmament. Gorbachev felt it was 'important
that the leaders of the superpowers should have a chance to
get a close look at each other'.[17] Wanting to understand the
character of the man he was about to meet, Gorbachev even
went back into Reagan's Hollywood days and viewed one of
his classic films, *Kings Row* from 1942. When this came out in
conversation, Reagan was particularly delighted.[18]

Reagan, Shultz and the large US delegation flew into
Geneva on 17 November. In a national television address
before departing, Reagan had stated that this was a special

moment in history with the opportunity 'to set a steady, more constructive course to the twenty-first century'. He spoke of his 'mission for peace' in Geneva and 'that the arms race must be stopped'. But he acknowledged the 'deep differences between us'.[19] He did not want to raise impossible hopes for what could be achieved. When he arrived in Geneva he had a day to acclimatise. He and Nancy were staying in a luxury villa loaned by the Aga Khan with a spectacular view over the lake, and the President and his wife toured the nearby château where he would meet the Soviet leader. Reagan felt in a confident mood and later wrote 'The juices were flowing', but he was undoubtedly anxious. This was his long-awaited opportunity to meet a Soviet leader one-on-one. For years he had been certain that many of the problems between the United States and the Soviet Union could be solved if only he could sit down and talk with the Soviet leader. He later admitted that he and Nancy did not sleep well that night.[20]

In the publicity war, Reagan won the first round. It was a bitterly cold morning on 19 November as Gorbachev's limousine drew up outside the entrance to the Maison Fleur d'Eau, but Reagan bounded out hatless and without his coat to greet the Soviet leader, who emerged from his car wrapped in a heavy scarf and overcoat. The cameras of the world's press recorded that despite his twenty years over the Soviet leader, the President looked more vigorous and youthful. It was a visual triumph. In shaking Gorbachev's hands, Reagan immediately felt 'there was something likeable' about him. 'There was warmth in his face and style, not the coldness bordering on hatred I'd seen in most senior Soviet officials I'd met until then.'[21]

Reagan wanted to begin with a private talk with Gorbachev, so after some photographs he took him into a side room. They planned to spend twenty minutes together there in a quick 'get to know you' session with no one else present but their interpreters. Reagan began by saying that they had both come from humble beginnings but now were the only two men in the world who 'could start World War Three or bring peace to the world'. Both men laid out their ideological positions. In another unmistakable reference to the November 1983 war scare, Gorbachev said there had been great 'fear of mutual destruction', that they both must now focus on 'the central issue at the present time, that is, the question of war and peace' and that this was 'the question that was on the minds of everyone' in the Soviet Union.[22] After about forty minutes an aide suggested to Shultz, who was waiting outside, that he should interrupt them to give the President an opportunity to break up the meeting. 'If you're dumb enough to do that you shouldn't be in your job,' said Shultz. The two world leaders talked for another half an hour, and when they emerged, after overrunning by nearly an hour, both men were smiling. Shultz could see that Reagan and Gorbachev had 'hit it off well'.[23] They had broken the ice.

Then, with their experts and advisers around them, the two leaders began the first plenary session. Now the plain talking began. Gorbachev opened with an attack on the power of the military-industrial complex over US politics that stirred up hostility to Soviet Russia, he claimed, in order simply to sell more weapons. Reagan attacked the Soviet Union for its position on human rights and related a long history of Soviet aggression from 1917 onwards, especially in regional affairs over recent years. He said the US people and its government did not want war with anyone. Gorbachev replied that the Soviet Union did not attempt to export revolution to the Third World but he pointed out that the United States tried to control regions of the world where they had strong vested interests. This first session was more confrontational on both sides than the private meeting.

When they broke for lunch, Gorbachev returned to his

residence and reported back to his delegation that Reagan appeared to him as 'not simply a conservative, but [as] a political "dinosaur"'.[24]

When the talks started again in the afternoon, they moved on to discuss arms control. Reagan vigorously defended his support for SDI and offered to share the new technology in what he called an 'open labs' policy. Gorbachev simply did not believe that the US would share such sensitive technology and suspected a trick. He told Reagan 'the Soviet Union strongly opposes an arms race in space' but added that if forced to, they would instruct their scientists to work on developing a shield in space that would be 'as effective and far more efficient than your project'. After a while an angry Gorbachev concluded, 'It looks like a dead end,' and an uneasy silence fell on the room.

Reagan suggested that the two leaders take a short walk and leave the other delegates to carry on with the detailed negotiations. He took him down to the boathouse on the lake, and there the two men, accompanied only by their interpreters, sat beside the roaring log fire that had been prepared. They discussed the idea of a 50 per cent reduction in nuclear weapons. Gorbachev said he was prepared to negotiate on the terms of such a reduction. They continued to disagree on SDI but, despite everything, the cosy atmosphere helped create a warmth between them. Neither leader wavered from his prepared position, and Reagan pointed out that on the escalation of nuclear weapons 'I have to tell you that if it's an arms race you must know it's an arms race you can't win', because the US would simply outspend the Soviet Union.[25] Gorbachev made it clear that his principal fear of space weapons was that it would provide the US with a defensive shield and so encourage them to make a first-strike assault against the Soviet Union, safe in the knowledge that they could survive any retaliation.

*Reagan and Gorbachev chat by the log fire at the boathouse in
Geneva. They struck up a rapport but still disagreed
over many issues of principle.*

Although no specific progress was made, the men continued to get along well and began to learn about each other's
strongly held positions: Reagan's sincere belief that a strategic
defence could help to prevent nuclear war, and Gorbachev's
intense hostility to the idea of weapons in space fearing that it
gave the US a first-strike capability.[26] Gorbachev later ascribed
the fact that although they disagreed bitterly they seemed to
get along well to the 'human factor' that had come into play,
and that both men realised they must 'maintain contact and
try to avoid a break'.[27]

By the time they rejoined the main group Reagan had
invited Gorbachev to Washington and Gorbachev had invited
Reagan to Moscow. That evening over dinner, hosted by the
Gorbachevs at the Soviet Mission, they did not discuss political issues but personal and social matters in a relaxed, friendly

way. They talked about the Soviet film industry and Russian history. Gorbachev told Nancy about his six-year-old grand-daughter who watched all the television news programmes and knew the names of every world leader. Nancy and Raisa had also met that day, and although they did not get along as well as their husbands, they too had invited each other to their respective capitals. There were jokes that if President Reagan would not go to Moscow then Nancy could go without him.[28]

The following day saw two more plenary sessions of the full negotiating teams and another two private meetings between the two leaders. Again the main sticking point preventing an agreement on arms control was Reagan's insistence on continuing with Star Wars research, and Gorbachev's bitter opposition to this. In their private meeting, Reagan again attacked Gorbachev over the Soviet Union's record on human rights. The Soviet leader refused to be lectured by the President on this subject, responding that many black people in the US lacked equal rights with whites. Over dinner that evening, the two delegations were deputed to draft a joint communiqué but could not agree. When they returned after dinner both leaders took charge and, realising that if they could not agree a communiqué it would look as though they had failed, they agreed a form of words in less than fifteen minutes.[29]

The following morning, before the world's media, Reagan and Gorbachev shook hands and signed the joint communiqué. Their body language showed the world that the two men had got on well. They had spent more than five hours together in private conversation. Some of the discussions had been heated and at times emotional. But they were talking. There was not a great deal of substance in the communiqué but both sides had pledged that arms control talks would continue towards the objective of reducing nuclear arsenals by one half. New exchanges would be started between the US and the Soviet Union. Moreover, the communiqué contained the phrase 'a nuclear war cannot be won and must never be fought'. And they had agreed that 'the parties will not seek military superiority'. This was a different Reagan to the strident President who had called for dramatic increases in military spending four years before. Both sides also agreed that the dreadful threat of nuclear confrontation that had run throughout 1983 and had come to a head that November must never be allowed to happen again. The crisis that had caused the Soviet Union to put its nuclear arsenal on to full alert and which Reagan had found 'really scary' had helped to bring the leaders of the superpowers together. They had begun a dialogue. They had got to know and understand each other a little. A miscalculation or accident was less likely now.

20

Endgames

On the afternoon following the signing of the Geneva joint communiqué, Ronald Reagan reported on the summit to the NATO General Council in Brussels and was received with strong applause. Then he flew back to the US and addressed a joint session of Congress in the House of Representatives. 'I can't claim that we had a meeting of the minds on such fundamentals as ideology or national purpose,' he said, 'but we understand each other better, and that's a key to peace ... we have a long way to go but we're heading in the right direction.' He was met with enthusiastic cheering and stomping in the chamber, almost like a conquering hero. He wrote in his diary, 'I haven't gotten such a reception since I was shot.'[1] The whole world was relieved that after the desperate tensions of 1983 the leaders of the two superpowers were at last talking to each other, and were talking about peace, not threatening nuclear war.

In Washington there was a feeling that the US had come out of the summit well. They had got their point of view across clearly and had made no concessions over the Star Wars programme. They could rest on their laurels. Reagan wrote to a friend, 'I'm not going to let myself get euphoric but still I have a feeling we might be at a point of beginning. There did seem to be something of a chemistry between the General Secretary and myself.'[2] In Moscow, Gorbachev was more sceptical, and when he addressed the Communist Party Central Committee he spoke about Reagan's 'manoeuvring'. He told colleagues in private that the President was still full of stereotypes about the Soviet Union but that he could see Reagan was genuine in wanting peaceful relations. However, there was a feeling in Moscow that they had only just begun the process of agreeing arms control. There was a lot more to be done.

So in January 1986, Gorbachev and Shevardnadze launched their so-called 'peace offensive'.[3] The Soviets offered to remove *all* intermediate nuclear weapons from Europe. They suggested that the Pershing IIs, Cruise and SS-20s should all go, along with reductions in troop numbers. They proposed a moratorium on the testing of nuclear weapons. And most dramatically, they called for the elimination of all nuclear weapons by 2000. But the price was that the US must give up on Star Wars. This 'offensive' was eagerly supported at the Party Congress in Moscow the following month along with a whole series of other reforms that would characterise the next phase of Gorbachev's leadership.

In Washington, Reagan wrote of the proposals as 'a h—l of a propaganda move'.[4] Indeed this characterised the US response to the offensive. It was seen as a publicity stunt and was denounced as 'lacking seriousness'. As ever, the Reagan administration was split. The National Security Advisors and the hawks in the CIA and the Department of Defense were totally hostile to the Soviet proposal which, it was argued, left the Soviets with an overwhelming advantage of land-based strategic nuclear missiles for some time to come. George Shultz and the State Department chiefs were more enthusiastic and wanted to examine the details of the proposals. Reagan himself shared the goal of a long-term removal of nuclear weapons but was suspicious of the short-term consequences.

Once again, Reagan acted tough in public but in private spoke of peace. He entered into a long correspondence with Gorbachev, continuing their dialogue of the previous year, with lots of talk about the quest for peace. Meanwhile, US warships including an electronic intelligence-gathering destroyer sailed along the Crimean coast recording the Soviet response in an action reminiscent of PSYOPS a few years before. Similar exercises along the Libyan coast provoked return fire and resulted in a US bombing raid on Gaddafi's bases in Benghazi and Tripoli. In Afghanistan, the US increased its secret military aid to the Mujahideen in their struggle against Soviet forces, arming them with hand-held Stinger anti-aircraft missiles that had the capacity to shoot down a helicopter. And in the Nevada desert the US tested a 19-kiloton nuclear bomb.

To Moscow, all this, along with the lack of support for the peace offensive, came across as unexpectedly belligerent. Gorbachev imagined various scenarios. He suspected that the military-industrial complex had become alarmed at the progress in Geneva and had got at the President. He wondered if the hawks felt the President had already made too many concessions to the Soviets and had put him under pressure. Or perhaps there was fear in Washington of a renewed, dynamic Soviet Union talking peace on the world stage. But none of it made much sense in the light of the bonhomie at Geneva. 'Try as I would, I simply could not understand this behaviour,' he wrote.[5]

Then, early on the morning of 26 April, an explosion tore apart a nuclear reactor at the huge Chernobyl power plant in the Ukraine. The amount of radioactive fallout over a large area was equivalent to a small nuclear bomb going off. The Soviet bureaucracy once again reacted slowly and revealed minimal information. When a radioactive cloud was picked up over Sweden, officials were forced into admitting the scale of the disaster that had taken place. Dozens died as a direct consequence of the Chernobyl accident. Some 135,000 people were eventually evacuated and resettled. The clean-up cost the Soviet economy billions of roubles. The secrecy, complacency and lack of safety culture within the Soviet nuclear industry so outraged Gorbachev and the reformers that it encouraged him to speed up his policy of *perestroika*, reconstruction or restructuring, and *glasnost*, openness or transparency. The Soviet system had to change, to become more accountable and responsive to people's needs. The nuclear tragedy made that even more clear. 'Chernobyl,' as Gorbachev said, 'made me and my colleagues rethink a great many things.'[6]

Annoyed with what he saw as a revived aggressiveness in the US, and with the Geneva negotiations having stalled, Gorbachev decided that there was no point in a second summit until the prospects for arms control had improved. But, frustrated with the slow progress of domestic reform and with a growing need to cut back on the nation's vast military expenditure, he changed his mind. While on holiday in the Crimea that autumn, Gorbachev sent an urgent message to Reagan suggesting another quick meeting, a small affair, one-on-one, with only principal advisers present. In early October the two leaders agreed on a venue: Reykjavik in Iceland, midway between the two countries. It would be a low-key affair in comparison to the Geneva summit, with far fewer reporters and journalists present.

By now, Gorbachev wanted to move at speed. It was clear to him that for *perestroika* to succeed the arms race had to be slowed and savings made in the vast Soviet defence budget. Chernobyl had both shown up the need for reform and given Soviet citizens a hint of what a nuclear explosion would be like. With his new adviser on foreign affairs, Anatoly Chernyaev, he planned fresh, wide-ranging offers on arms reductions to circumvent the negotiations in Geneva. Together they also threw out many of the socialist dogmas that had underlined Soviet thinking for decades. They rejected the notion of the international class struggle and the ultimate triumph of international socialism over capitalism. They binned the previous building up of America as an 'imperialist threat'. Instead they tried to focus on the search for new approaches to global security while being able substantially to reduce Soviet spending on arms and defence. Chernyaev summed up the situation: 'The main goal of Reykjavik ... is to sweep Reagan off his feet with our bold even "risky" approach to world politics.' Gorbachev told the Politburo, 'Our main goal is to prevent the arms race from entering a new stage [by going into space] ... If we don't back down on some specific, maybe important issues, if we don't budge from the positions we've held for a long time, we will lose in the end. We will be drawn into an arms race we cannot manage. We will lose because right now we are already at the end of our tether.'[7]

The two delegations arrived in Iceland in the winter darkness. Moonlight revealed a bleak, rugged, volcanic landscape. Reagan did not know how to prepare for Reykjavik because the Americans were unclear as to what Gorbachev would bring to the table. The day before the meeting, Soviet expert Jack Matlock stood in for Gorbachev in some role-playing with Reagan, teasing out some of the issues they anticipated would come up.[8] The President prepared his responses on a set of cards. Hofdi House, where they were to meet, was a small, isolated property, far less luxurious than the grand mansions in Geneva. Local legends claimed it was haunted. There were no proper facilities for a secretariat who had to work out of a bathroom for most of their stay. The view in the American camp was that this was going to be nothing more than a meeting to prepare for the real summit to come in Washington at some later date.

The first morning of their meeting, 11 October 1986, began with a private one-on-one between Reagan and Gorbachev. The Soviet leader took the initiative and began to outline a dramatic proposal of a 50 per cent reduction of each side's total nuclear arsenals, including the heavy intercontinental ballistic missiles, and the elimination of all intermediate nuclear missiles in Europe. Reagan once again spoke about human rights in the Soviet Union and repeated the Russian proverb he had learned: *doveryai no proveryai* – 'trust but verify'. Gorbachev grew irritated and a little angry. Reagan became flustered and dropped his cue cards on the floor, then could not find the right card for his response to Gorbachev. The Soviet leader thought he had no answer as 'the American President and his aides had been preparing for a completely different conversation'.[9] So he suggested that Shevardnadze and Shultz join them.

During the rest of the morning session, Gorbachev continued to outline his proposals for nuclear weapons reductions. Shultz remembered that he was 'brisk, impatient, and confident, with the air of a man who is setting the agenda and taking charge of the meeting'.[10] The two leaders and their foreign secretaries went back and forth on the arithmetic of arms reductions. But the Americans could see that Gorbachev was making substantial concessions. As ever, the sticking point was Reagan's Star Wars proposal. The Soviets wanted to prohibit any weapons in space but agreed to permit research and development only in the 'laboratory', so that the testing of weapons would not be allowed. This, they argued, was in accordance with the ABM Treaty. Reagan responded cautiously to the range of proposals. When they broke for lunch, Shultz remembered that 'Excitement was in the air . . . Perhaps we were at a moment of breakthrough after a period, following the Geneva summit, of stalemate.' The veteran Soviet expert Paul Nitze told the others, 'This is the best Soviet proposal we have received in twenty-five years.'[11]

During the afternoon session, Reagan outlined his passionate belief in the need for a strategic defence system in space. He said that once this had been constructed, all ballistic missiles could be eliminated. He pointed out that some rogue leader might get his hands on a nuclear missile and attack America at some point in the future so there was still a need for a defensive shield in space.

Gorbachev became angry. 'You will take the arms race into space and could be tempted to launch a first strike,' he said.

'That's why I propose to eliminate ballistic missiles and share SDI with you,' Reagan responded.

Gorbachev said that he frankly did not believe the US would share such technology with the Soviet Union. 'If you will not share oil drilling equipment or even milk processing factories, I do not believe that you will share SDI,' he scoffed.

Tempers began to flare. Reagan insisted that agreement on human rights and on the many regional disputes around the world must all be part and parcel of a US–Soviet agreement and could not be separated out. It was agreed that working parties would strive through the evening and into the night to draw up specific proposals.[12]

The following day, the talks continued in an atmosphere of constructive problem solving. The Soviets continued to make concessions. They agreed to include their SS-20s located in Asia along with the reductions of intermediate nuclear weapons in Europe. They agreed to leave aside the British and French nuclear arsenals as a separate issue. They agreed to include the question of human rights in any broad agreement. Reagan wrote, 'George and I couldn't believe what was happening. We were getting amazing agreements. As the day went on I felt something momentous was occurring.'[13] But Gorbachev would not concede that research for Star Wars could carry on outside the laboratory. It came down to how strictly the ABM Treaty was to be interpreted.

The talks were due to end at noon but continued into the afternoon. The American team drafted a specific proposal. There would be two five-year periods. In the first five years there would be a 50 per cent cut in 'strategic offensive arsenals';

in the second five years a 50 per cent cut in 'offensive ballistic missiles', both land-based and sea-based. The definitions were purposely kept a little vague. But 'research, development and testing' of space weapons could continue throughout the ten-year period. The Soviets drafted a revised version in which there could be no testing of space weapons. And then the Americans redrafted this. They were inching towards a dramatic agreement but still could not reach a final form of words satisfactory to both parties. There was disagreement over the meaning of 'strategic arms' versus 'ballistic missiles'. Gorbachev claimed that the American President wanted to be a 'winner' but in this negotiation there could be no 'winners and losers'. The 'loser' would simply take steps to undermine any agreement and it would be worthless.

In exasperation, late in the afternoon, Reagan suddenly said, 'It would be fine with me if we eliminated all nuclear weapons.'

Gorbachev shot back, 'We can do that. Let's eliminate them. We can eliminate them.'

'Let's do it,' added Shultz.

It was an extraordinary moment in the Cold War. The leaders of the two superpowers were talking together about abolishing nuclear weapons. Reagan had frequently spoken about this but his staff had never taken him seriously. Now he had departed from the script and had made the proposal at a US–Soviet summit. But instead of signing an outline agreement there and then they started to argue again over Star Wars. Gorbachev insisted that research could only continue in the laboratory. Reagan said they were arguing over 'a question of one word'. Gorbachev said it was more than a word, it was a principle, and if he went back to the Politburo and the Soviet people and told them that he had conceded SDI he would be called 'a dummy and not a leader'. 'It's "laboratory" or goodbye,' he insisted.[14]

There was a pause. Reagan passed Shultz a note on which he had scribbled 'Am I wrong?' Shultz whispered back, 'No, you are right.'[15]

Reagan stood up and gathered his papers. Gorbachev did the same, and said, 'Please pass on my regards to Nancy.'

As they walked out of Hofdi House it was dark, but the lights of the waiting television crews soon lit up the scene revealing the massive disappointment on the faces of the two leaders. Both men were angry. They looked fatigued and disappointed. Reagan's teeth were clenched and his face had lost much of its colour. As they walked away their body language was totally different from Geneva, eleven months earlier.

When they parted, Reagan turned to Gorbachev and said, 'I still feel we can find a deal.'

'I don't think you want a deal,' Gorbachev replied. 'I don't know what more I could have done.'

'You could have said yes,' said the President.

'We won't be seeing each other again,' remarked Gorbachev as they bid each other farewell. He meant in Reykjavik, as they were both scheduled to depart that evening. But the phrase was overheard by some of the press and a rumour flashed out that US–Soviet relations had collapsed.[16]

The leaders of the two superpowers had for the first time imagined a future without nuclear weapons. They had been one word away from going down in history as the greatest peacemakers of all time. But they had failed to agree on how to achieve this vision and by ending in bitter acrimony had come away without *any* agreement on arms reductions. The US team felt they were right. SDI was their big strength, one that would keep the Soviets negotiating. If they gave up on that they would have no leverage. Gorbachev had wanted to kill off SDI. Despite making major concessions that had changed the nature of arms reduction talks, he had failed. Both men later described the annoyance and disappointment they felt.[17]

Reagan and Gorbachev emerge after their Reykjavik meeting.
The body language shows that the leaders were
angry and frustrated with each other.

Gorbachev had been instructed by the Politburo that if the negotiations failed he should denounce the President and make clear to the world how intransigent he had been. He should berate Reagan as a threat to world peace. As he walked the 400 metres to the press centre he thought about what he would say. He felt shattered by what had happened but knew their progress was too important to be sacrificed 'for the sake of a momentary propaganda advantage'. When he walked into the press centre a thousand journalists stood up in silence, waiting for his verdict on the talks. He later wrote, 'I sensed the anxiety in the air. I suddenly felt emotional, even shaken. These people standing in front of me seemed to represent mankind waiting for its fate to be decided.' Instinctively, Gorbachev gave a positive spin to the meeting and came up with a phrase that made headlines worldwide. He memorably said, 'In spite of all its drama, Reykjavik is not a failure – it's a breakthrough, which allowed us for the first time to look over the horizon.'[18] At first the Americans called the summit a failure, but within days they too were starting to call it a 'breakthrough'. Shultz felt that an important threshold had been crossed. 'I recalled the fear and tension in 1983 when INF [Intermediate Nuclear Force] missiles had been deployed, and I knew that we were doing the right thing in trying to achieve drastic reductions in these vast nuclear arsenals.'[19]

Reykjavik had shown that a broad agreement on arms reduction was possible. Both leaders had displayed statesman-like qualities, Gorbachev in conceding several points that had been integral to the Soviet position for years, Reagan in proposing a broad abolition of nuclear weapons. But differences remained, and forty years of traditional Cold War suspicion and mistrust could not be talked away in an afternoon. The irony is that the possibility of a nuclear-free world had been lost because of American enthusiasm for a technology that would never be realised, along with Soviet fears that America's technological superiority meant such a system was just around the corner. But at Reykjavik the time had simply not been right. The twenty-first century would not dawn with a nuclear-free world.

Not everyone was delighted with the prospects raised at Reykjavik. America's allies in western Europe were not at all happy about the removal of American nuclear weapons, without even having been consulted. The NATO allies feared that this would leave them wide open to the Warsaw Pact's vast superiority in conventional forces. Margaret Thatcher was incandescent with rage when she heard the reports from Reykjavik, fearing British security was about to be surrendered. She felt 'as if there had been an earthquake beneath my feet'. In her view, 'The whole policy of nuclear deterrence which had kept the peace for forty years was close to being abandoned ... Somehow I had to get the Americans back onto the firm ground of a credible policy of nuclear deterrence.'[20] She was partly assuaged when on a visit to Washington she was promised full American support for the modernisation of the UK's independent deterrent with the Trident nuclear missile system. Chancellor Helmut Kohl in West Germany was also opposed to what he saw as the US abandonment of Germany's defence. He insisted on keeping the seventy-two West German Pershing II missiles even if the US withdrew theirs. It took all of Reagan and Shultz's diplomatic skills to dissuade him from this, later.

In Moscow, Gorbachev denounced Reagan to the Politburo as 'a representative of the class enemy' who exhibited 'extreme primitivism, a caveman outlook and intellectual impotence'.[21] But to his closest aides he began to show more respect for the American President and suggested that a deal would soon be possible. 'A spark of understanding was born between them, as if they had winked to each other about the future,' wrote Chernyaev.[22] Gorbachev was still a man in a hurry, needing to relieve the burden of defence spending on the Soviet economy to allow for his other reforms. After advice from his scientists that Reagan's Star Wars programme was still years or even decades from realisation, Gorbachev made a profound decision. In February 1987 he announced that he would no longer insist on linking restraints to SDI as a condition for an arms control agreement. Gorbachev effectively abandoned holding on to the 'one word' that had prevented a historic agreement at Reykjavik. It was a major climbdown.

For much of 1987 Reagan was distracted with trying to control the impact of the Iran-Contra scandal. Illegal arms sales to Iran had been used to fund the Contra guerrillas who were fighting the Marxist regime in Nicaragua. This was all part of Reagan's strategy of trying to roll back communist advances in the Third World. Several senior US officials were involved in a shady network of deals involving agents and arms dealers across the Middle East and the use of secret Swiss bank accounts. Admiral John Poindexter, who had replaced Bud McFarlane as National Security Advisor, took the hit and resigned over the issue. But it was Lieutenant-Colonel Oliver North, an NSC official, who took most of the blame in the public eye. The illegal deals and cover-ups cast the Reagan administration in a bad light and the President's approval rating sank to its lowest level. He was lucky that the scandal, potentially on the scale of a Watergate, did not bring him down.

In April 1987, George Shultz visited Moscow and in meetings with Eduard Shevardnadze laid the foundations for what would become the Intermediate Nuclear Force (INF) Treaty, which would remove both sides' nuclear missiles from Europe. A series of meetings between the two followed in Washington and Moscow to iron out the details. Meanwhile, Reagan came under pressure from the hawks within his administration and from right-wing pressure groups across the country who feared he was trading away America's security out of his desire to reduce nuclear weapons. Within his administration, Casey in the CIA, Weinberger in Defense and others did everything they could to oppose, frustrate or slow up the progress of events towards the signing of the new treaty. Outside, Richard Nixon denounced Reagan's approach and predicted it would cause a crisis within NATO. Others who had supported his hard-line stance during his first term accused him of going soft on communism. Some even called him Gorbachev's poodle.

Partly to counter these charges, Reagan decided to visit Berlin. On the city's 750th anniversary, on 12 June 1987, he made one of his most memorable speeches. Echoing President Kennedy's great speech in the same city in 1963 in which he announced that all free men could be proud to say they were

Berliners, Reagan addressed a crowd of about 20,000 people just to the west of the Brandenburg Gate, in the very shadow of the Wall that had divided Berlin for more than a quarter of a century and become one of the great symbols of Cold War division. To the crowd, Reagan proclaimed, 'General Secretary Gorbachev, if you seek peace, if you seek prosperity for the Soviet Union and eastern Europe, if you seek liberalisation, come here to this gate! Mr Gorbachev, open this gate.' Then, reaching his climax, and to growing cheers from the Berlin crowd, Reagan, with his actor's sense of timing, called out, 'Mr Gorbachev, Mr Gorbachev, tear down this wall!'[23] The speech did much to revive his reputation as a Cold War warrior. And it forever linked Reagan with the fall of the Wall, even though this came two years later, in very different circumstances and well after he had left the White House.

The result of the intense diplomacy between Shultz and Shevardnadze came in the Washington summit, held more than two years after the first in Geneva. Reagan had hoped to invite Gorbachev to a triumphant tour of the US, starting in Washington and culminating in a few days on his ranch in California. Gorbachev made it clear he would come to Washington for summit diplomacy but there was no time for anything else. The meetings finally took place over three days from 8 December 1987. The centrepiece was the signing of the INF Treaty in the East Room of the White House. It was covered live on television in the US, the Soviet Union and around the world. The proposal Reagan had initially made for a zero-zero option in 1981, rejected then by an ageing Soviet leadership, was finally achieved. All the Pershing IIs and the Cruise missiles which had provoked such protest in western Europe would be withdrawn. To Gorbachev, agreeing to abolish the SS-20s was final acceptance of the flawed Soviet policy that had brought about their deployment in the 1970s. And freeing the Kremlin from the risk of missiles that could arrive in Moscow in a matter of minutes 'removed a pistol to our head', wrote Gorbachev, echoing the words of his predecessor.[24] It was the first time that an entire class of nuclear weapons would be removed and destroyed. Alongside the removal of the missiles came a process of verification that was far more advanced than anything that had gone before. Officials from both sides were authorised to visit missile sites, factories and destruction plants to ensure that everything was done precisely by the book. Television cameras were called in to film the destruction of the redundant missiles. Reagan spoke about the INF Treaty as not the end but the beginning of a new working relationship that would help to create a new world. In his short speech at the signing ceremony, Gorbachev said he was proud to be 'planting this sapling which may one day grow into a mighty tree of peace'.[25]

However, beyond this historic agreement, the Washington summit did not deliver on the opportunity offered at Reykjavik. Reactions from hostile factions in both Washington and Moscow had brought the two leaders back from the brink of total nuclear disarmament. Again, there was argument about whether weapons in space would keep the peace or add to global insecurity. Again, Reagan prodded Gorbachev about human rights in the Soviet Union. At one point Gorbachev became so resentful of a Reagan lecture that he said, 'Mr President, you are not a prosecutor and I am not on trial here. Like you, I represent a great country, and therefore expect our dialogue to be conducted on a basis of reciprocity and equality. Otherwise there simply will be no dialogue.'[26] It was an indication of how well the two men got on together that despite moments like this they did continue to talk. In this instance, Gorbachev joked that if the US was so keen on the free movement of peoples, why did their border guards constantly arrest Mexicans trying to get into their country? There were also discussions on regional disputes, especially

Nicaragua, and Gorbachev made it clear that he had decided to withdraw the Soviet Army from Afghanistan.

In many ways, the historic signing of the INF Treaty in Washington was overshadowed by the public relations triumph of Gorbachev's first visit to the United States. 'Gorbymania' swept America. Gorbachev brought with him a strong delegation of leading Soviet scientists, intellectuals and artists. He hosted a series of receptions at the Soviet embassy to which he invited top American businessmen, politicians, artists and media moguls to meet him and their Soviet counterparts. Raisa was also immensely popular, and as she travelled around Washington by car crowds came out to cheer her. On the third day of the summit, Mikhail and Raisa were driving back to the Soviet embassy when the Soviet leader ordered the driver of his limousine to stop. To the horror of his bodyguards, Gorbachev and his wife dived into the assembled crowd on Connecticut Avenue to shake hands and acknowledge the well-wishers. The American public loved it. *Time* magazine made Gorbachev 'Man of the Year'. Polls showed that 65 per cent of Americans had a good impression of Gorbachev – higher than Reagan's own approval rating, which had risen back up to 58 per cent.

In April 1988, a series of accords were signed leading to the Soviet Army's withdrawal from Afghanistan. The army had lost 13,000 men dead and 30,000 wounded during the war, which had dragged on for nearly nine years. Probably a million Afghans had lost their lives, and many more were wounded and homeless. The US had spent $2 billion arming the Mujahideen, and by equipping the Islamic fundamentalists with advanced technology they left a legacy of violence that carried on throughout the 1990s with the establishment of the Taliban and well into the twenty-first century and the war on terror.

From 29 May to 2 June 1988, Reagan travelled to Moscow

for the reciprocal summit agreed in Geneva. It was mostly a piece of theatre, stage-managed as a show of unity. There was no real progress on talks about further arms reductions. Reagan still clung on to support for his Star Wars programme. The Soviets still pushed for agreements on the reduction of strategic arsenals. When they proposed a sweeping declaration to denounce war as a means of resolving disputes, the Americans rejected it, fearing it would undermine the defence budget. Reagan made a speech at Moscow State University about living in a world without nuclear weapons in freedom. After a standing ovation he answered questions from students. He met various eastern Church leaders and Soviet citizens from all walks of life whom he chatted freely with. He got on very well with the Gorbachevs and told them that he and Nancy regarded them as friends.

On the morning of 31 May, Reagan and Gorbachev went on a walkabout in Red Square. It was a bright spring day. They ambled comfortably through the crowds, many of whom were wearing Wrangler jeans and colourful jackets. There were Red Flags alongside the Stars and Stripes flying from every lamp post. The bells of St Basil's were ringing. Below the podium where Stalin and Brezhnev had watched endless lines of Soviet weaponry pass by, the leaders of the two superpowers looked like genuine equals enjoying a relaxing day in the city – two elderly tourists soaking up the scene. Reagan picked up a baby and held him aloft.[27] The British television journalist Jon Snow called out, 'Do you still think you're in an "evil empire", Mr President?' Reagan replied, smiling, with the single word 'No'. When asked why not, the President said, 'I was talking about another time and another era.'

It had indeed been another time. Since he had first described the Soviet Union as an 'evil empire', aggressive American behaviour and Soviet paranoia had taken the world to the brink of a nuclear precipice. But the scare this had provoked helped eventually to bring the leaders of the two superpowers together in mutual cooperation. There was a genuine new understanding, even a friendship, between them. Nothing symbolised this more than that morning in Red Square. If Reagan felt he had been correct in describing the Soviet Union as an 'evil empire' five years before, he could see that things had changed and the country under Gorbachev with *glasnost* and *perestroika* was now a different place. The war scares of 1983 had brought the world to the brink but, remarkably, had ended up by helping to deliver at least a level of nuclear disarmament. Most importantly, the world had survived. And the end of the Cold War itself was in sight.

Epilogue

Vice President George H. W. Bush watched coverage of President Reagan's walkabout in Red Square on television at his home in Maine. He was not as excited or upbeat about the end of the 'evil empire' as his commander-in-chief. He was far more sceptical about the changes going on inside the Soviet Union. When running for the presidency later in 1988 he stressed a more hard-headed approach. 'I think the jury is still out on the Soviet experiment,' he said in a televised debate with Democrat nominee Michael Dukakis.[1]

When he took over as President in January 1989, Bush brought in a new foreign affairs team with James Baker as Secretary of State, Brent Scowcroft as National Security Advisor and Richard Cheney as Secretary of Defense. Like all new administrations, they began a review of US foreign policy, and at the forefront of this was Washington's relationship with Moscow. It took some months to complete the review. The new policy was more cautious and pragmatic than that of Reagan's administration. As a previous US representative to the UN, chief of the diplomatic mission to China and one-time director of the CIA, Bush had a great deal more experience of foreign affairs than most Presidents (and certainly far more than Reagan), but he was no visionary. He proudly said he was suspicious of what he called 'the vision thing'. The decision was made to come up with no new initiatives and offer nei-ther help nor hindrance to Gorbachev's reforms. There was a nagging fear that if the US lined up too closely with the Soviet leader then he might be forced out in a coup and replaced by a hard-liner who would take the whole situation back to where it had been before the arms reduction agreements.

However, this meant that Bush's administration was left constantly struggling to keep up with the dramatic pace of events. Gorbachev was still a man in a hurry and 1989 would prove to be a turning point in world history.[2] In December 1988, at a speech at the UN, he promised a stunning unilateral reduction of Soviet forces in eastern Europe including a cut of half a million soldiers along with the removal of 10,000 tanks and 800 combat aircraft. This was the only way he could see of reducing the burden of defence spending on the Soviet economy. He also offered freedom of choice to the Soviet allies in eastern Europe. And as he eased up on Soviet control, a revolution quickly followed.

In January 1989, the Hungarian Parliament agreed to allow freedom of association and assembly. This was followed in May by multi-party elections. No doubt many Hungarians, remembering the massacre of 1956, looked anxiously over their shoulder at Moscow's reaction. But Gorbachev announced his support for the reforms. In Poland, too, the seven-year ban was lifted on the Solidarity trade union, and in the country's first free election in June it won 99 of the 100 seats available in the senate and a majority in the lower house. In a long phone call with the Polish communist leader in August, Gorbachev recommended that the party should form a coalition with Solidarity. For the first time in history, a Communist Party willingly gave up power. And it did so with Soviet support. Gorbachev wrote, 'Let everyone make his own choice and let us all respect that choice.'[3] A Rubicon had been crossed.

Thousands of East Germans began flooding through Hungary, once it had opened its border into Austria, and from there to West Germany. When Gorbachev visited East Berlin in October he had talks with the ultra-conformist 77-year-old East German communist leader Erich Honecker. Gorbachev suggested to Honecker that he should introduce *perestroika* into East Germany but the German leader would have none of it. At a huge rally in East Berlin to mark the fortieth birthday of the German Democratic Republic, the party called out the faithful to line the streets. To the amazement of party bosses they started chanting 'Gorby! Gorby!' Some even heard calls of 'Gorby Save Us!' The days of communist East Germany were numbered.

In the Soviet Union there were also reforms. In March the first largely free elections were held for a new Congress of People's Deputies. One third of the seats were reserved for communists but there was a significant move away from the party in the other seats. For the first time, if there was only one candidate, crossing out the name on the ballot paper was counted as a vote against. Gorbachev was elected President of the Congress. But other players began to build up significant popular power bases. Five million voted for dissident communist Boris Yeltsin as mayor of Moscow. His policy was clear: he wanted to abolish the Communist Party, dismantle the Soviet Union and make Russia an independent, democratic state. These first moves to democracy soon prompted a nationalist revival in the Asiatic provinces of the Soviet Union. But Gorbachev insisted that liberalisation did not mean a weakening of the Union. Soldiers confronted rioters, and in Georgia twenty protesters were shot dead. Regardless, a huge popular movement called for the independence of the three Baltic states, Lithuania, Latvia and Estonia, on the fiftieth anniversary of their annexation by Stalin.

Gorbachev also went to China, the first Soviet leader in thirty years to visit Beijing. He discussed reducing tensions between the two countries and drastically cutting his forces in Manchuria and along the border. The Chinese leaders went along with this but were determined that they would remain steady on their own path of communism despite growing opposition. Emboldened by Gorbachev's visit, one million supporters of the Democracy Movement came out in Tiananmen Square. On the day after Gorbachev left, martial law was declared. Loyal troops were ordered to clear the square and a bloodbath followed, televised live around the world. The massacre was followed by the arrest of thousands of pro-democracy activists and was effectively the end of the Democracy Movement. China went on with liberal economic reforms while maintaining its outward allegiance to communism and centralised political control. But the scenes from Tiananmen Square discredited the Chinese regime and showed other governments that in the new age of 24/7 television news, sent by satellite live around the world, violent repression of popular protest was not viable.

Washington found itself merely watching the rapid developments in Europe and Asia but maintained its policy of cautiously standing back from events. Soviet Foreign Minister Eduard Shevardnadze appealed to his opposite number James Baker to take a more energetic and supportive line. When he visited the US in September, Shevardnadze got on well with Baker and for the first time he convinced a leading US policy-maker that the changes in the Soviet Union were real, permanent and irreversible. Baker concluded, 'The situation has the makings of a whole new world.'

The last few weeks of the year saw a dramatic climax to events. In Berlin, Honecker was replaced by a younger leader, but it was too little, too late. A confused announcement about granting exit visas for East Berliners prompted crowds to gather along the Wall on the night of 9 November. Not sure what to do, the border guards asked for orders but received none. With huge crowds building up, at the Bornholmer Strasse crossing the guards took it upon themselves to open the border gates. A few wary East Berliners began very cautiously to pass through to West Berlin; after all, 200 had been shot trying to cross the Wall. But as the word spread, the remaining border guards stood aside, and the other crossing points were opened. The trickle became a flood. Hundreds, then thousands poured through to be welcomed with open arms, kisses and hugs by West Berliners. Chisels and hammers appeared and people started to hack at the ugly wall that had been a scar across the city for nearly thirty years. It was all screened live on television and watched around the world. People everywhere cheered this ultimate and very symbolic victory of people power.[4]

The triumph of people power. Thousands crossed from East to West Berlin on the night of 9 November 1989. Mallets and hammers appeared and the Wall soon came down.

The year ended with a so-called Velvet Revolution in Czechoslovakia in which nearly a million people marched against the government. Opposition leader and playwright Václav Havel was released from prison and elected President. In Bulgaria, too, reformers took control. Only the repressive communist regime of Nicolae Ceauşescu in Romania remained. He and his wife Elena had ruled with an iron fist for more than twenty years. But when the Securitate (secret police) fired on demonstrators, killing ninety-seven people, huge crowds came out in protest. Ceauşescu addressed a rally of specially assembled supporters in Bucharest, intending to show that he was still in charge. But to his amazement he was interrupted by catcalls, boos and whistles. Visibly shaken, he retired from the balcony and the following day fled by helicopter. He was captured, charged with treason and put before an impromptu military tribunal. Ceauşescu and his wife were summarily put up against a wall and shot on Christmas Day. Their bodies were shown on television. It had been an extraordinary year.

Bush finally agreed to meet Gorbachev on neutral territory. The summit was intended to take place on two warships in Malta harbour but a wild winter storm blew up and neither leader was able to get to the guided-missile cruisers. Instead they met on a Russian cruise liner, which had been adapted as a floating hotel. For once the weather outside was the reverse of the calmness of the meeting. In a series of agreements, Gorbachev assured Bush that the Soviet Union would never start a war against the United States. For many this seemed to mark the end of the Cold War. Others saw the reunification of Germany in October 1990 and the final casting aside of the Iron Curtain that had descended over Europe after the Second World War as the true end.

By now the genie of reform was out of the bottle and it was hard for anyone to put a stop to momentous political changes. Shock waves from eastern Europe crossed the USSR. In the summer of 1991, the Soviet Union finally broke up and became a Commonwealth of Independent States. The Baltic republics declared their independence from Moscow, as did the republics of Ukraine, Belarus, Moldavia, Azerbaijan, Kazakhstan, Uzbekistan, Kirghizia, Tadzhikistan and Armenia. In August there was an attempted coup against Gorbachev by those who thought reform had gone too far. Among the conspirators was Vladimir Kryuchkov, the paranoid KGB leader who had directed Operation RYaN. The coup failed, but it still marked the political end for Gorbachev. Power passed into the hands of Boris Yeltsin, who won the popular vote to be leader of the Russian Federation. On 25 December 1991, the Soviet Union ceased to exist as the Red Flag with its hammer and sickle, prophesying the workers' revolution, was lowered at the Kremlin for the last time. Gorbachev had never intended this but the reforms he had started had unleashed a tsunami of change that he could not hold back.

There were still several issues to resolve. The political reform was seismic. But economic reform was very slow. The transition from a centrally controlled economy to a market economy in the former Soviet Union was a difficult process. The centralised apparatus of the state was sold off but this did little to help the lot of most people. Many lost secure jobs, and once reliable pensions were overtaken by inflation. Economic change was a chaotic and distressing process for millions of citizens. Corruption became endemic. The shelves in most shops remained bare.

And then there was the question of the nuclear arsenal. Who would take hold of the briefcase with the codes to launch nuclear weapons? The 1990s began with the dismantling and destruction of intermediate nuclear weapons in Europe as a result of the treaty signed by Reagan and Gorbachev in Washington in 1987. There was another agreement to reduce conventional forces in Europe as the Soviet Union withdrew its military units. While still in power, Gorbachev signed START 1 with Bush, in July 1991. It reduced the nuclear warheads of the two powers to fewer than 9000 each with just 1500 delivery vehicles. Two years later this was decreased further. The reduced Soviet nuclear stockpile was now shared between Russia (with the lion's share), the Ukraine, Belarus and Kazakhstan. The new leaders of all these states agreed to abide by the terms of START 1. This was a far cry from the total abolition of nuclear weapons at which Reagan and Gorbachev had stared over the horizon in Reykjavik. And the bi-polar world of the second half of the twentieth century prepared to transition awkwardly into the multi-polar and arguably even more dangerous world of the twenty-first century.

Spies had played a leading role in the events of the tense year of 1983, as we have seen. Despite the end of the Cold War, the spying of Aldrich Ames and Robert Hanssen carried on for some years with both men selling secrets to the Russian Federation. Ames was finally tracked down by an internal CIA inquiry and was arrested in February 1994. He initially declared he was innocent but later admitted his guilt and was given a life sentence without remission. His wife Rosario was given a five-year sentence for tax evasion. At the time of writing he is still being held in a high-security penitentiary in Indiana. Hanssen carried on passing information to the SVR, the Russian organisation newly formed out of the KGB, until 2001. As the net slowly closed around him, he planned one final drop in a Virginia park. On this occasion he was followed and spotted by FBI officers who moved in and arrested him. 'What took you so long?' he is supposed to have asked them. He pleaded guilty to fifteen counts of espionage and was given fifteen consecutive life sentences. At the time of writing Hanssen is in a secure prison in Colorado and spends twenty-three hours of each day in solitary confinement.

*Aldrich Ames, CIA officer and double agent who sold secrets
to the KGB, in chains after his trial in 1994.*

With the collapse of East Germany, in January 1990 an
angry crowd stormed the offices of the Stasi in the Lichtenberg
district of East Berlin. The name of the ex-head of the HVA,
Markus Wolf, was made public. The 'man without a face' was
now a very public figure with his picture regularly in the
papers. After a spell as an exile in Russia, the East German
spymaster returned to a unified Germany, was arrested and
put on trial for treason. He was found guilty in a glaring case
of victor's justice in which former West Germans judged the
activities of an East German who had been on the 'losing'
side of the Cold War. Wolf appealed by asking how could he
have committed treason against the state for which he had
worked for forty years, the German Democratic Republic? His
sentence was annulled by the German supreme court. In his
memoirs he wrote, 'The Cold War was not a time of blacks and
whites, but of many shades of grey.'[5]

The West German government offered immunity to intelligence agents in return for information. An ex-HVA officer passed on details about the work of their agent in the highest echelons of NATO. All he knew was his codename, 'Topaz'. NATO counter-intelligence began a search for who this could be. Rainer Rupp even heard about the search himself, but with the Cold War over he became fatalistic about what would happen to him. Rewards were offered to ex-HVA officials to name Topaz but no one took up the offer. The CIA eventually got a database of names of HVA agents, all efficiently listed on a computer disc. This finally led the investigators to Rupp in 1993.[6] They did not want to arrest him in Belgium, where he still worked, so they waited until July when he visited Germany for his mother's birthday. When he and his wife arrived at his mother's house for the celebrations they immediately became suspicious that something was up. But he was by now exhausted and had no wish to spend the rest of his life as a fugitive so Rupp did not resist arrest. He was found guilty of espionage in a German court and sentenced to twelve years in prison. He was freed after seven years. But he is convinced that the Americans would still like him 'not only to be in gaol but to throw the key away'.[7] He is now a free man.

After his daring exfiltration in July 1985, when Oleg Gordievsky arrived in Britain he became a celebrity within intelligence circles. His initial debriefing lasted for eighty consecutive days and then carried on less intensely for another eighteen months as MI6 squeezed every morsel of information they could from him about how the KGB was structured, how it functioned, and about the 1983 war scare. His debriefings resulted in 6000 pages of notes that were circulated to intelligence and political analysts in London.[8] He told them about KGB operations, the political, military and strategic thinking of the Kremlin, and tried to explain

Soviet psychology. In September 1985, Bill Casey, the CIA chief, flew from Washington to meet and interview him. After MI6 had fully debriefed him, Gordievsky visited several other Western intelligence agencies in France, Germany, Canada, Israel and New Zealand to exchange information, give lectures and offer advice. He met Margaret Thatcher on several occasions, and in July 1987 he visited the United States and had a meeting with President Reagan in the White House. He made several other journeys to the US to brief groups of CIA specialists. At many of these sessions he sat opposite a man with large glasses and a friendly smile with whom he got on well and grew to respect. It was none other than Aldrich Ames, the man whom he did not then realise had sold his name to the KGB. Ames still had several years of selling secrets ahead of him.[9]

Oleg Gordievsky, the only senior KGB double agent ever smuggled out to the West, meets Reagan in the Oval Office, July 1987.

Gordievsky later worked for several years with a leading historian of intelligence, Christopher Andrew from Cambridge, and collaborated on a detailed account of the inside history of the KGB. In this book came the first limited revelations in public about the Soviet war scare of November 1983.[10]

Although Gordievsky never wanted to return to live in the Soviet Union he grew desperate to be reunited with his family. The KGB had put his wife, Leila, under close observation for several years after her husband disappeared. They dictated letters that she had to write telling him to come home, that he would receive an official pardon and all would be forgiven. He realised these were all lies. When the letters failed to bring him back, they told Leila he had taken up with a British woman and no longer wanted to see her. Although he was living a busy life and travelling extensively, Gordievsky began to feel everything had been in vain and he yearned to see Leila and his daughters again. Despite intense pressure from British and later American diplomatic sources, the Russians were extremely reluctant to allow Gordievsky's wife and daughters to leave the Soviet Union and join him in Britain. Both Reagan and Thatcher personally asked Gorbachev to release the family. When Thatcher asked him directly, Gorbachev pursed his lips and refused to discuss the subject.[11] His escape was clearly still a humiliating and painful episode for the KGB.

After the failed coup in 1991, the power of the KGB went into decline and Boris Yeltsin granted the family permission to leave Russia. Gordievsky was finally reunited with his wife and daughters Maria and Anna, who were by now teenagers, in September 1991. It was more than six years since he had last seen them at the sanatorium outside Moscow. However, the marriage did not survive the long separation or the hurt Leila understandably felt that for decades her husband had deceived her by never telling her of his work for the British. Two years after their reunion they were divorced.

In November 1985, a Soviet military tribunal found Gordievsky guilty of treachery and sentenced him to death in
absentia. The threat of assassination by a visiting Russian
hit squad has hung over his life ever since, particularly in
recent years. The intelligence Gordievsky brought to Britain
and the West is impossible to value but certainly in terms of
security alone was unique and priceless. In 2007 he was made
a Companion of the Order of St Michael and St George (CMG)
for 'services to the security of the United Kingdom'. Some
wits noted that this was the same award as that given to the
fictional James Bond. At the time of writing, Gordievsky still
lives as a guest of the British state in a safe house in the south
of England.

The US intelligence establishment had not come out of the end
of the Cold War well. No one had predicted how quickly events
would unravel or how rapidly the demise of the Soviet Union
would come about. Moreover, the CIA was still in denial about
the events of 1983 and what Robert Gates later came to call
'the most dangerous year'.[12] It was an ultra-top-secret report
from outside the world of intelligence, produced for the Bush
White House in February 1990 from the President's Foreign
Intelligence Advisory Board (PFIAB), that first made clear the
scale of the crisis. It reported, 'We believe that [in 1983] the
Soviets perceived that the correlation of forces had turned
against the USSR, that the US was seeking military superiority, and that the chances of the US launching a nuclear first
strike – perhaps under cover of a routine training exercise –
were growing.' It concluded unequivocally that in November
1983 'we may have inadvertently placed our relations with the
Soviet Union on a hair trigger'.[13]

In the mid-1990s the CIA decided to open its own investigation into whether it really had missed one of the most
frightening moments of the Cold War. Were the Soviets

actually about to launch a nuclear strike against the West? There was still controversy within the CIA over whether this was a real crisis or simply an example of Soviet disinformation. Robert Gates asked, 'To what degree was our skepticism about the war scare prompted by the fact that our military didn't want to admit that one of its exercises might have been dangerously if inadvertently provocative, or because our intelligence experts didn't want to admit that we had badly misread the state of mind of the Soviet leadership?'[14] Ben Fischer had been an analyst and an operations officer in the CIA all his life and was by the mid-nineties acting as CIA historian. He spent a year studying documents related to the events and produced an account in 1996 for the secret in-house journal of the CIA, *Studies in Intelligence*, entitled *A Cold War Conundrum: The 1983 War Scare in US-Soviet Relations*. His essay appears to have been written without access to the PFIAB report, but his conclusions were broadly similar. He decided the scare was real. He built up a picture of Operation RYaN slowly ticking all the boxes within the Soviet intelligence establishment that a US attack was imminent. The PSYOPS that had been going on for some time had 'spooked the Russians'; the aggressive language of the US leadership had outraged and disturbed them; the Star Wars announcement had 'touched a sensitive nerve'; the shooting down of the Korean airliner, the military alert after the Beirut truck bomb, increased communication between London and Washington after the Grenada invasion – all these events brought the Soviet leadership to the brink. And then came Able Archer 83. Fischer concluded that 'RYaN was real', and that while Soviet fears of a US first strike were exaggerated, 'they were scarcely insane'.[15]

Nearly three decades have passed since the end of the Cold War. In the 1990s there was a honeymoon period during which the US offered economic aid to the former states of the

Soviet Union and military advice on winding down, storing and managing its decaying nuclear arsenal that threatened a vast ecological catastrophe if not supervised properly. But this help was accepted reluctantly and only grudgingly. The people of Russia and the other states that had once been part of the USSR were still proud. They might not have the wealth of America (although some Russian oligarchs rivalled American billionaires) but they were aware of having had a long and glorious history. They were not to be pushed around. Vladimir Putin was appointed Prime Minister in 1999 and has been elected President and appointed Prime Minister continuously for nearly twenty years since. He has successfully played on these feelings within Russia, and the people's apparent love of a strong leader.

Putin grew up in Leningrad (St Petersburg) in the 1950s and 1960s. In 1975, after leaving university, he joined the KGB, then under Yuri Andropov. He was a junior officer in counter-intelligence before moving on to the First Chief Directorate under Kryuchkov. At the end of the Cold War he was based in East Germany and helped to burn KGB files after the fall of the Berlin Wall to prevent them falling into the hands of hostile demonstrators. He resigned having reached the rank of lieutenant-colonel in 1991 but retains some of the paranoia and suspicion about foreign influences that he picked up during his formative KGB years. In this sense there is a direct link between the Soviet Union of Andropov and Kryuchkov and the Russia of Vladimir Putin. During the first two decades of this century he has grown the economy and rebuilt Russian influence in areas where it had long disappeared, most notably in the Middle East. After a short war with Georgia in 2008, Russia modernised and upgraded its military resources. In 2014, Putin seized the Crimea from Ukraine in an act that was widely denounced as illegal.

Western powers have seen this as a trend backwards

towards a Soviet-style aggressive state and have responded with economic sanctions and expressions of outrage about corruption and the abuse of human rights. Fears have grown about Russia's ability to conduct a form of hybrid warfare using cyber attacks against Western systems and deploying fake news against its enemies. This came to a head in the US presidential election in 2016 when accusations were made that Russia had tried to rig the election against Hillary Clinton and in favour of Donald Trump, just as in 1984 there were allegations of Soviet meddling in Reagan's mid-term election.

Russia can still bring hard military power to bear, and not only in conflicts with its neighbours. NATO grew anxious in September 2017 when a military exercise called Zapad 17 seemed to threaten the Baltic states. The exercise was the largest military mobilisation since the 1980s and involved troops, artillery, tanks and fighter jets from Russia and Belarus. Weapons were fired alarmingly close to Russia's border with the European Union.[16] NATO sent small-scale reinforcements to Poland and the Baltic to reassure these governments of Western support. The US moved 600 paratroopers to the Baltic as a demonstration of its resolve. If Able Archer 83 had once been provocative, Russian military exercises like Zapad 17 have taken its place in recent years.

But all this is still a far cry from the economic, political, ideological and military divide of the Cold War years. Russia is again a powerful nation, politically and militarily, but it cannot rival the one superpower, the United States. The US still runs the world's biggest economy and in 2015 spent $600 billion on its annual defence budget (more than the next eleven highest-spending nations combined).[17] What America has lost in recent years is the will to play the superpower role. The military incursions of President George W. Bush in Afghanistan and Iraq proved enormously divisive at home and internationally. They culminated in political failure despite military success. Many of the weapons developed and showcased in the 1980s to threaten the Soviet Union had their baptism of fire in the deserts of the Middle East, providing the 'shock and awe' sought by Bush. Under President Obama there was a reaction against the military operations of his predecessor. Maybe President Trump's mission to 'Make America Great Again' will lead to a US revival of strength similar to that under Reagan thirty-five years ago. But it seems unlikely that Trump can provide the leadership to guide the Western world in the way Reagan did.

Elsewhere, although the number of nuclear warheads has reduced as a consequence of further disarmament talks, the number of nuclear powers has increased dramatically. As well as the US, Russia, China, Britain and France during the Cold War, Pakistan and India also admit to having nuclear arsenals, and Israel is known to possess nuclear weapons, as are some of the former Soviet states. Several other countries have toyed with developing a nuclear capability, including Egypt and Saudi Arabia. Many states have the technology to build nuclear power plants, and it is not impossible to transfer this know-how into the production of weapons. Many nations resent the idea that only a few 'top dog' states are reliable, honest and transparent enough to possess nuclear weapons. Military strategists have pointed out that only one country has ever dropped nuclear bombs and that is the United States, to end its war with Japan. Very few countries, once they have started, have turned their back on developing nuclear weapons, although Iran might be one.

The latest member of the nuclear club is North Korea. Its strangely remote and unpredictable leadership terrifies its neighbours and provokes the late-night ire of the tweeting President Trump. All this heightens the possibility of a limited nuclear war breaking out somewhere on the planet. The trouble if or when this happens is that not only will millions lose their lives, but it might also prove impossible to prevent the dispute from escalating. The world of Mutual Assured Destruction did in its mad way maintain the peace between the superpowers, although it came desperately close to failing in a series of errors, false alarms and miscalculations, most spectacularly in 1962 and in 1983. The world was lucky to have survived. Very lucky.

Was the 1983 war scare the most dangerous moment in Cold War history? The Cuban missile crisis of October 1962 was very publicly played out, at least in the West. It usually holds the accolade as the most perilous episode of the Cold War. By contrast, the Able Archer 83 incident was not reported at the time and is not well known outside specialist circles. But it too could lay claim to being the most dangerous few days of the Cold War period.[18]

All sides had reason to be embarrassed by the events of November 1983. The Soviets nearly launched a nuclear war as a consequence of their paranoia and miscalculation. NATO played out a highly provocative war game without realising that it nearly sparked a devastating nuclear exchange. The Americans missed completely, or at the very least underestimated, one of the most alarming chapters of the Cold War. With the revelations of the last couple of years we are only now coming to realise how close those events of 1983 came to provoking World War Three. Ben Fischer has described this war scare as 'the last paroxysm of the Cold War'. The man who learned many of its lessons and, along with President Reagan, was determined that it should never be repeated was Mikhail Gorbachev. He summed it up neatly in early 1986, 'Never, perhaps, in the post-war decades was the situation in the world as explosive and hence more difficult and unfavourable as in the first half of the 1980s.'[19]

After several decades of political, economic, ideological and military confrontation, the Cold War ended peacefully. The events of 1983 show that it might not have been that way.

Acknowledgements

I first came across the November 1983 war scare when researching and writing the book to accompany the Ted Turner/CNN/Jeremy Isaacs twenty-four-part television series *Cold War* in 1996–7. Very little was known about the story then. And many historians were sceptical that there was much of a war scare. The series did not have time to cover the story and the book contains only a passing reference to it.[1]

But the incident stuck with me. The idea that the world nearly came to an abrupt end on 9 November 1983 astonished me. I looked up in my business diary what I'd been doing that day. Little did I know then what a dangerous moment we were all living through. I kept going back to the events and trying to find out more. In the early 2000s a little more information crept out. When President Clinton left office, as happens with most Presidents on their departure from the White House, his administration declassified a large bunch of documents, and included in them was the essay *The 1983 War Scare: A Cold War Conundrum* by in-house CIA historian Ben Fischer, investigating the episode to discover how close to World War Three we had really come. I only later found out it was a modified version of a report he had written for the classified CIA journal *Studies in Intelligence*. Every time I visited Washington I met with Ben, who had just retired, luckily for me as he felt more able to talk. I remember that when we met he always sat with his back to the wall, usually in a corner with a full view of everyone in the café, bar or restaurant. I learned a lot during these discussions, and not just about how ex-spies locate themselves in a public space. There was much that he could not tell me. But plenty that he could.

Eventually I put a proposal together for a documentary feature on the subject through the production company of which I was managing director, Flashback Television. Discovery US showed a lot of interest in the subject from the start; Channel 4 in the UK eventually came on board as well. Backed by these two broadcasters, after a year or so of negotiations we finally raised a reasonable budget. Henry Chancellor joined as producer-director and did a superb job, making a truly gripping ninety-minute drama-documentary feature. The Channel 4 version was called *1983 – The Brink of Apocalypse*; the Discovery version was called *The Soviet War Scare, 1983*. In the UK, the film won a highly prestigious Grierson Award for Best Historical Documentary of 2008.[2]

Usually when starting work on a documentary like this you look around and find the best historians who have written about the subject and ask them to become advisers. They will direct you to the key sources and perhaps some of the most interesting participants to interview. On the *Cold War* series in the mid-1990s a distinguished team of scholars from the US, the UK and Russia gave invaluable advice, viewed the cuts of each episode and checked every word of commentary.[3] But when Henry and I started pre-production in 2007 and were looking for historical advisers we could find no one. Many specialists were unsure about what had taken place and how serious it had been. Most historians said to us, 'If you find out what really happened, please come back and tell us!' We felt it was still a blank canvas and that (to mix metaphors) we were writing a first draft of history. NATO was still a little embarrassed by the events. The CIA felt they would be accused of missing one of the most dangerous moments in the Cold War. And Russian military and intelligence officials did not want to admit how scared they had become.

But a reasonable production budget allows for proper research. A good team came on board who had the time to dig deep. Eventually we were able to interview a range of top American generals and intelligence officials. And we had a big break when we interviewed Robert Gates. He had been deputy head of the CIA at the time (Bill Casey, the director, had died in 1987). We couldn't afford to go to Texas where Gates was president of the Texas A&M University and had a very full schedule, but we found out that he was in Washington while we were there filming. He agreed to do an interview. He was very relaxed and gave us a gripping couple of hours of material and a real insight into the strengths and weaknesses of the intelligence establishment. Within days we heard in the news that President George W. Bush had appointed him Secretary of Defense. That was why he had been in Washington. A couple of days later and he would never have had the time to spend with the likes of us.

Also, we had a good team in Moscow led by the Dutch investigative journalist Margreet ter Woerds. In addition to several senior military and intelligence officials from 1983, she was able to track down many of the military men who had gone on to combat alert in early November. No one had ever found and interviewed people like this, those who had had their fingers very literally on the nuclear buttons. Their memories were good. They all recalled without difficulty the terrifying time when they went on to maximum nuclear alert. Their testimony is unique.

It was a big team that worked on the documentary, too many to list here, but in addition to Henry and Margreet I would like to thank for their contributions Jeff Baynes, Steve

Bergson, Cherry Brewer, Richard Bright, John Hughes-Wilson, Ian MacPherson, Maurice O'Brien, Sam Organ, Svetlana Palmer, Owen Parker and Ben Taylor.

There the story might have rested for me had it not been for the tenacious interest in the subject of the war scare of the National Security Archive in Washington. The NSA is a remarkable organisation. Located within George Washington University in the capital, the archive adheres to impeccable academic standards. But it is devoted to making official papers from around the world during the latter part of the twentieth century available to scholars. Their métier is to use the Freedom of Information Act to crowbar out of an often reluctant bureaucracy key and revealing historical documents. I had the privilege of working with Tom Blanton and William Burr at the NSA during the making of the *Cold War* series and the writing of the book. In those days they worked alongside the Cold War International History Project with Jim Hirshberg and Vlad Zubok, who regularly produced giant bulletins, each one as big and as thick as an old-fashioned telephone directory, packed with documents and translations of documents. They brought into the public domain top secret reports, internal memoranda, and transcripts of meetings, conversations and telephone calls that literally rewrote the established history of the Cold War.

In recent years, Nate Jones has driven the assault on finding out more about the events of 1983 and the November war scare. His work has been extraordinary. In the last couple of years he has pried loose from secret files around the world more than a thousand pages of documents relating to Operation RYaN, Able Archer 83 and the background to the events of that year. These include Freedom of Information Act releases by the CIA, the National Security Agency, the Defense Department and the State Department, as well as research findings from other American and British archives, previously declassified

Soviet Politburo and KGB files, and records from other communist eastern European states and from NATO. Not only do the NSA doggedly track down such material, but they are utterly committed to making it all available.[4] Nate Jones and the others at the NSA are scholars in their own right but also archivists dedicated to making as much material as possible accessible to the maximum number of people. Everyone who studies and researches the Cold War owes them a great debt of gratitude.

The jewel in the crown of recently revealed evidence on the November war scare is the ultra-top-secret report produced for the Bush White House in February 1990, from the President's Foreign Intelligence Advisory Board (PFIAB) chaired by Anne Armstrong, and written by Nina Stewart. The board studied hundreds of top secret intelligence documents and interviewed seventy-five officials from the US and Britain. The ninety-four-page typed report stated, 'There is little doubt in our minds that the Soviets were genuinely worried by Able Archer', and it established that Soviet fears were 'real' not exaggerated. Moreover, the 'US intelligence community did not at the time, and for several years afterwards, attach sufficient weight to the possibility that the war scare was real'. As a consequence 'the President was given assessments of Soviet attitudes and actions that understated the risks to the United States'. In other words, the President was not given a realistic account of how near the Soviet Union came to launching a nuclear attack on the US. By underplaying the Soviet fears, the US intelligence community made the 'especially grave error [of assuming] that since we know the US is not going to start World War Three', the leaders of the Kremlin would also believe that.[5] The PFIAB report was thorough in its investigation and powerful in its conclusions. It should have clearly troubled those charged with advising the President on matters of national security. The problem was that the report was available only to a tiny select group, a few Washington insiders who had the highest possible security clearance.[6] The NSA only heard about the existence of the PFIAB report thirteen years after it was presented. It then took twelve years of fighting to get the report declassified, which finally happened in October 2015.

I'm grateful to many others who have given their time and with whom I have enjoyed discussions on the war scare and related matters over many years. I would especially like to include Sir Jeremy Isaacs, Professor Lawrence Freedman, Professor Jeremy Black and Henry Chancellor. Svetlana Palmer helped (again) with Russian translations.

At Little, Brown I have been lucky to work with an excellent and very professional team including Nithya Rae as editor, Linda Silverman who found the photographs, and Daniel Balado as copy-editor. Richard Beswick led the team and has been a great editor to work for.

And, as always, my final thanks are to Anne who helped to keep me sane while studying the MAD world of 1983.

Bibliography

Collections of Documents/Official Reports

The Committee for the Compilation of Materials on Damage Caused by the Atomic Bombs in Hiroshima and Nagasaki (tr. Eisei Ishikawa and David Swain), *Hiroshima and Nagasaki: The Physical, Medical, and Social Effects of the Atomic Bombings*. London: Hutchinson, 1981.

Fischer, Ben, *A Cold War Conundrum: The 1983 War Scare in US Soviet Relations*. Langley, Virginia: CIA, 1996.

Hines, John G., *Soviet Intentions 1965-1985: Volume II, Soviet Post-Cold War Testimonial Evidence*. Washington: BDM Federal, INC. for the Office of the Secretary of Defense Net Assessment, 1995. Unclassified with portions 'retroactively' classified. See: NSA.

International Civil Aviation Organisation (ICAO), *Final Report of Investigation as Required by Council Resolution of 16 September 1983* on the shooting down of flight KAL 007; published by the ICAO as C-WP 7809, Montreal, 1984.

International Commission to enquire into reported violations of International Law by Israel during its invasion of the Lebanon [in 1982], Chair Sean MacBride, *Israel in Lebanon*. London: Ithaca Press, 1983.

Johnson, Thomas R., *American Cryptology during the Cold War*. National Security Agency, 1999.

Primary Accounts, including Memoirs, Diaries, Recollections

Anderson, Martin, *Revolution: The Reagan Legacy*. New York: Harcourt Brace Jovanovich, 1988.

Andrew, Christopher and Oleg Gordievsky, *KGB: The Inside Story of its Foreign Operations from Lenin to Gorbachev*. London: Hodder & Stoughton, 1990.

Andrew, Christopher and Vasili Mitrokhin, *The Mitrokhin Archive: The KGB in Europe and the West*. London: Allen Lane, 1999.

Chernyaev, Anatoly (tr. and ed. Robert D. English and Elizabeth Tucker), *My Six Years with Gorbachev*. Pennsylvania: Pennsylvania State University Press, 2000. Translation of Russian original *Shest' let s Gorbachevym: po dnevnikovym zapisiam*, published in Moscow in 1993.

Combs, Dick, *Inside the Soviet Alternate Universe: The Cold War's End and the Soviet Union's Fall Reappraised*. Philadelphia: University of Pennsylvania Press, 2008.

Dobrynin, Anatoly, *In Confidence: Moscow's Ambassador to America's Six Cold War Presidents*. New York: Times Books, 1995.

Fisk, Robert, *Pity the Nation: Lebanon at War*. Oxford: Oxford University Press, 2001.

Gates, Robert M., *From the Shadows: The Ultimate Insider's Story of Five Presidents and How They Won the Cold War*. New York: Simon & Schuster, 1996.

Gorbachev, Mikhail, *Memoirs*. London: Doubleday, 1996.

Gordievsky, Oleg, *Next Stop Execution: Autobiography*. London: Macmillan, 1995.

Hachiya, Michihiko (tr. Warner Wells), *Hiroshima Diary: the journal of a Japanese Physician August 6 – September 30, 1945*. London: Victor Gollancz, 1955.

Haig, Alexander, *Caveat: Realism, Reagan, and Foreign Policy*. New York: Scribner, 1984.

Heseltine, Michael, *Life in the Jungle: My Autobiography*. London: Hodder & Stoughton, 2000.

Howe, Geoffrey, *Conflict of Loyalty*. London: Macmillan, 1994.

Matlock, Jack F., *Reagan and Gorbachev: How the Cold War Ended*. New York: Random House, 2004.

Morris, Edmund, *Dutch: A Memoir of Ronald Reagan*. London: HarperCollins, 2000.

Reagan, Ronald, *An American Life*. New York: Simon & Schuster, 1990.

—— (ed. Douglas Brinkley), *The Reagan Diaries*. New York: HarperCollins, 2007.

—— with Richard G. Hubler, *Where's the Rest of Me?* New York: Duell, Sloan and Pearce, 1965.

Reed, Thomas C., *At the Abyss: An Insider's History of the Cold War*. New York: Random House, 2004.

Shultz, George, *Turmoil and Triumph: Diplomacy, Power and the Victory of the American Ideal*. New York: Charles Scribner's Sons, 1993.

Snow, Jon, *Shooting History: A Personal Journey*. London: HarperCollins, 2004.

Speakes, Larry, *Speaking Out: The Reagan Presidency from Inside the White House*. New York: Charles Scribner's Sons, 1988.

Teller, Edward with Judith Shoolery, *Memoirs: A Twentieth Century Journey in Science and Politics*. Oxford: Perseus Press, 2001.

Thatcher, Margaret, *The Downing Street Years*. London: HarperCollins, 1993.

Wolf, Markus with Anne McElvoy, *Man Without a Face: The Autobiography of Communism's Greatest Spymaster*. London: Jonathan Cape, 1997.

Secondary Accounts

Aldous, Richard, *Reagan and Thatcher: The Difficult Relationship*. London: Hutchinson, 2012.

Beschloss, Michael, *Kennedy Versus Khrushchev: The Crisis Years, 1960–1963*. London: Faber & Faber, 1991.

Black, Jeremy, *The World of James Bond: The Lives and Times of 007*. London: Rowman & Littlefield, 2017.

Braithwaite, Rodric, *Afgantsy: The Russians in Afghanistan, 1979–89*. London: Profile Books, 2011.

—— *Armageddon and Paranoia: The Nuclear Confrontation*. London: Profile, 2017.

Cannon, Lou, *Reagan*. New York: Puttnam, 1982.

—— *President Reagan: The Role of a Lifetime*. New York: Simon & Schuster, 1991.

Dannatt, Richard, *Boots on the Ground: Britain and Her Army Since 1945*. London: Profile, 2016.

Dobbs, Michael, *One Minute to Midnight: Kennedy, Khrushchev and Castro on the Brink of Nuclear War*. New York: Alfred A. Knopf, 2008.

Fisher, Beth, *The Reagan Reversal: Foreign Policy and the End of the Cold War*. Columbia: University of Missouri Press, 2000.

Fitzgerald, Frances, *Way Out There in the Blue: Reagan, Star Wars and the End of the Cold War*. New York: Simon & Schuster, 2000.

Freedman, Lawrence, *The Evolution of Nuclear Strategy*. London: Macmillan, 1981.

—— *The Cold War: A Military History*. London: Cassell & Co, 2001.

Fursenko, Alexandr and Timothy Naftali, *'One Hell of a Gamble': Khrushchev, Castro and Kennedy 1958–1964*. New York: Norton, 1997.

Gaddis, John Lewis, *The Cold War*. London: Allen Lane, 2005.

—— *Strategies of Containment: A Critical Appraisal of American National Security Policy During the Cold War*. Oxford: Oxford University Press, 2005, revised and updated edition.

Garthoff, Raymond, *The Great Transition: American-Soviet Relations and the End of the Cold War*. Washington: The Brookings Institution, 1994.

Hersh, Seymour M., *The Target is Destroyed: What Really Happened to Flight 007 and What America Knew About It.* New York: Vintage Books, 1987.

Hoffman, David E., *The Dead Hand: Reagan, Gorbachev and the Untold Story of the Cold War Arms Race.* New York: Doubleday, 2009.

—— *The Billion Dollar Spy: A True Story of Cold War Espionage and Betrayal.* New York: Doubleday, 2015.

Holloway, David, *Stalin and the Bomb.* Yale: Yale University Press, 1994.

Isaacs, Jeremy and Taylor Downing, *Cold War: For Forty-Five Years the World Held its Breath.* London: Abacus, 2008; originally published by Bantam Press, 1998.

Johnson, R. W., *Shootdown: The Verdict on KAL 007.* London: Chatto & Windus, 1986.

Jones, Nate, *Able Archer 83.* New York: The New Press, 2016.

Kahn, Herman, *On Thermonuclear War.* Princeton: Princeton University Press, 1960.

Maydew, Randall C. and Julie Bush, *America's Lost H-Bomb: Palomares, Spain, 1966.* Manhattan, Kansas: Sunflower University Press, 1997.

Medved, Harry and Randy Dreyfuss, *The Fifty Worst Films of All Time (And How They Got That Way).* New York: Warner, 1978.

Miller, David, *Olympic Revolution: The Biography of Juan Antonio Samaranch.* London: Pavilion, 1992.

Miller, David, *The Cold War: A Military History.* London: John Murray, 1998.

Morgan, Iwan, *Reagan: American Icon.* London: I. B. Tauris, 2016.

Oberdorfer, Don, *From the Cold War to a New Era: The United States and the Soviet Union, 1983-1991.* Baltimore: Johns Hopkins University Press, 1998; originally published as *The Turn* in 1991.

Pry, Peter, *War Scare: Russia on the Nuclear Brink.* Westport: Praeger, 1999.

Remnick, David, *Lenin's Tomb: The Last Days of the Soviet Empire*. London: Random House, 1993.

Rhodes, Richard, *The Making of the Atomic Bomb*. New York: Simon & Schuster, 1986.

Sagan, Scott D., *The Limits of Safety: Organizations, Accidents and Nuclear Weapons*. Princeton: Princeton University Press, 1993.

Service, Robert, *The End of the Cold War: 1985-1991*. London: Macmillan, 2015.

Steele, Jonathan and Eric Abraham, *Andropov in Power: From Komsomol to Kremlin*. Oxford: Martin Robertson, 1983.

Stokes, Gale, *The Walls Came Tumbling Down: The Collapse of Communism in Eastern Europe*. Oxford: Oxford University Press, 1993.

Thompson, Robert Smith, *The Missiles of October: The Declassified Story of John F. Kennedy and the Cuban Missile Crisis*. New York: Simon & Schuster, 1992.

Volkogonov, Dmitri, *The Rise and Fall of the Soviet Empire: Political Leaders from Lenin to Gorbachev*. London: HarperCollins, 1998.

Voslensky, Michael (tr. E. Mosbacher), *Nomenklatura*. London: The Bodley Head, 1990.

Wise, David, *Spy: The Inside Story of How the FBI's Robert Hanssen Betrayed America*. New York: Random House, 2002.

Zubok, Vladislav, *A Failed Empire: The Soviet Union in the Cold War from Stalin to Gorbachev*. Chapel Hill: University of North Carolina Press, 2009.

Key Sources

NSA   The National Security Archive is a non-governmental research and archive organisation located at George Washington University, Washington DC. The NSA publishes vast numbers of documents in series of Workbooks, many of which are available online. See: www.nsarchive.gwu.edu

REAGAN   The Public Papers of Ronald Reagan are held in the Ronald Reagan Presidential Library. All his speeches can be found online in date order. See: www.reaganlibrary.archives.gov/archives/speeches

CARTER   The key speeches of Jimmy Carter are available online at the American Presidency Project at the University of California. See: www.presidency.ucsb.edu/

BUSH   The key speeches of George H. W. Bush are available online at the American Presidency Project at the University of California. See: www.presidency.ucsb.edu/

THATCHER   The Margaret Thatcher Foundation in the
           Thatcher Archive at Churchill College, Cam-
           bridge, lists thousands of speeches online. See:
           www.margaretthatcher.org

CIA   The Central Intelligence Agency based in Langley,
           Virginia, now makes some of its own studies and
           historical reports available online. See: www.cia.
           gov/library/center-for-the-study-of-intelligence/
           csi-publications

FLASHBACK Interviews conducted during the course of 2007
           by Flashback Television with participants –
           including leading Soviet, American, British
           and German players – in the events of 1983 for
           the television documentary *1983 – The Brink
           of Apocalypse* (in the US: *The Soviet War Scare,
           1983*) (producer-director Henry Chancellor;
           executive producers Taylor Downing and
           Sam Organ). Copies of the transcripts of the
           interviews are held at the NSA in Washington
           and at the Basil Liddell Hart Military Archives
           in the War Studies Department of King's
           College, London.

Notes

Prologue

1   Michihiko Hachiya, *Hiroshima Diary*, p.13.
2   Quoted in Richard Rhodes, *The Making of the Atomic Bomb*, p.714.
3   *Hiroshima and Nagasaki: The Physical, Medical, and Social Effects of the Atomic Bombings*, pp. 363–84.
4   Hachiya, *Hiroshima Diary*, p.21.
5   *Hiroshima and Nagasaki: The Physical, Medical, and Social Effects of the Atomic Bombings*, p.340.
6   An excellent account of the development of the Soviet bomb is David Holloway, *Stalin and the Bomb*. He concludes that the intelligence supplied by science spies like Klaus Fuchs, the German-born British physicist who had been part of the Manhattan Project, was useful to the Soviets but probably only brought things forward by a few months. The development of Soviet atomic technology was primarily limited by the ability to mine and process uranium ore. Overall he argues the speed of the development of the Soviet atom bomb was remarkable.
7   The nuclear strategist was Herman Kahn in *On Thermonuclear War*.
8   Lawrence Freedman, *The Evolution of Nuclear Strategy*, p.235.
9   Jeremy Isaacs and Taylor Downing, *Cold War*, pp.161–83.
10   It was this scenario that Stanley Kubrick satirised in his black comedy movie *Dr Strangelove, Or: How I Learned to Stop Worrying and Love the Bomb* (1964) in which an American air base commander goes berserk and issues the go-codes for his B-52s to launch a nuclear attack on the Soviet Union. By the time the film came out this possibility had been closed off, allowing the US Air Force to claim that events depicted in the film could never happen.
11   Excellent accounts of the Cuban missile crisis can be found in Michael Dobbs, *One Minute to Midnight*; Michael Beschloss, *Kennedy Versus Khrushchev*; Robert Smith Thompson, *The Missiles of October*; and from the Soviet side Aleksandr Fursenko and Timothy Naftali, *'One Hell of a Gamble'*.

12 Freedman, *The Evolution of Nuclear Strategy*, p.245ff.
13 Ronald Reagan, *An American Life*, p.257 & p.13.
14 See the Acknowledgements for a more detailed outline of the making of the television documentary and the work of the National Security Archive.
15 *Octopussy*, directed by John Glen, produced by Albert Broccoli, written by George MacDonald Fraser, Michael G. Wilson and Richard Maibaum, and starring Roger Moore and Maud Adams with Steven Berkoff as General Orlov; see Jeremy Black, *The World of James Bond*.

1 Reagan

1   REAGAN: Inauguration Address, 20 January 1981; and see Edmund Morris, *Dutch: A Memoir of Ronald Reagan*, pp.410–12.
2   The films were *Knute Rockne, All American* (1940), in which he played a football player, George Gipp, who died of pneumonia, and which gave him one of his most famous lines – 'Win one for the Gipper'; *Santa Fe Trail* (1940); and *Kings Row* (1942), during which, after awaking from an operation in which both his legs had been amputated by a sadistic doctor, he screamed the famous question 'Where's the rest of me?' All three films were genuine A-movies.
3   Ronald Reagan and Richard Hubler, *Where's the Rest of Me?*, p.162; and Frances Fitzgerald, *Way Out There in the Blue*, p.50.
4   Reagan, *An American Life*, p.110.
5   Iwan Morgan, *Reagan: American Icon*, pp.51–4.
6   The film was *Johnny Belinda* and she won the Best Actress Oscar in 1949.
7   The film was *That Hagen Girl* (1947), a vehicle for the transition of child star Shirley Temple into an adult actress. Despite Reagan's own concerns, Jack Warner insisted he play the part of the man who was Temple's love interest although he was twice her age. See Harry Medved and Randy Dreyfuss, *The Fifty Worst Films of All Time*.
8   The film was *Bedtime for Bonzo* (1951).
9   This famous GE slogan was actually the pay-off line from the introduction to *General Electric Theater* hosted by Reagan: 'In engineering, in research, in manufacturing skill, in the values that bring a better, more satisfying life, at General Electric, progress is our most important product.' See: http://adage.com/article/adage-encyclopedia/general-electric/98667/
10 Morgan, *Reagan*, pp.64–5.
11 Reagan and Hubler, *Where's the Rest of Me?*, pp.257–65; and Morgan, *Reagan*, p.65.
12 Lou Cannon, *Reagan*, p.20.
13 This statement was made repeatedly on the campaign trail; see Morgan, *Reagan*, p.90.
14 The quote is from Lyn Nofziger, his director of communications, and is quoted in Fitzgerald, *Way Out There in the Blue*, p.64.
15 Morgan, *Reagan*, p.99ff.

16 The quotations are from the Committee on the Present Danger pamphlet *Alerting America*, quoted in Fitzgerald, *Way Out There in the Blue*, pp.87–8.

17 Fitzgerald, *Way Out There in the Blue*, p.109ff.

18 Robert Gates, *From the Shadows*, p.191.

19 Larry Speakes, *Speaking Out*, p.68.

20 Thomas Reed, *At the Abyss*, p.259.

21 Until January 2017: Donald Trump was already seventy at the time of his inauguration.

2 Andropov

1   Dmitri Volkogonov, *The Rise and Fall of the Soviet Empire*, p.329.

2   Some have argued that Mao Zedong should hold the dubious distinction of being the greatest mass murderer of the twentieth century because of the starvation and deaths that followed his economic reforms.

3   From the *International Herald Tribune*, 18 November 1982, quoted in Jonathan Steele and Eric Abraham, *Andropov in Power*, p.2.

4   Ibid., p.3.

5   Isaacs and Downing, *Cold War*, p.25.

6   Christopher Andrew and Oleg Gordievsky, *KGB: The Inside Story*, p.355.

7   For a fuller account of events in Poland and Hungary in 1956 see Isaacs and Downing, *Cold War*, pp.140–60.

8   Christopher Andrew and Vasili Mitrokhin, *The Mitrokhin Archive*, p.7.

9   Volkogonov, *The Rise and Fall of the Soviet Empire*, p.336.

10 Ibid., p.337.

11 Mikhail Gorbachev, *Memoirs*, p.11.

12 Volkogonov, *The Rise and Fall of the Soviet Empire*, p.343.

3 Reagan Rearms

1   Fitzgerald, *Way Out There in the Blue*, p.159ff; and John Lewis Gaddis, *Strategies of Containment*, pp.393–4.

2   *Washington Post*, 23 January 1981.

3   Raymond Garthoff, *The Great Transition*, p.33ff.

4   David Miller, *The Cold War: A Military History*, p.196ff.

5   NSA: Thomas R. Johnson, *American Cryptology during the Cold War, 1945–89: Book IV, Cryptologic Rebirth 1981–89*, National Security Agency, 1999, Top Secret, p.271ff.

6   Lawrence Freedman, *The Cold War*, p.190ff.

7   Garthoff, *The Great Transition*, p.35.

8   NSA: *Reagan's Nuclear War Briefing Declassified*; and Reed, *At the Abyss*, p.242.

9   Reagan, *An American Life*, p.258.

10 Speakes, *Speaking Out*, p.8.

11   There was some confusion over exactly what Weinberger had done, as he had put SAC on a higher alert but had not increased the DEFCON standing of the military as a whole; see Fitzgerald, *Way Out There in the Blue*, pp.170 & 515.

12   Reagan, *An American Life*, p.269.

13   Ronald Reagan, *The Reagan Diaries*, pp.14–15.

14   Reagan, *An American Life*, pp.272–3.

15   NSA: *Reagan's Nuclear War Briefing Declassified*, Briefing Book no. 575: Documents 12 & 13.

16   Reed, *At the Abyss*, p.243.

17   Ibid., p.244.

18   Ibid., p.244.

19   NSA: *Reagan's Nuclear War Briefing Declassified*, Briefing Book no. 575: Documents 15, 16 & 17.

20   Reagan, *An American Life*, p.13.

21   Ibid., p.550.

22   Ibid., p.257.

23   REAGAN: Address at Commencement Exercises at Eureka College, Illinois, 9 May 1982.

24   Anatoly Dobrynin, *In Confidence*, p.502.

25   Reagan, *The Reagan Diaries*, p.75.

26   Nate Jones, *Able Archer 83*, p.9.

27   REAGAN: Address to Members of the British Parliament, 8 June 1982.

28   REAGAN: Remarks at the Annual Convention of the National Association of Evangelicals in Orlando, Florida, 8 March 1983.

29   Reagan, *An American Life*, p.570.

4 Operation RYaN

1   The story was later told by General Adrian Danilevich to American Defense officials after the Cold War; see NSA: John G. Hines, *Soviet Intentions 1965–1985: Volume II, Soviet Post-Cold War Testimonial Evidence*, p.27.

2   See Michael Voslensky, *Nomenklatura*.

3   Dick Combs, *Inside the Soviet Alternate Universe*, p.70.

4   The interview with Marshal Ogarkov was by Leslie Gelb in the *New York Times* and is quoted in CIA: Ben Fischer, *A Cold War Conundrum*, p.12.

5   FLASHBACK: Interview with Oleg Kalugin.

6   Andrew and Gordievsky, *KGB: The Inside Story*, p.445.

7   Ibid., p.448.

8   CARTER: The State of the Union Address Delivered Before a Joint Session of the Congress, 23 January 1980.

9   Rodric Braithwaite, *Afgantsy*, p.263ff.

10   Andrew and Gordievsky, *KGB: The Inside Story*, p.482.

11   REAGAN: The President's News Conference, 29 January 1981.

12   Dobrynin, *In Confidence*, p.486.

13 NSA: Hines, *Soviet Intentions 1965–1985*; interview by Vitalii Kataev with American Defense officials after the Cold War.

14 Gaddis, *The Cold War*, p.212.

15 NSA: The President's Foreign Intelligence Advisory Board (PFIAB), *The Soviet 'War Scare'*, Top Secret, p.53.

16 Gates, *From the Shadows*, p.259.

17 Andrew and Gordievsky, *KGB: The Inside Story*, p.488.

18 Jones, *Able Archer 83*, p.14.

19 Andrew and Gordievsky, *KGB: The Inside Story*, pp.488–9.

20 NSA: KGB Chairman Yuri Andropov to General Secretary Leonid Brezhnev, *Report on the Work of the KGB in 1981*, 10 May 1982.

21 NSA: Deputy Minister Markus Wolf, *Stasi Note on Meeting with KGB Experts in the RYAN Problem*, 14–18 August 1984.

22 FLASHBACK: Interview with Oleg Gordievsky.

23 Andrew and Gordievsky, *KGB: The Inside Story*, p.489. In the event this might not have been so absurd. It was said in January 1991 that the launch of the Gulf War could have been predicted by noting the increase in the number of evening pizza deliveries to the Pentagon in the run-up to war; see Jones, *Able Archer 83*, p.309.

24 FLASHBACK: Interview with Oleg Gordievsky.

25 FLASHBACK: Interview with Oleg Kalugin.

26 Jones, *Able Archer 83*, pp.19–20.

27 Markus Wolf, *Man Without a Face*, p.222.

28 NSA: PFIAB, *The Soviet 'War Scare'*, Top Secret, p.52.

29 Dobrynin, *In Confidence*, p.512.

30 Volkogonov, *The Rise and Fall of the Soviet Empire*, pp.346–9.

31 NSA: Top Secret Memorandum from Moscow Centre to London Resident, *Permanent operational assignment to uncover NATO preparations for a nuclear missile attack on the USSR*, 17 February 1983.

32 Morgan, *Reagan*, p.215.

5 Star Wars

1 The account of Reagan's visit to NORAD comes from Martin Anderson, *Revolution*, pp.80–3.

2 Anderson, *Revolution*, pp.83–8; and David Hoffman, *The Dead Hand*, p.29.

3 Gaddis, *The Cold War*, p.196.

4 See Chapter 3 and Reagan, *An American Life*, pp.13 & 547.

5 Anderson, *Revolution*, p.88; and Hoffman, *The Dead Hand*, p.31.

6 Alexander Haig, *Caveat: Realism, Reagan, and Foreign Policy*, p.105.

7 Reagan, *An American Life*, pp.550–1.

8 Morgan, *Reagan*, p.213.

9 Michael Heseltine, *Life in the Jungle*, pp.244–53; the quote is on p.253.

10 Fitzgerald, *Way Out There in the Blue*, pp.180–91.

11 Reed, *At the Abyss*, pp.244–5.

12 Hoffman, *The Dead Hand*, pp.49–50. In his memoirs Teller describes being disappointed at the meeting as he felt he had not been able to

get his message across to Reagan, of whom he was a great admirer: see Edward Teller, *Memoirs*, p.530.

13 Reagan, *The Reagan Diaries*, p.100.

14 Anderson, *Revolution*, p.97; and Hoffman, *The Dead Hand*, p.50.

15 Lou Cannon, *President Reagan*, pp.329–30; Hoffman, *The Dead Hand*, p.52; and Fitzgerald, *Way Out There in the Blue*, p.197. There are slightly different accounts of this meeting by those present but the gist is exactly the same, that the Joint Chiefs of Staff were keen to find a way around the MX impasse and eagerly put forward the defence initiative, that McFarlane took this up with enthusiasm, and that Watkins used the final phrase about 'protecting' rather than 'avenging' the American people.

16 Reagan, *The Reagan Diaries*, p.130.

17 Cannon, *President Reagan*, pp.330–1.

18 Reagan, *The Reagan Diaries*, p.139.

19 REAGAN: Address to the Nation on Defense and National Security, 23 March 1983.

20 Reagan, *The Reagan Diaries*, p.140.

21 Fitzgerald, *Way Out There in the Blue*, p.210ff; and Morgan, *Reagan*, p.218.

22 Dobrynin, *In Confidence*, p.528.

23 *Pravda*, 27 March 1983, quoted in Isaacs and Downing, *Cold War*, pp.390–1.

6 Lack of Intelligence

1   NSA: *CIA Biographical Profile of Yuriy Vladimirovich Andropov*, 11 January 1983.

2   Gates, *From the Shadows*, p.199.

3   Ibid., pp.203–7.

4   Ibid., p.238.

5   Reagan, *An American Life*, p.551.

6   FLASHBACK: Interview with Robert Gates.

7   Gates, *From the Shadows*, p.259.

8   George Shultz, *Turmoil and Triumph*, p.5.

9   Ibid., p.165.

10 Dobrynin, *In Confidence*, pp.484–5.

11 Reagan, *The Reagan Diaries*, p.131.

12 Dobrynin, *In Confidence*, pp.517–22.

13 Reagan, *An American Life*, p.551.

14 Gates, *From the Shadows*, p.264.

7 Double Agents

1   In line with most of the Soviet bloc intelligence organisations, officers in the KGB held military ranks. Although the KGB was a civilian organisation and officers only rarely (on ceremonial occasions) wore

uniforms, a form of military discipline prevailed in which orders had to be obeyed.

2 Oleg Gordievsky, *Next Stop Execution*, p.244.

3 Ibid., pp.249–52

4 Ibid., p.248.

5 Ibid., pp.170–212.

6 Ibid., pp.253–4.

7 FLASHBACK: Interview with Oleg Gordievsky; and Gordievsky, *Next Stop Execution*, p.263.

8 Andrew and Gordievsky, *KGB: The Inside Story*, p.490.

9 FLASHBACK: Interview with Oleg Gordievsky.

10 Gordievsky, *Next Stop Execution*, pp.261–2.

11 Andrew and Gordievsky, *KGB: The Inside Story*, p.477.

12 The case was given by the KGB's Third Department to Kim Philby, the British double agent, then living in Moscow, to analyse. They would occasionally ask him to review cases where a problem had arisen. After a careful study he concluded that Haavik must have been named by a mole operating within the KGB. He was of course absolutely correct.

13 Gordievsky, *Next Stop Execution*, p.223.

14 Andrew and Gordievsky, *KGB: The Inside Story*, pp.477–8.

15 FLASHBACK: Unless otherwise stated the details about Rainer Rupp are taken from his interview.

16 Wolf, *Man Without a Face*, p.299.

17 Steve Vogel, 'The Spy Who Loved Her', *Washington Post*, 16 November 1994.

18 Wolf, *Man Without a Face*, p.317; and FLASHBACK: Interview with Rainer Rupp.

19 FLASHBACK: Interview with Rainer Rupp.

20 Wolf, *Man Without a Face*, p.300.

21 Ibid., pp.xi & 222.

8 PSYOPS

1 R. W. Johnson, *Shootdown*, p.55.

2 Seymour Hersh, *The Target is Destroyed*, p.25.

3 Ibid., pp.24–5.

4 CIA: Ben Fischer, Intelligence Monograph, *A Cold War Conundrum*, p.8.

5 Ibid., p.7.

6 Ibid., p.7.

7 NSA: Johnson, *American Cryptology during the Cold War*, National Security Agency, 1999, Top Secret, p.318.

8 NSA: Johnson, *American Cryptology during the Cold War*, National Security Agency, 1999, Top Secret, p.331.

9 Reed, *At the Abyss*, p.267.

10 Ibid., p.268.

11 Ibid., p.269.

12 NSA: *The 1983 War Scare Briefing Book, Vol I*, No. 426, Document 12: *Harriman Papers*, Library of Congress, Manuscript Division, Box 655.
13 His wife was Pamela Churchill Hayward, the former wife of Winston Churchill's son Randolph. Harriman had had an affair with Pamela during the war years.
14 NSA: *The 1983 War Scare Briefing Book, Vol I*, No. 426, Documents 13 & 14: *Harriman Papers*, Library of Congress, Manuscript Division, Box 655.

9 Shootdown

1 The black box was recovered by the Soviets but its recovery was never revealed to the West. Ten years after the incident, the Russian Federation handed the black box to International Civil Aviation Organisation (ICAO) investigators. It failed to answer any of the key questions about the flight.
2 This interpretation was put together after much research and use of flight simulators by Howard Ewing, a pilot with immense experience of flying over the north Pacific who became fascinated by what could have happened on the flight deck of KAL 007; see Hersh, *The Target is Destroyed*, p.277ff. It is only one of several versions of what might have happened. Each one explains some of what happened but not all. Several explanations assume that KAL 007 was on some sort of spying mission; see also Johnson, *Shootdown*, p.xff. This author has gone for a single interpretation of events, but if the reader wants to explore the other versions then they should consult Hersh, Johnson or others.
3 Johnson, *Shootdown*, p.7ff.
4 ICAO, *Final Report of Investigation as Required by Council Resolution of 16 September 1983*, p.56.
5 Hersh, *The Target is Destroyed*, p.50ff.
6 The Soviets later reported that one pilot did catch up with KAL 007, and he said it was flying without lights and took evasive action. This seems highly unlikely and was possibly some sort of excuse offered for failing to take action against the errant airliner. It still leaves this question unanswered: if a fighter pilot had caught up with the aircraft while it was still in Soviet airspace, why did it not take action? See Johnson, *Shootdown*, p.17ff.
7 NSA: Johnson, *American Cryptology during the Cold War*, National Security Agency, 1999, Top Secret, p.321ff; and Hersh, *The Target is Destroyed*, p.64ff.
8 In the press conferences held by the Soviets after the event his name was withheld and he appeared anonymously. He was later named by the Soviets as Major Kasmin. The quotes that follow are from FLASHBACK: Interview with Gennady Ossipovich.
9 This was recorded in the black box that was analysed in the late 1990s.
10 The fishermen did not come forward with this evidence for several weeks as they were terrified of being prosecuted for illegally fishing in Soviet waters. By the time they told their story all possibility of

American or Japanese vessels tracing the spot where KAL 007 had crashed and trying to retrieve the black box had passed; see Hersh, *The Target is Destroyed*, pp.32–3.

10 Outcry

1 KAL 007 had crossed the International Date Line, so it had been shot down in the early morning of 1 September, but it was still the evening of 31 August in the USA.

2 Shultz, *Turmoil and Triumph*, p.361.

3 NSA: Johnson, *American Cryptology during the Cold War*, National Security Agency, 1999, Top Secret, p.321ff.

4 Ibid., pp.323–4; and Hersh, *The Target is Destroyed*, p.88ff.

5 NSA: Johnson, *American Cryptology during the Cold War*, National Security Agency, 1999, Top Secret, p.324ff.

6 Hersh, *The Target is Destroyed*, pp.107–23.

7 Shultz, *Turmoil and Triumph*, p.361.

8 Gates, *From the Shadows*, p.267.

9 Shultz, *Turmoil and Triumph*, p.362; Speakes, *Speaking Out*, pp.119–20; and Hersh, *The Target is Destroyed*, pp.143–6.

10 REAGAN: Remarks to Reporters on the Soviet Attack on a Korean Civil Airliner, 2 September 1983.

11 *New York Times*, 2 September 1983.

12 Gates, *From the Shadows*, p.267; and NSA: Johnson, *American Cryptology during the Cold War*, National Security Agency, 1999, Top Secret, pp.325–8.

13 Shultz, *Turmoil and Triumph*, p.364.

14 Volkogonov, *The Rise and Fall of the Soviet Empire*, p.363.

15 Dobrynin, *In Confidence*, pp.537–8.

16 Volkogonov, *The Rise and Fall of the Soviet Empire*, pp.365–9; and Hoffman, *The Dead Hand*, pp.84–5.

17 Hersh, *The Target is Destroyed*, pp.186–8.

18 REAGAN: Address to the Nation on the Soviet Attack on a Korean Civil Airliner, 5 September 1983.

19 Hersh, *The Target is Destroyed*, pp.235–7. The US had tidied up some of the language in its translation so the words 'Yolki palki' were translated not as 'What the hell' or 'Holy shit' but 'Fiddlesticks'.

20 NSA: Johnson, *American Cryptology during the Cold War*, National Security Agency, 1999, Top Secret, pp.329–30.

21 FLASHBACK: Interview with Gennady Ossipovich.

22 Dobrynin, *In Confidence*, pp.539–40.

23 NSA: Johnson, *American Cryptology during the Cold War*, National Security Agency, 1999, Top Secret, p.333.

24 Dobrynin, *In Confidence*, p.540; and Hersh, *The Target is Destroyed*, pp.251–2.

25 NSA: Johnson, *American Cryptology during the Cold War*, National Security Agency, 1999, Top Secret, pp.331–4.

26 Reagan, *An American Life*, p.584.

11 False Alerts

1   NSA: *The 3 AM Phone Call*, Briefing Book No. 371; and Gates, *From the Shadows*, p.114.
2   For this and the following accidents and failures see Isaacs and Downing, *Cold War*, pp.268–72; see also Scott Sagan, *The Limits of Safety*.
3   See Randall Maydew and Julie Bush, *America's Lost H-Bomb*.
4   Hoffman, *The Dead Hand*, pp.7–9.
5   FLASHBACK: Interview with Stanislav Petrov; the quotations that follow are from this interview.

12 Truck Bomb

1   Reagan, *An American Life*, p.407ff.
2   Robert Fisk, *Pity the Nation*, p.199ff; and Shultz, *Turmoil and Triumph*, p.44.
3   Reagan, *An American Life*, p.410.
4   Andrew and Gordievsky, *KGB: The Inside Story*, p.455.
5   Reagan, *An American Life*, p.422.
6   The Soviets responded by installing a new generation of SA-5 surface-to-air missiles in Syria. During the installation a series of Soviet advisers and technicians were sent to Syria. This author spent a night at the Damascus Sheraton in September 1982 and was surprised to find a Soviet athletics team, all in matching tracksuits, relaxing in the bar. It did not take much detective work to spot that very few in the team looked like athletes: it was the first of the Soviet military advisers in rather poor disguise.
7   Reagan, *The Reagan Diaries*, p.98; Shultz, *Turmoil and Triumph*, p.69ff; and Reagan, *An American Life*, pp.427–9.
8   Report of the International Commission, *Israel in Lebanon*, pp.51–65.
9   Ibid., p.162ff.
10   Footage of bulldozers pushing bodies of Jewish Holocaust victims into mass graves at Bergen-Belsen and Buchenwald after the liberation of these Nazi camps in April 1945 had shocked the world.
11   The Kahan Commission reported in February 1983 that Israeli forces should have known of the risk of allowing Phalangist troops into the Palestinian refugee camps and should have done something to stop the massacre once it had started. The Commission concluded, 'the Jewish public's stand has always been that the responsibility for such deeds falls not only on those who rioted and committed the atrocities but also on those who were responsible for safety and public order, who could have prevented the disturbances and did not fulfill their obligations in this respect'. Quoted in Shultz, *Turmoil and Triumph*, p.113.
12   Reagan, *The Reagan Diaries*, p.101.
13   This author filmed the French and Italian peacekeeping forces who proudly landed at Beirut docks in September 1982, the Italians with feathered plumes in their helmets, and then filmed the US Marines,

who chose to make a show of coming ashore from landing craft, Iwo Jima-style, on the beaches to the south of the city.

14 Reagan, *The Reagan Diaries*, 23 April 1983, p.147.

15 Morgan, *Reagan*, p.226.

16 Hansard, 24 October 1983, quoted in Richard Aldous, *Reagan and Thatcher*, p.144.

17 Margaret Thatcher, *The Downing Street Years*, p.331.

18 Thatcher, *The Downing Street Years*, pp.332–3; and Aldous, *Reagan and Thatcher*, pp.151–3.

19 Reagan, *An American Life*, pp.457–8 and 466.

13 Kremlin Paranoia

1 Igor Andropov is quoted in Volkogonov, *The Rise and Fall of the Soviet Empire*, p.371.

2 Ibid., p.370.

3 Chazov's untranslated Russian memoirs, published in 1991, are quoted in Volkogonov, *The Rise and Fall of the Soviet Empire*, pp.375–6.

4 Gorbachev, *Memoirs*, p.151.

5 Geoffrey Howe, *Conflict of Loyalty*, pp.349–50.

6 Thatcher, *The Downing Street Years*, p.450.

7 Gates, *From the Shadows*, pp.290–1.

8 Volkogonov, *The Rise and Fall of the Soviet Empire*, pp.376–8.

14 Able Archer 83

1 Richard Dannatt, *Boots on the Ground*, p.191.

2 NSA: *The 1983 War Scare, Vol II*, Briefing Book No. 427, Documents 3 & 4 *Autumn Forge 83*; and Jones, *Able Archer 83*, pp.25–6.

3 NSA: PFIAB, *The Soviet 'War Scare'*, 15 February 1990, Top Secret, p.xii.

4 NSA: *The 1983 War Scare, Vol II*, Briefing Book No. 427; Documents 6a & 6b *NATO Exercise Able Archer 83 Scenario*, NATO Historical Files; and see also Jones, *Able Archer 83*, pp.1–2.

5 NSA: Air Force Seventh Air Division, Ramstein, *Exercise Able Archer 83, SAC ADVON, After Action Report*, 1 December 1983, p.5.

6 FLASHBACK: Interview with Spike Callender.

7 FLASHBACK: Interview with Eugene Gay.

8 Andrew and Gordievsky, *KGB: The Inside Story*, pp.502–3.

9 Jones, *Able Archer 83*, p.26.

10 NSA: *The 1983 War Scare, Vol II*, Briefing Book No. 427, Documents 6a & 6b *NATO Exercise Able Archer 83 Scenario*, NATO Historical Files.

11 CIA: Fischer, *A Cold War Conundrum*, p.69.

12 FLASHBACK: Interview with Robert McFarlane.

13 Jones, *Able Archer 83*, p.30.

14 Ibid., p.33–4.

15 Combat Alert

1   Gorbachev, *Memoirs*, p.151.
2   FLASHBACK: Interview with Robert Gates.
3   Isaacs and Downing, *Cold War*, p.391.
4   CIA: Fischer, *A Cold War Conundrum*, p.17.
5   Romanov's speech was reported in *Pravda* on 6 November 1983; see Jones, *Able Archer 83*, p.37.
6   NSA: PFIAB, *The Soviet 'War Scare'*, Top Secret, p.64ff.
7   NSA: Interview with Vitalii Tsygichko in December 1990 by John G. Hines, *Soviet Intentions 1965–1985*.
8   FLASHBACK: Interview with Oleg Kalugin.
9   FLASHBACK: The details and quotes from this story are taken from the interview with Viktor Tkachenko.
10 FLASHBACK: The quotes are taken from the interview with Ivan Yesin.
11 Miller, *The Cold War*, pp.120–1.
12 FLASHBACK: The quotes are taken from the interview with Sergei Lokot.
13 FLASHBACK: The quotes are taken from the interview with Maxim Devetyarov.
14 NSA: PFIAB, *The Soviet 'War Scare'*, Top Secret, p.79.

16 Night

1   Andrew and Gordievsky, *KGB: The Inside Story*, p.502.
2   Ibid., p.503; and Gordievsky, *Next Stop Execution*, p.272.
3   FLASHBACK: Interview with Oleg Gordievsky.
4   FLASHBACK: The quotes are from the interview with Rainer Rupp.
5   Jones, *Able Archer 83*, p.37.
6   NSA: PFIAB, *The Soviet 'War Scare'*, Top Secret, pp.28–9.
7   FLASHBACK: Interview with Spike Callender.
8   FLASHBACK: Interview with Robert Gates.

17 'Really Scary'

1   First to analyse in detail what had happened was the ninety-four-page report for the President's Foreign Intelligence Advisory Board (PFIAB), chaired by Anne Armstrong, *The Soviet 'War Scare'*, in February 1990, but this top secret report was not declassified until October 2015. The first analysis that was declassified was by CIA historian Ben Fischer in *Studies in Intelligence*, a CIA in-house journal, in 1996 entitled *The 1983 War Scare in US-Soviet Relations: A Cold War Conundrum*.
2   Jones, *Able Archer 83*, pp.39–40.
3   NSA: CIA, Special National Intelligence Estimate, *Implications of Recent Soviet Military-Political Activities*, Top Secret, 18 May 1984; and PFIAB, *The Soviet 'War Scare'*, Top Secret, pp.11–14.
4   Howe, *Conflict of Loyalty*, p.350.

5   NSA: PFIAB, *The Soviet 'War Scare'*, Top Secret, p.11.
6   FLASHBACK: Interview with Robert McFarlane (McFarlane did not know of Gordievsky by name at this point, he just knew him by a codename – his real name came out much later).
7   Jones, *Able Archer 83*, pp.45–6.
8   Reagan, *The Reagan Diaries*, p.186.
9   Ibid., p.199.
10 FLASHBACK: Interview with Robert McFarlane.
11 Reagan, *The Reagan Diaries*, p.199.
12 NSA: *Small Group Meeting of 19 November 1983, 7.30am*, The Secretary of State's Dining Room, Secret, p.4.
13 Jones, *Able Archer 83*, p.3.
14 NSA: CIA Memorandum from CIA Director William Casey, *US/Soviet Tension*, 19 June 1984, Secret; and PFIAB, *The Soviet 'War Scare'*, Top Secret, p.17.
15 FLASHBACK: Interview with Robert McFarlane.
16 Thatcher, *The Downing Street Years*, p.458; and Howe, *Conflict of Loyalty*, pp.353–4.
17 Hoffman, *The Dead Hand*, p.155.
18 Reagan, *An American Life*, p.588.
19 Jones, *Able Archer 83*, p.49.
20 REAGAN: Address to the Nation and Other Countries on US-Soviet Relations, 16 January 1984.
21 Gaddis, *The Cold War*, p.228. Gaddis says he heard the story from two well-placed White House sources. The handwritten addition appears in Jones, *Able Archer 83*, pp.301–2.
22 NSA: Johnson, *American Cryptology during the Cold War*, National Security Agency, Top Secret, p.319.
23 Reagan, *The Reagan Diaries*, p.247.
24 Reagan, *An American Life*, pp.595–8.
25 The USA won more than twice the number of gold and silver medals in Los Angeles in 1984 as in the following Olympics in Seoul in 1988 where there was full global attendance. Juan Antonio Samaranch, the IOC president, formally protested to ABC Television about the jingoistic nature of its coverage of the 1984 Los Angeles Games – see David Miller, *Olympic Revolution*, p.109.
26 NSA: PFIAB, *The Soviet 'War Scare'*, Top Secret, pp.5 & 18.
27 Morgan, *Reagan*, pp.231–6.
28 Howe, *Conflict of Loyalty*, pp.355–7.
29 Gordievsky, *Next Stop Execution*, pp.305–13.
30 NSA: *The Gorbachev File*, Briefing Book No. 544; Document 1: *Memorandum of Conversation between Mikhail Gorbachev and Margaret Thatcher, December 16 1984* by Charles Powell; and Thatcher, *The Downing Street Years*, p.459.
31 Thatcher, *The Downing Street Years*, pp.459–63; Howe, *Conflict of Loyalty*, pp.358–60; and Gorbachev, *Memoirs*, pp.160–2.
32 Thatcher, *The Downing Street Years*, pp.461–3; and THATCHER: TV Interview with BBC, 10 Downing Street, 17 December 1984.
33 Gorbachev, *Memoirs*, pp.164–5.

18 Spy Wars

1   Interview with Aldrich Ames in Ted Turner/CNN/Jeremy Isaacs Productions, *Cold War*, episode 21, 'Spies 1944–94'.
2   Gates, *From the Shadows*, p.17.
3   The following account comes from Gordievsky, *Next Stop Execution*, pp.319–43.
4   Andrew and Gordievsky, *KGB: The Inside Story*, p.xxviii.
5   See David Hoffman, *The Billion Dollar Spy*.
6   Hoffman, *The Dead Hand*, p.198.
7   See David Wise, *Spy: The Inside Story*.
8   This account is taken from both Gordievsky, *Next Stop Execution*, pp.1–24, and FLASHBACK: Interview with Oleg Gordievsky.
9   Howe, *Conflict of Loyalty*, p.436.
10 FLASHBACK: Interview with Oleg Gordievsky.

19 Pay-off

1   Reagan, *An American Life*, p.611.
2   NSA: *The Gorbachev File*, Briefing Book No. 544; Document 5: *Impressions of the Man, His Style and His Likely Impact upon East-West Relations* in May 1985, John Browne MP, twenty-page note to President Reagan about Gorbachev.
3   Reagan, *Reagan Diaries*, p.337.
4   NSA: *The Gorbachev File*, Briefing Book No. 544; Document 2: *Letter from President Reagan to General Secretary Gorbachev, 11 March 1985*.
5   NSA: *The Gorbachev File*, Briefing Book No. 544; Document 3: *Letter from Gorbachev to Reagan, 24 March 1985*.
6   Gates, *From the Shadows*, pp.331–2.
7   Shultz, *Turmoil and Triumph*, p.532.
8   Jack F. Matlock, *Reagan and Gorbachev*, pp.112–13. According to an autopsy, it seemed that Major Nicholson had been shot through the heart and so would have died instantly. Even immediate medical attention could not have saved him.
9   Schultz, *Turmoil and Triumph*, pp.563–4.
10 Ibid., p.575.
11 Reagan, *An American Life*, p.631.
12 Reagan, *Reagan Diaries*, p.355.
13 Matlock, *Reagan and Gorbachev*, p.153.
14 Shultz, *Turmoil and Triumph*, pp.576–7.
15 Speakes, *Speaking Out*, pp.131–2.
16 Matlock, *Reagan and Gorbachev*, p.147; and Gates, *From the Shadows*, p.358.
17 Gorbachev, *Memoirs*, pp.403–5.
18 Reagan asked Gorbachev to correct Georgy Arbatov, who repeatedly claimed that he was just a B-movie actor, and tell him that he had starred in A-movies as well, of which *Kings Row* was one.

19 REAGAN: Address to the Nation on the Upcoming Soviet-US Summit Meeting in Geneva, 14 November 1985.
20 Reagan, *An American Life*, p.634.
21 Ibid., p.635.
22 NSA: *The Geneva Summit*, Briefing Book No. 172; Document 15: *Memorandum of Conversation, Reagan-Gorbachev, Geneva, 19 November 1985; First Private Meeting.*
23 Shultz, *Turmoil and Triumph*, p.600.
24 Gorbachev, *Memoirs*, p.406.
25 Reagan, *An American Life*, p.637.
26 NSA: *The Geneva Summit*, Briefing Book No. 172; Document 19: *Memorandum of Conversation, Reagan-Gorbachev, Geneva, 19 November 1985; Second Private Meeting.*
27 Gorbachev, *Memoirs*, p.408.
28 NSA: *The Geneva Summit*, Briefing Book No. 172; Document 20: *Memorandum of Conversation, Reagan-Gorbachev, Geneva, 19 November 1985; Dinner Hosted by the Gorbachevs.*
29 Shultz, *Turmoil and Triumph*, pp.602–6; Reagan, *An American Life*, pp.638–40; and Gorbachev, *Memoirs*, pp.408–10.

20 Endgames

1 Reagan, *An American Life*, p.641; and Reagan, *The Reagan Diaries*, p.371.
2 Morgan, *Reagan*, p.293.
3 Rodric Braithwaite argues that some of the ideas behind the 'peace offensive' began with the Soviet military: the previous spring two senior members of the General Staff had been asked to come up with ideas for the elimination of nuclear weapons within fifteen years. See Braithwaite, *Armageddon and Paranoia*, p.360ff.
4 Reagan, *The Reagan Diaries*, p.383.
5 Gorbachev, *Memoirs*, p.413.
6 Ibid., p.193.
7 Anatoly Chernyaev, *My Six Years with Gorbachev*, pp.81–4.
8 Matlock, *Reagan and Gorbachev*, p.217.
9 Gorbachev, *Memoirs*, p.416.
10 Shultz, *Turmoil and Triumph*, p.758.
11 Ibid., p.760.
12 Gorbachev, *Memoirs*, pp.416–18; and Shultz, *Turmoil and Triumph*, pp.760–2.
13 Reagan, *An American Life*, p.677.
14 NSA: *The Reykjavik File*, Briefing Book No. 203; Document 15: *US Memorandum of Conversation, Reagan-Gorbachev, Final Meeting, 12 October 1986.*
15 Shultz, *Turmoil and Triumph*, pp.772–3.
16 Ibid., pp.773–4.
17 Reagan wrote 'I was very disappointed – and *very* angry' in *An American Life*, p.679; Gorbachev wrote that as they left Hofdi House 'Everyone was in a bad mood', *Memoirs*, p.418.

18 Gorbachev, *Memoirs*, p.419.
19 Shultz, *Turmoil and Triumph*, p.777.
20 Thatcher, *The Downing Street Years*, pp.471–2.
21 NSA: *The Reykjavik File*, Briefing Book No. 203; Document 21: *Session of the Politburo, 14 October 1986, About the Results of the Meeting in Reykjavik by the General Secretary*, p. 1.
22 Chernyaev, *My Six Years with Gorbachev*, p.85.
23 REAGAN: Remarks on East-West Relations at the Brandenburg Gate in West Berlin, 12 June 1987.
24 Gorbachev, *Memoirs*, p.444.
25 REAGAN: Remarks on Signing the Intermediate-Range Nuclear Forces Treaty, 8 December 1987; and Gorbachev, *Memoirs*, p.443.
26 Gorbachev, *Memoirs*, p.447.
27 Jon Snow, *Shooting History*, p.300.

Epilogue

1 There are several powerful accounts of the end of communism in eastern Europe including Gale Stokes, *The Walls Came Tumbling Down*, David Remnick, *Lenin's Tomb*, and Robert Service, *The End of the Cold War*; see also Isaacs and Downing, *Cold War*, pp.428–81.
2 It is ironic that the change in the world order in 1989 marked the 200th anniversary of the French Revolution in 1789 and the sweeping away of the *ancien régime*, and with it the idea that governments could base their legitimacy on inherited and divinely approved power.
3 From Gorbachev's book *Perestroika*, published in the Soviet Union in 1987, quoted in Gaddis, *The Cold War*, p.235.
4 Stokes, *The Walls Came Tumbling Down*, pp.136–41. Turner/CNN/Jeremy Isaacs Productions, *Cold War*, episode 23, 'The Wall Comes Down 1989' provides a very graphic account of these events.
5 Wolf, *Man Without a Face*, p.340.
6 Ibid., pp.330–3.
7 FLASHBACK: Interview with Rainer Rupp.
8 CIA: Fischer, *A Cold War Conundrum*, p.22.
9 Gordievsky, *Next Stop Execution*, pp.344–87.
10 Andrew and Gordievsky, *KGB: The Inside Story*, pp.xix–xxi.
11 Thatcher, *The Downing Street Years*, p.774.
12 Gates, *From the Shadows*, p.258.
13 NSA: PFIAB, *The Soviet 'War Scare'*, Top Secret, pp. vii and xii.
14 Gates, *From the Shadows*, p.273.
15 CIA: Fischer, *A Cold War Conundrum*, p.71.
16 'Baltic alarm as large-scale Russian war games near final phase', *The Guardian*, 19 September 2017.
17 According to figures assembled by the International Institute for Strategic Studies in *Top 15 Defence Budgets, 2015*.
18 During a January 2000 Congressional testimony, Peter Pry, a former

CIA analyst, asserted that Able Archer 83 was 'more dangerous than the Cuban Missile Crisis' – see Pry, *War Scare*; and Jones, *Able Archer 83*, p.318.
19 CIA: Fischer, *A Cold War Conundrum*, p.61.

Acknowledgements

1 Isaacs and Downing, *Cold War*, pp.399–400.
2 Taylor Downing, 'The Cold War: A Personal View', in the *Journal of British Cinema and Television*, Vol. 10.1, January 2013, pp.93–105.
3 Taylor Downing, 'History on Television: The Making of *Cold War*', in the *Historical Journal of Film, Radio and Television*, Vol. 18:3, August 1998, pp.325–32.
4 Some of the latest evidence uncovered is published in Jones, *Able Archer 83*.
5 NSA: PFIAB, *The Soviet 'War Scare'*, Top Secret, pp.1–30.
6 The PFIAB report was classified as Top Secret UMBRA GAMMA WNINTEL NOFORN NOCONTRACT ORCON, which translates into normal speak as: Communications Intelligence (UMBRA), Signals Intelligence (GAMMA), Sources and Methods (WNINTEL), For the eyes of no foreign nationals (NOFORN), For the eyes of no contractors or consultants (NOCONTRACT), and Originator Controlled (ORCON), meaning of very limited and controlled distribution.

Index

Page numbers in *italics* refer to illustrations